My Dead Parents

My Dead Parents

A MEMOIR

Anya Yurchyshyn

CROWN
NEW YORK

Copyright © 2018 by Anya Yurchyshyn

All rights reserved.
Published in the United States by Crown, an
imprint of the Crown Publishing Group, a division
of Penguin Random House LLC, New York.
crownpublishing.com

CROWN is a registered trademark and the Crown
colophon is a trademark of Penguin Random House
LLC.

Library of Congress Cataloging-in-Publication Data
is available upon request.

ISBN 978-0-553-44704-0
Ebook ISBN 978-0-553-44705-7

Printed in the United States of America

Book design: Elina D. Nudelman
Jacket design: Elena Giavaldi
Jacket photographs: (parents) courtesy of the author;
(typed letters) George Yurchyshyn/courtesy of the
author; (handwritten letter) Anita Yurchyshyn/
courtesy of the author

10 9 8 7 6 5 4 3 2 1

First Edition

"Whereas the beautiful is limited, the sublime is limitless, so that the mind in the presence of the sublime, attempting to imagine what it cannot, has pain in the failure but pleasure in contemplating the immensity of the attempt."

—IMMANUEL KANT

НА КОНЯ!
(Onto the horse!)

CONTENTS

Part One

Part Two

My Dead Parents

$\mathcal{M}$y mother, Anita, died in her sleep in 2010, when she was sixty-four and I was thirty-two. The official cause of death was heart failure, but what she really died from was unabashed alcoholism, the kind where you drink whatever you can get your hands on, use your bed as a toilet when you can't make it to the bathroom, and cause so much brain damage you lose the ability to walk unsupported. The cause of her death was herself, and her many problems.

The month after she died, I began cleaning out her house, my childhood home, in downtown Boston. As a kid, my house sometimes seemed enchanting, filled to the ceiling with items my parents had collected on their many trips around the globe. But when my father, George, was killed in a car accident in Ukraine in 1994, my mother lost interest in our home, and it started to die as well. By the time she passed away, treasured rugs were being eaten by moths and mice, the fire escape was dangling off the back, and some windows wouldn't open, while others wouldn't close. Everything that once seemed special was chipped or cracked and buried under sticky dust. I saw cleaning out the house as my last goodbye to her and my dad, and I was eager to finally be rid of them. I thought I would box up what I wanted, toss what I didn't, and avoid being caught by what had become its most potent force—sadness.

My parents were intellectuals with exciting careers, but

that wasn't what mattered to me as their child. My father had been emotionally distant and occasionally abusive. My mother hadn't protected me. She was resentful and selfish, and this was before her drinking brought out, or created, qualities that were much worse. My parents were married for twenty-seven years, but rarely seemed to even like each other. I believed that they'd never been in love.

I began my work in my mother's large study. Growing up, it had been the part of the house that was specifically hers, an area where the air was still and sacred. It was where she wrote and practiced her speeches for the Sierra Club, kept her favorite books and special jewelry. But during the last ten years, it became a haphazard storage room for everything from stained sheets to months of unopened mail. I spent days sorting the clothing piled on the room's red couches and the incredible amount of panty hose she'd purchased from Filene's Basement and never worn. I'd anticipated this task for years, and getting rid of things so banal and expected was both boring and surreal: *There goes that stained cotton turtleneck, that long pink coat she made my father buy her because she thought it made her look regal.*

I split the wall of books between boxes that would be donated and boxes that I'd bring back to Brooklyn. I reached deep into her closet and, when I came across something that my sister and I might want to keep—silk kimonos, a leopard jacket—I brought it into my mother's room and placed it on her bed, which had been stripped by her aide the morning she'd been found dead in it.

I tried to summon a memory of getting rid of my father's belongings after he died, but couldn't. Then I remembered that my mother's best friend, Sylvia, had traveled from Chicago to help with the job, sparing me from having to fold his suits and throw away his underwear, and from seeing my mother doing it. Although the house had been my parents' and they'd acquired the majority of its contents together, I'd gotten used to thinking of it as my mother's. What I was going through those first few days was the soggy life she'd lived after my father died.

Once I'd pried loose this first layer, I began to move more slowly. I had to pay attention to what was passing through my fingers—my mother's work files, broken necklaces with beads my sister might want to repurpose, our grade-school report cards. At the bottom of a small wooden chest, I found a collection of letters bound by a cracked rubber band. After I'd managed to remove it, I unfolded the letter on top of the pile. It was typed on thin, crinkly paper, dated 1966, and addressed to my mom, who would have been twenty-one.

I miss you, I miss you, I miss you, I miss you, I miss you, I miss you, I (sorry I ran off the end of the line, I meant to say: I miss you). It's so hard to convince myself that you are so terribly far away. I have such a desire to just call you up, run over to the dorms and pick you up so that we could run along the beach, roll on the Midway, sail our boat, fly a kite, goose each other down the street . . .

I laughed. Who'd write such goofy things to her? I scanned the pages that followed, but it was only the signature, handwritten in blue ink, that revealed the author's identity: George.

"What?" I whispered. My father would have never written such silly things or have been so free with his affection.

I made my way through the rest. In 1971, my father wrote, "Whenever I leave you I feel a powerful and wonderfully terrible series of emotions . . . there is an emptiness inside me, a true aching of the heart. It is a longing and a dull sorrow for leaving behind that which I love."

In 1973, my mother told him that she'd "never be fully able to write what loving you has meant. Our love is wondrous; it has a life almost of its own which encompasses us whether we are together or apart." Her tight, Catholic school script was barely legible, but the ink was steady and bold. She'd transcribed her devotion in a fever. When I flipped the page over and ran my fingers across it, I felt the force of the words she'd pressed into it.

What I was reading contradicted what I'd long ago decided: that my parents had never been happy with each other, never had hope. I couldn't believe that my father could have been so articulate and vulnerable, or that my mother had ever adored him so intensely. My brain was in revolt. What I was reading seemed to have been written by strangers, not the people I'd known. I read their letters again and again, arguing with what I found. But as I continued to find proof of their love, I realized that I was defending the story I'd arrived with against mounting counter-evidence, and losing.

There were many more letters, as well as postcards, faxes, and trunks full of pictures and slides. Each offered a window into my parents' lives and revealed parts of them I'd never seen. Almost every year of their relationship was accounted for in their own words. It was intimate and foreign territory, unfathomably vast. The space I'd cleared had filled up again; the whole house could not contain everything I didn't know.

I sat in my mother's study for days, trying to take in my parents' lives and relationship, to see them for who they really were. When my sister called to ask how the cleaning was going, I cheerfully said "Great," but it had come to a sharp stop. I was picking at our parents' remains like a vulture, more concerned with what I could consume than what I should discard.

I had so many questions, and I couldn't ask my parents any of them. I wanted to wave their letters in their faces and shout, "Hey, what the hell is this? And what the hell happened to you?"

I searched and gathered and read and reread, until I slowly began accepting what was so obviously true: I didn't know my parents at all. The stories I'd told myself about them were wrong. Instead of pushing them away as I'd planned, I worked to bring them closer, hoping I could learn who they'd really been and what had happened to their love.

CHAPTER ONE

Unhooked

$\mathcal{M}$y parents traveled with empty suitcases. Black, with stiff plastic shells, their luggage was scuffed and dotted with stickers from airports around the world. These suitcases banged hollow against the ones that held my parents' clothes as they hurried out of our Boston home to their next destination, where they knew they'd fall in love with objects large and small. The suitcases were heavy when they returned weeks later; sometimes it took both of them to carry one.

The night they came back from wherever they'd been, they gathered my sister, Alexandra, and me in the living room so we could watch them unpack their new treasures. My father unfolded a coarse rug and said he'd spent six hours drinking tea with its seller in Lebanon. My mother held up a statue and said that the dealer who'd sold it to her in Zimbabwe had tried to swap it with a fake when he delivered it to her hotel room. A small embroidered hat was placed on my head; it had belonged to the son of a Syrian imam. These unveilings happened so frequently throughout my childhood that eventually they looped into a single evening, one longer and more interesting than any day, where my parents talked over each other, shared jokes my sister and I didn't get, and delighted in their acquisitions as well as in each other. My father traveled more than my mother, and when he returned from a trip he'd taken alone, he'd make a similar presentation. But those evenings lacked the intimate electricity of the ones that followed a trip they had taken together.

As my mother studied their purchases, she sucked on a Kent Golden Light and sipped a martini that dangled loosely from her hand. She'd crouch down and ask my sister and me what we thought of the things we were seeing, while my father remained upright with his hands on his hips and a smile on his face. We gave our assessments: pretty, ugly, scary, weird. As we spoke, they found a home for each new prize above the fireplace or on a chest, situating a Chinese snuff bottle between an Afghan dagger and a Hopi basket. I'd fall asleep on the floor before they finished unpacking, sprawled on a rug procured on an earlier excursion, momentarily happy, and even grateful, to be their child.

Our house was a cramped testament to my parents' curiosity. There was no television in the living room, but there was an African statue in every corner, Iranian kilims and Indonesian textiles hanging off every wall, and shelves crowded with books. I had little knowledge of the context or craftsmanship of what my parents collected, but each item gave me a jolt when I touched it. They were all from the same place: far away. I couldn't wait to get there.

My father took his battered Nikon camera and at least ten rolls of slide film on every one of their trips. A few days after their acquisitions were unveiled, the four of us gathered again in the living room as he fought with the slide projector, fussed with the carousel, and steadied the pull-down screen on its stand so Alexandra and I could see where they'd been.

In the dark of our skinny row house a few blocks from the Charles River, he showed us ancient cities, rain forests, market stalls with pyramids of bright fruit. My parents smiling as they rode camels or held each other in front of an ornate fountain. My mother alone as she glanced seductively at my father or into the distance with a look of humble contempla-tion. Attuned to the distinct vibrations of my father's silences, she knew when he was plotting a candid photo and made sure he got her best angle. When we came to a picture of my mom bathing under a waterfall or perched on a desert rock, my fa-ther paused the show. He'd remove a bunch of slides and study them in front of the projector's lens, put a few back in, but set more to the side. Pictures of my mother usually came in a series; with each photo that clicked by, pieces of her clothing disappeared.

During these presentations, I looked at the people in the photographs, at the people showing them to me, then back at the pictures again, searching for glimpses of my parents in each. The couple in the room and the couple on the screen matched only in the days after they returned. When the slide show was over and the projector put away, this couple transformed back into people I recognized; they became my parents again. The cozy bubble had popped, and life would return to its normal state. I'd go back to looking over my shoulder, to shuffling through the house in fear.

When I wanted to travel, I studied copies of *National Geographic* or went on "safari" in our Junk Room, where items not currently on display, or that my parents had forgotten they owned, were stored: wooden masks too scary to touch, knives with horn handles, a shrunken head with hair on it. The overhead light had burned out long ago, and boxes and trunks were stacked so high that the thin beams of sunlight that shot between them could only lift the musty dark to dusk. Entering the Junk Room was like pushing through Lewis's wardrobe and finding myself in Narnia. I was on an adventure in a mysterious world, one where I saw myself whacking through thick jungle vines and creeping into forgotten tombs. My expeditions were more frequent than my parents', but I could always discover something new by creating a fresh path or having grown the inch necessary to finally be able to reach a certain shelf. When I heard them calling my name, I returned, covered in scratches and dust, and unsure of how much time had passed.

A desire for adventure wasn't the only reason that I set off into the Junk Room; I also went there to hide from my father. My father as I knew him wasn't the man in the pictures, a man who was relaxed, happy. He was a bully with a temper as destructive as a wildfire, one I seemed fated to spark. He was the commanding force in my life. His moods controlled its weather; his words crushed and corralled me. To him, I was always doing something wrong, and that made me so nervous that I'd inevitably trip or slip, drop glasses and plates, fall out of chairs. At any moment, I knew I could do something to ignite his anger and he'd unleash a storm of insults: messy, clumsy, stupid, a crybaby. I was an emotional, skinless kid, and his words, delivered with rage or in whispered disgust, hurt more than any physical punishment.

A small child in a family of small people, I spent my youth not wanting to be bigger but to be smaller still. I wished I could be absorbed into walls, contort my limbs to fit through mouse-size cracks. I hid in the dark of the Junk Room and in my closet but was never able to make myself fully disappear from my father's radar. I was terrified of his rage and hated that he saw my tears as a reason to yell more, not less. Though my mother was affectionate and never yelled the way he did, I was scared of her as well, because she didn't, or couldn't, protect me from him.

If I had to be near my father, I'd unhook my heart and retreat to a secret place within myself. My eyes still blinked, and I could answer questions when asked, but I wasn't really there. I thought that he wasn't angry about whatever bad or stupid thing I'd done; he was angry because of me. I was the bad thing that had happened, the thing that was wrong. My simple, stupid existence was the problem. I thought he'd correctly determined that I was innately deficient, too broken to fix. I knew that it was mean to yell at me the way he did, but I also thought I deserved it. How frustrating for him to be burdened with such a defective daughter.

When I was two, I fell down the flight of wooden stairs

that led to our kitchen, tumbling over and over until my face hit the landing.

I'd been looking for my parents, who were drinking coffee and eating grapefruit. My father ran over as I howled. He lifted me to my feet and shook me. "What's wrong with you, dummy? Don't you look where you're going?"

I put my hands on my hips and shouted, "Don't call me a dummy," then ran to my mom and took shelter in her robe.

I don't remember this moment, but my mother spoke of it many times. She'd do an impression of me, scrunching her face in anger, stomping her foot, growling "dummy." She was proud that I'd stood up to my father, who was shocked by the force of my response. I was shocked by it, too; I never defended myself, never yelled back.

A moment I do remember: I am four and in the pantry, a tight space off the living room where my parents stored alcohol and plates reserved for company. The pantry had a stove that was different from the one in our kitchen. It was flat and embedded in a countertop. I was playing with it as my parents prepared for a dinner party, grabbing its knob and turning it hard enough so the button went red. My father told me to stop, then told me again, and again. He said it was dangerous, to leave it alone, that it was something only grown-ups could touch. Anya! What? *Stop!*

I couldn't. I was too mesmerized by how the metal got hot without any fire. He stalked over and grabbed my hand. I watched as he pressed my finger to the stove's shiny surface. When the pain hit, I screamed. My mother ran to me and screamed, too, but that didn't make him stop. When he finally released my finger, he flipped over my hand, and we watched the blister form and fill.

I wrenched my wrist from his grip and took off for my room, where my mother soon delivered an ice pack and a stack of Oreos. I stayed quiet. I wanted the Oreos, but I didn't want to need them, or an ice pack, either. My father had taught me the lesson he'd wanted, and a few more I wouldn't forget.

Alexandra, who was five years older than me, never seemed to provoke his anger the way I did—further proof that I was the problem, not him. Sure, he yelled at her, but not like he did at me. The reason was obvious: She was smarter and better behaved. And prettier. And cleaner. She had long, straight brown hair. I idolized her because she was older and had a room full of barrettes and magazines. When her friends came over, I'd sit outside her bedroom and whine until my mother forced them to play with me. But I didn't consider her an ally; I resented her ability to avoid our father's wrath, and for not crumpling under it like I did.

I wasn't afraid of my dad all the time. When he came home from his job at the Bank of Boston and shouted "I'm home," I ran to him almost as often as I ran from him. The direction depended on how recently and severely I'd been shouted at. If it had been a few days, I'd jump up and down while he took off his black coat and stood in the living-room doorway. I'd hop on one of his legs and wrap myself around it, and he'd swing me back and forth until his foot cramped. On many weekend mornings, I'd creep into my parents' dark room, made hot by their bodies, and slither into their bed. I'd climb on top of my father, who pretended to be a raft on the "great, grey-green, greasy Limpopo River" from Kipling's *Just So Stories*. As I balanced on his belly, he'd rock back and forth and identify the creatures he saw on the river's edge: cheetahs and crocodiles, hippos submerged to their nostrils. I'd inevitably hit a patch of rapids, and if they didn't succeed in capsizing me, a current I couldn't fight sent me over a booming waterfall that dumped me onto the floor.

My father also took my sister and me skiing in New Hampshire, where we had a small cabin that my parents had decorated with Native American and Western antiques. Wherever we were, if we found an arcade, he'd spend ten bucks playing Centipede and Skee Ball with me. If we couldn't get a good-enough prize with the tickets we'd earned, he'd offer up ten more. At Christmas, my father was usually able to control his temper for at least two days, which led me to think that the holiday, its decorations and traditions, might have magic powers. But those easy moments were erased by the ringing chaos that normally engulfed me.

I studied my small world and wondered why my parents were the way they were. I thought that they, my sister, the people down the street at the 7-Eleven orbited around only me. If my parents left the room, or I ran out of it, they froze in place. They haunted my thoughts, but they didn't continue living, acting, or being acted upon, and had come into existence when their children did.

I knew only the most basic elements of their lives. My mother worked; she did something with oceans and also maybe trees. Later I understood that she was the international vice president of the Sierra Club. Her position was unpaid and allowed her to work from home, but she traveled often to the club's headquarters in San Francisco and attended environmental conferences all over the world. She stood out in our WASP-y neighborhood with her multicultural collection of jewelry and clothing, and the cigarette dangling from her mouth. I thought she was beautiful. She was petite and blond, and she carried herself like a model though she had crooked, tobacco-stained teeth and a mole on her chin.

One of her favorite pieces of clothing was a black silk bomber jacket that she'd gotten in China, which had a fire-breathing dragon embroidered on its back. When she wore it to pick me up from nursery school or kindergarten, other kids would shout "Dragon Lady!" They'd turn to me. "Your mom is here. The Dragon Lady is here."

I'd demand they shut up, but they weren't scared of me, only of my mother. When she opened the gate to the playground, they'd stop. As we walked home, she held my hand in her left and a cigarette in her right, and I'd pull on her arm.

"Don't wear that jacket anymore," I'd beg. "Kids make fun of me. And you."

"Well that's not nice, but you should just ignore them."

"I can't!" I'd wail.

She laughed. "This jacket is very chic, Anya. I'm wearing it."

Though I hated that kids joked about my mom, I loved how she dressed and that she was different. My mother didn't do a lot of things that my friends' mothers did. It was my father who helped my sister and me get ready in the morning, who fed us and walked us to school. My mother spent her mornings sleeping, snoring loudly behind their bedroom door. I accepted that my mother slept late, just as I accepted that, if I had a nightmare, it was my father who arrived to comfort me with a Ukrainian lullaby, although the person I'd been crying for was my mother. I was attentive to the nuances of gender at a young age and understood why she rarely cooked or cleaned; it was boring. The few times the four of us ate dinner together, my father would end up screaming at my sister and me because we were slow, fussy eaters. Sometimes he chanted "Chew, chew, swallow, swallow, faster, faster," or turned off the light and left us to eat in the dark after he and my mother had finished and gone upstairs.

When he was away, and sometimes when he was home, my sister and I were in charge of feeding ourselves. At five and ten, we became experts with can openers and microwaves so we could eat our Chef Boyardee and Hungry-Man dinners. I wasn't mad that my mom didn't cook. I hated eating with my family and preferred eating alone. I would have swapped my parents for a completely new set if I could have, but since I couldn't, I liked being able to avoid them.

My mother's style matched her personality. When she and I ran into someone she knew, she laughed extra hard and rolled her eyes or hugged me tightly like a mom in a happy family sitcom. She was always telling stories and constantly repeated ones that I, and the rest of her audience, had heard before. Her best bits supported her two most important beliefs about herself: that she was a wonderful person and mother, and that she was a victim who'd suffered many injustices. The first relied on her tales of how, when she was a teenager, a stranger had spat on her Jewish friend, and she'd righteously stood up for him; and of how when Alexandra was three, she told her that "it doesn't really matter what color you are, just what kind of

person you are," and later heard my sister singing those lines to herself in the bath.

Strangers often complimented my name or said they'd never heard it before. If my mother was around, she'd chirp, "Thank you, I made it up." I believed her until I met another Anya in a pottery class when I was eight. I told my mother about it, but she dismissed me before I could ask all the questions that I suddenly had. She continued to tell people that she'd come up with the name herself, poof! When I later found a novel on her bookshelf with my name as its title, I brought it to her and waved it indignantly. "You didn't make up my name. This book is called *Anya*!" She told me it was a coincidence. I kept at her, desperate to have her admit she'd been lying, but she wouldn't give in.

Realizing that my mother lied took away not only her credibility but my belief that she was special. It suggested that she thought she needed to be more, a better woman than she was. I wondered why she had to tell her stories over and over. What was she asking of me, or her other listeners, by repeating these anecdotes until we could recite them along with her? She never even seemed to consider how they might land; she thought the meaning or moral that was obvious to her was what we'd take away, too. But that wasn't true of the story of me falling down the stairs. From that, I got not that I was brave but that when my father was cruel to me, my mother didn't stop him, a conclusion that was solidified when my father burned me.

Although she smiled and laughed a lot, I didn't believe my mom was happy. She looked like she was performing joyfulness, not feeling it. At home, I saw a cloud hovering around

her, and even when she was with people, I could sometimes see loneliness in her face when she glanced away or the light shifted. She was quick to obscure these shadows with a joke or a bark of laughter, but something trembled within her, and I didn't trust whatever it was.

The stories about the injustices of her life were even more practiced, such as the one she often told about the visit she made to her father, Roman, when she was twelve. He'd been in and out of mental institutions and had abandoned his family the day after my mother was born. When she appeared on his doorstep years later, he told her to leave. He and his new wife had company, and their guests didn't know about his other family. The first few times I heard this story, I was sad for my mother. Her dad was "crazy" and so mean he wouldn't even let her inside his house. Tales like these were presented less like stories than requests, or sometimes demands, for sympathy.

Though she was articulating one of the sources for the pain I'd glimpsed, I didn't believe that Roman was responsible for it. The explanation I chose was my own father. He was the reason for my heavy unhappiness, so I decided he was also the cause of hers. My mother broadcast her craving for attention and affection to him as often as she did to others, but he always seemed too uninterested or distracted to respond. She would talk to him with need or frustration in her voice as he frowned and leafed through whatever stack of papers he'd brought home, until her sentences trailed off into an exasperated "George!" My mother seemed to accept their dynamic; to me, this was further proof that they didn't love each other, and that my mother was weak.

A few days before Halloween, when I was eight, my father tried to help me carve a pumpkin. We fought about the design, and when I didn't give in, he dropped the knife abruptly and left the room. Having failed as a referee, my mother let me crawl into her lap and drench her shirt with tears.

"Mom," I whispered, "sometimes I don't love my daddy."

"That's all right," she said. "It's not always easy to love people."

I thought she was speaking to herself as well as to me.

I watched my father as closely as I did my mother but knew even less about him. I knew that he worked at a bank in a tall building downtown, and that his job was the reason he traveled so often to the Middle East and Africa. Though he sometimes made jokes, overall, he was serious. His skin and hair were darker than mine; he wore silver glasses and had a short, coarse beard. He wasn't tall, but to me he seemed huge.

Besides his temper, my father's most obvious attribute was that he was Ukrainian. He'd been born there and spoke the language with his parents and friends. I knew I was also Ukrainian, but only half, because my mother was Polish American. Being Ukrainian meant that my family made varenyky and borscht from scratch on Christmas; painted pysanky, the traditional Ukrainian Easter eggs; and went to a Ukrainian church on both holidays. Occasionally my father tried to teach me a bit of the language using cheap picture books, but he always gave up when I couldn't pronounce any of the words correctly or retain them. These details amounted to what being Ukrainian meant to me, but I didn't know what it meant to him.

My father told me three stories about his childhood. Unlike my mother, he only told his stories once. They all happened in Ukraine, where he was born in 1940 and which his family fled four years later. Two were about being attacked by farm animals, and one was about his family's rushed escape from their village in a horse-drawn cart. I couldn't conjure an image of his family's escape, a cart, danger. It didn't seem real and neither did Ukraine. Ukraine sounded like a setting for a dark fairy tale that offered no magic or redemption, a place that had nothing to do with me.

I learned much more about being Ukrainian from my father's younger sister, my aunt Lana; her husband, Gene; and my younger cousins, Larissa and Natalie. We spent holidays and occasional weekends at their home in Connecticut. Unlike my father, Lana married a Ukrainian, and their daughters were raised with a strong sense of cultural identity. When my grandfather Dymtro, whom we called "Did," died, my grandmother Irene, "Babtsia," moved in with them, and she contributed to and monitored the household's Ukrainianness.

Larissa and Natalie seemed foreign because they were so Ukrainian. They'd grown up speaking the language, going to a Ukrainian church, and attending Ukrainian scouts and summer camp. From them, I concluded that being Ukrainian meant being purposely distinct and dorky. I felt lucky that my father had raised me differently, but when my sister and I were with Aunt Lana's family, I noticed that he compared us to our cousins and that we didn't measure up.

Every Easter, as my father drove us to Connecticut for church and my aunt's traditional lunch of kovbasa, eggs, and babka, he'd drill us on the appropriate Easter greeting: *"Khrystos voskres"* (Christ is risen!), and its response, *"Voistynou voskres!"* (Indeed, He has risen!). We'd not only forgotten it from the year before but still couldn't get it right. He'd become more frustrated with every mile, repeating "*Khrystos voskres! Voistynou voskres!*" over and over as we sank into our seats and mangled the words. He'd slow down so he could safely drive while looking back at us, shouting "*Khrys-tos vos-kres!*" while my mother begged him to focus on the road. We'd have the phrase down when we pulled into my aunt and uncle's driveway, but we'd forget it by the time they opened their door. We'd mumble distant approximations until our father groaned and pushed us inside.

Babtsia was sweet to my sister and me, but she never missed an opportunity to remind us that we should speak Ukrainian like our cousins, who were the products of an appropriate union. She treated my father like a visiting dignitary; after giving him a formal hug, she sat him on the couch, brought him coffee or water and a plate of food, then sat close by and asked about his work, his take on current events. She was polite to my mother but rarely pleasant. My mother had told me that his parents had opposed their wedding and threatened not to attend because she was Polish. I didn't know why that was so important to them, or what risk they thought my father was taking or fate they believed he was courting by committing to my mom. I wouldn't find out until many years later.

In my memories of childhood, my father was always around, working at our long living-room table, reading an American or Ukrainian newspaper on the couch, or screaming at me. He felt inescapable. In truth, he was often gone—to Nigeria, Zimbabwe, or Turkey—for weeks at a time. My body relaxed in the easy quiet that settled in our home. My mom and I watched reruns of *Cheers* and *I Love Lucy* as we lay on their bed, and I could run through the house without being yelled at. I looked forward to my father's departures, but when my mother was going away for Sierra Club work, I'd follow her around hiccupping from the fear. I didn't want to be left alone with my dad. When she was traveling, he was even harder on me and even more difficult to avoid.

When my mother was able to join him, or when they just wanted to travel together, my mother's mother, Grandma Helen, came from Chicago to stay with us. She was the person I loved most in my family. She wore soft cardigans and faded housecoats, and padded through our house in pink slippers. She played endless games of Connect Four and Scrabble with us, and made us Wheatena for breakfast. Babtsia babysat us only once. I don't remember what happened, but my mother told me she demanded they come home early because we were so wild.

I didn't miss my parents when they were gone, even when their trips were almost a month long. Their absences were normal to me, and they felt like vacations, a break from shouting and fighting, and hiding.

Sometimes when my father was away alone, my mother's friend Bob would visit. She was girlish in his presence and seemed genuinely happy when he was there. I was happy, too. I adored Bob because he was funny and affectionate and never got angry. I wished I had him as a father instead of my own.

Once, when he and my mother were trying to get me to nap, I threw a tantrum because I didn't want to stop hanging out with them. I started stomping my feet, and Bob tried joking with me. He said, "Do you want to have a stomping contest?" and started stomping, too. He and my mother laughed, and I began to cry. I understood that they wanted to be alone and to have fun without me. After he left, my mother asked my sister and me not to tell my father that Bob had stayed with us. She made the same request after each of his visits.

My mother enjoyed her prettiness and the attention she received for it, as well as for her flamboyant style, but I looked like an urchin. I'd inherited my parents' terrible vision. Both of my eyes were weak, but one was even weaker than the other, and I began wearing thick glasses in kindergarten. Far more embarrassing was that I sometimes had to wear a flesh-colored eye patch to strengthen my weaker eye and prevent it from becoming permanently turned in. Adults and children gawked at me when I wore it in public, and I would become so upset that I'd remove it and throw it on the ground. One of my parents would be prepared with an extra and would press it on as I protested.

My hair was dark, somewhere between curly and wavy, and my mother kept it short. I envied my sister's long hair because she could wear pigtails and barrettes, and because it told strangers that she was a girl. They often thought I was a boy, and addressed me as one. "I'm not a boy," I'd wail as they went red and apologized.

This mistake was easy to make because my mother dressed me in gender-neutral clothes. Denim overalls and plain turtle-necks, sneakers without any pink on them. She dressed my sister the same, but her hair marked her as a girl. I was jealous that my friends got to wear skirts and dresses. When I asked my mother why I couldn't, she told me that she wanted me to be able to play like a boy, to hang on the jungle gym without having to worry about showing my underwear. I wanted to play like a boy, but I also wanted people to see my underwear.

I was tiny, always the smallest in my class, and though I'd been a chubby baby, I quickly developed my mother's slight frame. Because my ribs stuck out, my sister called me "the Ethiopian," telling me that I looked like the starving children we saw on the news and who our parents invoked when we didn't finish our food. Doctors were concerned by my size and inability to gain weight, and X-rays of my hands or feet were a part of my annual checkups. I loved getting X-rays, wearing the heavy lead shirt, being in the room alone, and getting to see my bones. But in the films my doctors saw problems. They were worried because my hands were the size of a five-year-old's, not an eight-year-old's. Their assessments supported my father's: Something was wrong with me. I was supposed to be different, better than I was.

When I started school, my deficiencies became even more conspicuous. I was a slow reader, had terrible handwriting and spelling, didn't get math, and couldn't sit still. I started working with a specialist, but my work didn't improve. My problems in school sparked a new anger in my father. It was sharp and obsessive, wild and guaranteed.

When he was away, I did my homework on the living-room floor or on my bed. My mother would help me when I got confused and sometimes looked over my work to make sure it had been done, but she seemed happy to cede responsibility for my education to the school. When he was in Boston, my father was in charge of my homework, and doing it was a battle I came to dread. When he got home from work and was ready for me, he'd call my name and I'd limp toward him, queasy with despair.

He made me sit at the long wooden table my parents had bought when they'd lived in London. It was the same place where he worked on evenings and weekends. Under his tight gaze, I'd spread out my sheets of math problems and hand-writing exercises, a passage to read and respond to. I started with math. I'd clutch a yellow pencil and read the instructions aloud. My father was impatient before I even began, correcting my pronunciation and sighing. "Come on, you know that word."

I talked my way through each problem so he could understand my approach, and with every correction, I became more hesitant. I pulled my worksheet toward my chest. As his patience drained, his breath became short and fast. Sensing his annoyance, I started to rush, to get somewhere near an answer and jot down a number.

"Anya!" He grabbed the pencil and slammed it down. "That answer is wrong, and you know it. Do it again!"

I picked up the pencil, but I was so nervous that I blurted out another wrong answer.

He sighed and walked away, then returned. "Do the work."

What did it mean to "do the work"? You either knew the answer or you didn't. I guessed again.

"What are you, stupid?" he hissed.

Stupid. The word made my entire body ache. I cringed as my eyes filled with tears. I kept my head still, trying not to blink, and hoped that they wouldn't escape.

"Are you?"

"No," I bleated, and my tears, so many more than I'd thought could be in my head, leaked out.

"Stop," he yelled. "Don't be a crybaby."

I wanted to protest, but I couldn't. I was a crybaby. If my mother walked in, I'd slide off my chair, attach myself to her legs, and beg her to do my homework with me instead. My father would tell her to leave, and she would, but only after telling him to "go easy" on me in a voice so flat that I realized she knew he wouldn't. I'd crawl back to my seat feeling even more alone than before.

When we got to penmanship, my father pointed to the letter or word I was supposed to be copying, and to what I'd written below. "Does this look like that?"

I shook my head.

"Do it right."

"I can't."

"You can," he said. "Don't be stupid."

I tried again, but not really. I couldn't think clearly.

"What's wrong with you! You're not even trying."

I wailed, hoping my mother would hear me.

"Be quiet," he finally exploded, shouting as loudly as I just had. "You're such a crybaby!"

I hated myself for having so many flaws, and I tried to fix them. I filled countless black-and-white composition books with scribbly lines of "The quick brown fox jumped over the lazy old dog." I made math flash cards and tried to memorize them. I hoped I could change into a child he would love.

The fear I felt around him was unbearable, and I started

getting severe headaches. They happened at school most frequently, although sometimes they'd find me on weekends.
They started behind my forehead and radiated around my
skull. When they took hold, I'd whimper and rub my palms
against my temples.

Questions from the school nurse led to questions from
doctors. "Did you recently hit your head?" prompted me to
remember that I'd knocked my head against a wall during
recess the month before. I remembered the accident, but it
hadn't been bad. I'd gone to the nurse and gotten some ice and
children's aspirin. This was the only information they seemed
to find helpful. I underwent CAT scans and other tests, but
none of them revealed a problem. They weren't migraines,
there wasn't a tumor. No one was sure what to do, and I de-
tected a strain of suspicion beneath the questions. Were my
headaches real?

They were. What brought them on was encountering difficult schoolwork such as new math or grammatical concepts,
and my anxiety when my father saw me struggling to understand it. If I didn't get something the first time it was taught,
I believed it would stay hard for me. The pain felt like the result of my brain working really hard and swelling with stress.
Succumbing to it was a way to push off the inevitable for at
least a little while. My headaches were an exit, a way to not
hear whatever was being taught, so I wouldn't anger my father
when he saw that I'd failed to master the lesson.

I wanted to tell my mother that I didn't need to go to the
doctor or lie in strange machines. I knew the cause of my headaches. It was obvious: I was stupid, my brain was broken. I didn't

think I could change, but I wondered if my father could. She saw how he approached the problem of his daughter, and how it failed to produce the result he seemed to want—a breakthrough or flash of understanding, a daughter he could be proud of, a daughter he could love. I wished he'd accept the failure that I was and leave me alone.

CHAPTER TWO

Ghosts

*W*hen I was ten, I was walking home from the play-ground with my friends Hillary and Shira, along with Shira's nanny, a tired Irish woman whom I saw more frequently than Shira's parents. I'd known Hillary and Shira since preschool—we lived in the same neighborhood and played together often— but Hillary and I were much closer than either of us were with Shira. We were *best friends* and fixtures at each other's houses; she'd often come to New Hampshire with my family or I'd go to Martha's Vineyard with hers. Shira could be bossy and a little mean, but her parents regularly pressured us into includ-ing her—or worse, spending time with her alone. Shira often made fun of me for not doing well in school. She also reported the things her parents said about me, such as their surprise when she'd told them that I wanted to be a zoologist—they couldn't believe I wanted a career with such a complicated name. They thought their daughter was too good for me, but I was one of her few options.

As we made our way home, Shira's nanny asked if I had any siblings, and I told her that I had an older sister.

Shira perked up. "You had a brother, too. But he's dead."

"No, I didn't." I laughed and looked at her nanny. "I didn't have a brother."

"You did," Shira insisted. "My mom told me."

I was used to Shira making proclamations or correcting me with an adult's authority, and I knew that she lied. We all did, if we wanted to win an argument about who owned the most pairs of jeans or to make one of our fantasies sound real. Shira was a mermaid like Madison in *Splash* because she ate shrimp with their tails on; I was a witch because I'd asked my cat Mischa if he was a witch's cat, and he'd winked. But we lied about ourselves, not each other. I knew what she'd said wasn't true, but I didn't know how to prove it. I could call her a liar, but I couldn't call her mother one.

"I did not," I said again. "Stop."

"You did have one," Shira sang. "You did."

Her nanny moved between us and said, "That's enough, girls."

There was something different about this lie: the outrageousness of the claim, the tone of Shira's delivery, her mother's involvement. It lingered among my thoughts until it was replaced by more immediate concerns, like what snacks were at home and watching *ThunderCats*.

Grandma Helen came to visit a few weeks later. One afternoon, she, my mother, Alexandra, and I were goofing around in my sister's room, trying to recite a television commercial for long-distance phone service.

"Talk to your mother," my mom said.

"Talk to your plants!" I shouted.

"No!" My sister laughed. "Call your mother, call your brother."

Brother! The word summoned the memory of my conversation with Shira. I turned to my mother asked, "Did I have a brother?"

The question flew from my mouth like I was merely asking what time it was, but it landed with a thud and sucked everything in the room to it, including people's smiles. Alexandra, my mother, and Grandma Helen exchanged uncomfortable looks. My grandmother and sister left the room, and my mother joined me on the edge of the bed.

I didn't like what was happening or how it was happening: really slowly, but also really fast. The air was churning. I wanted to grab it and force it to be still.

"Yes," my mother said slowly, "you had a brother. His name was Yuri. He was born after Alexandra, while we still lived in London. He died two months before his first birthday."

I shut my eyes, found the edge of my sister's mattress beneath her sheets, and held on to it. I thought I'd mastered my unsteady environment by teaching myself to expect disasters and danger, and to never relax. But that had only been train-ing, and not a very good one. My mother had revealed that my immediate world was much bigger than I thought it was. It had a place, maybe many places, that I didn't know about. They'd always been there, I just hadn't been able to see them.

She guided me downstairs to her bedroom. I lay on the unmade bed while she collected two pictures of Yuri—one from the top of her dresser, another from its bottom drawer. The photograph on her dresser had always been there. In it, Yuri was around six months old, and Alexandra was offering him a red block as my mother beamed between them. I'd asked my mother who the baby was when I was very young, and she'd said his name, "Yuri. That's Yuri." She didn't tell me that he was my brother or that he was dead. In the other picture, the one I'd never seen, he was only a few days old. He was asleep in a hospital nursery, and my sister was peering down at him through a large window. I recalled a picture in my sister's photo album of my mother smiling over a double pram, and realized that Yuri had to be the other baby. He hadn't been hidden from me, exactly, but his true identity had never been revealed.

I looked at the photograph that I'd seen before. It had changed. That baby was now my brother. I was older than he'd ever been, but I was his younger sister. "Brother" didn't seem like the right word, since we'd never met. My sister had a brother, not me.

My mother explained that Yuri had died from pneumonia. She and my father were very sad when he died. My father had cradled his body and whispered "My son, my son, my son" as he wept. They'd been worried they wouldn't be able to conceive again. "You were our miracle baby," she told me. "Your father was hoping for another boy, but the second he held you, he was just so happy to have another child." She stroked my hair. "We didn't tell you about Yuri because we didn't want you to feel like you were a replacement."

She explained that she'd told Shira's mother about Yuri, assuming they were talking in confidence. She wondered why Shira's mother, a therapist and professor of psychology, thought it was appropriate to share the information with her daughter, who had "such a big mouth. But you shouldn't be mad at Shira," she said. "She didn't know what she was doing."

If there had been less agony in her voice, I might have been proud to be such a thing, a miracle, me. But I didn't want to be one. I was so sad for Yuri. I wanted him to be alive, and I wanted to be normal. A dead baby was terrible; it should have been impossible. I felt haunted by his presence as well as his absence. He was there, and he wasn't. He'd always been there, and I hadn't known. I didn't *want* to know about him. I wanted things to go back to the way they were before I'd asked my question, back to a way they'd never actually been.

We both cried, but I wanted to be the only one who was upset. My mother's pain indicated yet another world, one that was hers, one I didn't want to be in. If she needed comfort too, she wouldn't be able to take care of me. If she was that vulnerable, I was even more helpless and alone than I'd previously felt.

She told me that she was still sad about Yuri and thought about him every day. Then she shared a story. She'd once accompanied my father to dinner at his colleague's house in Zimbabwe. Afterward, the men went to smoke cigars and discuss work and politics, while the women drank tea and talked. The hostess complained that her maid was taking time off because she'd lost a child. My mother suggested that this woman might have some sympathy for her employee, and the woman said, "These people are used to losing children. It isn't a big deal to them."

"I wanted to *strangle* her," my mother said. "To slap her and say, 'How dare you? A mother *never* gets over losing her child.'" Although my mother loved showing me pictures of her trips and things she collected abroad, she didn't tell many long stories about what happened when she was away. Once this story had been introduced, it joined the canon.

My father was out of town when we had this talk, and though I assumed that my mother told him about it, he never spoke of Yuri to me. I found myself looking for Yuri over my shoulder, wondering if he'd always been following me, hiding under my bed or in my desk at school.

On a Sunday morning a few months later, while my family was spending the weekend in New Hampshire, my mother told me to eat breakfast quickly because we were going to church.

I looked up from my yogurt. "Why?"

"It's the anniversary of Yuri's death," she said. "Try to find a nice shirt."

I put on a fuzzy green sweater that had once been Alexandra's, the nicest thing I had in my collection of ski clothes, and zipped up my parka until the old lift tickets scraped my chin.

We went to a small brick church on the outskirts of the closest town. It was more like an office building than Boston's dramatic churches, which had spires, turrets, and stained-glass windows. It was a regular Sunday service. Families clustered in the middle of waxed pews, and people who'd come alone sat in the back or close to the aisle. I stood, sat, knelt, and said "Amen," but I didn't listen to the priest. I thought about how bored I was, and that I was cold, and wondered what we'd eat for lunch. Maybe we'd go to the town's one restaurant, since it was kind of a special occasion. Maybe I'd be allowed to get a sundae.

My attention was pulled back when I saw that the empty pew in front of me was shaking. I glanced at my father; he was clutching the back of it and convulsing with grief, his mouth contorted by gasps and groans. His pain was louder than my mother's had ever been. It wasn't pleading; it was violent. I shrank against the pew, horrified by his transformation. Like my mother's grief, his also scared me, but in a different way. Hers made me think that she might not be strong enough to ever be relied on, but his made me wonder what else he could do to me.

When I looked at him after the service, he was back to normal, but I knew that whatever force had overtaken him could come back. I thought that if I could examine his insides as I had my own, the X-ray would reveal that a calcified deposit of melancholy held his body together and not a frame of bones.

We didn't go to the restaurant. We drove the twenty minutes back to our cabin and each claimed our own space. I sat in the loft where my sister and I slept on the long, checkered futon that Velcroed together to make a couch, and put a book I'd already read in front of my face.

Thinking about that morning in church made me so

uncomfortable that I batted its images and sounds away as if they were flies. I tried to do the same with the conversation I'd had with my mother. I didn't want to think about that, either. All I knew was that a change had occurred because a truth had been exposed. Not only did I have a dead brother but my parents had secrets, and I didn't know everything about the world we shared. We were operating with different maps. Mine had blank spaces, entire continents I'd never heard of.

My life was the same, but I was different. I was listless and morose. I didn't attach these feelings to learning about Yuri as a person, my brother, a fact or event. I didn't attach them to anything, so they grew without my help or awareness as I wandered through my days. My father still yelled at me about homework, but my reactions, and my efforts to make him happy, were dulled. Only my headaches were sharp.

A few months later, when I was in fourth grade, I found myself alone in the girls' bathroom. After I peed, I looked over the white walls. They were bright and blank. I'd never seen anything on them, no scrawls or stickers. I found the short pencil I had in my pocket and wrote, "I hate me," in small letters next to the toilet.

I was working at my desk that afternoon when my teacher crouched next to me and whispered for me to come with her. I followed her into the bathroom and the red stall I'd occupied earlier, where she silently pointed at the wall. I'd already forgotten what I'd done just a few hours ago.

I froze. I'd done something really bad. My teacher was mad. She'd call my father, he'd be madder, and I'd be in trouble.

But my teacher wasn't angry. She put the toilet seat down,

sat on it, and opened her arms, then nodded when I hesitated. I got on her lap and exploded into tears. When I calmed down, she asked why I hated myself.

"Because I'm stupid." I sniffled.

"You're not stupid," she said.

I insisted that I was.

She shook her head, then took out a long pink eraser. She placed it in my hand, then watched as I made what I'd written disappear. I never told my parents what happened, and they never asked me about that incident. But soon I was taken to a hospital for an educational and psychological evaluation, the first of many I'd receive over the next few years.

As the three of us sat in a waiting room full of families and wooden toys, I tried to guess what was wrong with the other kids. Eventually a cheerful doctor arrived and called my name. Long, shiny hallways led to a series of small rooms where I was told to copy drawings, memorize sequences of shapes, and list as many words as I could that started with the letter *F* in one minute. Several doctors casually asked questions about my feelings and my family.

I found the results of this evaluation when I was cleaning out my mother's house. It gave detailed descriptions of my performance—I was able to identify single words up to a seventh-grade level on an oral reading test, but my active working memory was well below age expectations. It listed my different learning disabilities before going into a psychological assessment.

Anya, herself, is a very fidgety ten-year-old girl . . . She described in some detail how she cries when her daddy yells at her. She states that when dad is away on business trips, things are much quieter and that he yells at her too much for having messy handwriting. She states that sometimes she is scared more when her mother is out of the house, not for fear of any type of abuse, but rather that father would yell more at her. Her specific wish was that her father not yell at her and that she had more friends and better handwriting . . . She also felt that she felt sad more than other children and also felt that many other children were smarter than she was.

This lucid articulation of my unhappiness was devastating when I first read it. Typed tightly on a page I could hold, a page I knew my parents had held as well, those words chiseled me back to child size and soaked me in the terror that spilled out whenever I'd heard my father's voice. They also soothed me. I hadn't retrospectively fabricated or embellished how I'd felt as a kid from an adolescent or adult perch.

Doctors also spoke to my parents, who told them about my headaches and about Yuri. The report stated,

Prior to Anya's birth, parents had another male child who died in infancy. That fact was kept confidential from Anya until just recently. Approximately three to four months ago, a friend told Anya that, in fact, she had a brother who died.

I didn't know if I'd brought up Yuri when speaking with the doctors, or if my parents had told them. The evaluation simply states that I told the doctor I found out about Yuri from a friend, and that I went to church with my family on the anniversary of his death.

It continued,

> Anya admits to being sad at times, but does not have any persistent depression that lasts for any longer period than a day. She admits to spontaneously crying and stated that "everybody likes to pick on me." She has transient self-destructive ideation and has thought about hurting herself with either a knife or jumping into water, although she has never made any attempt to hurt herself. Notably, most of these thoughts were several months in the past and she currently denies any active suicidal ideation.

The doctors concluded that there were

> many potential psychological dynamics that may impact on Anya's headaches. This would include the report that Anya perceives that her father yells at her too much, that Anya was told about her brother's death after such a long time, as well as potential intrinsic depression characteristics that Anya has evidenced in the past.

I didn't associate my sadness with Yuri. To me, everything was about my father.

I was put into therapy immediately. My therapist was probably in her forties, but she seemed far older, ancient even, like a witch, not because she was wrinkled or hunched but because she was so cold. Her questions—"How are you feeling," "Tell me about your father"—were clinical and flat. I answered her as if I were being quizzed. I was honest but not open. I sat on my hands, swung my legs, and looked around the room and tried to do "well," but I didn't understand what talking to her was supposed to accomplish. She met with my sister once, and with my mother, and once with all three of us. If she met with my father, or with my parents together, I didn't know about it. She was fixated on my brother's death, seeming to think that was what was causing my headaches and depression. I didn't argue and say no, it was my father. I didn't think she'd believe me.

I stopped seeing that therapist after complaining that I didn't like her. My mother told me she didn't like her very much, either, and took me to another one, a man who was animated and liked to watch me play games. Though he was friendly, I felt the way I had with the first therapist: confused about why I was there and what was supposed to be happening. I never left therapy feeling hopeful or more prepared to handle my life. But I suppose some part of it must have been effective, because without my noticing, I stopped having headaches and didn't have to visit so many doctors.

The following year, the Bank of Boston dissolved their Middle East and Africa division. My father was given a chance to find a domestic position within the bank, but he couldn't find one he liked, so he started a consulting company. He no longer needed to take the long trips I depended on for the breaks they gave me. He was always around and was usually grumpy and short. His focus on finding clients and generating income became a sort of shield. He paid less attention to me and my homework, though I knew I could still do something, many things, to make him snap, and acted accordingly.

My mother left her job at the Sierra Club and began teaching ESL to adults in the workplace, so there was some money coming in. She loved teaching and told me stories about her classes. I pretended I wasn't interested because I didn't want to be interested in anything about her, but I liked hearing about her students—Cambodian refugees who became nurses, Iranian physicians who'd had to become janitors—and their questions: the best way to address a boss's spouse, what to wear to a work party, if Halloween was devil worship that would corrupt their children.

If my parents fought about money, I didn't hear them, but my mother worried about it in front of me. She told me that our family's income had plummeted, but that our expenses were increasing. My sister would be in college in a few years.

My father spent two years trying to establish a consulting business before finally finding a job with a company in Saudi Arabia that suited his background and interests. My mom had been pushing him to look for a "real job," but she told him he couldn't take this one. I didn't know what the job was, only that if he took it, he'd live in a compound, and when we visited, we'd live there, too.

My mother was incensed that he was even considering taking the position and told him that she'd divorce him if he accepted the offer. She tried to get my sister and me on her side by telling us a story we'd already heard many times. In the seventies, my parents were detained at the Riyadh airport when security found a small, old bottle of whiskey in my father's camera bag, something he'd probably swiped from a hotel mini-bar. They shouted at him as he apologized and explained that he wasn't trying to smuggle alcohol into the country, he'd simply forgotten he had it on him. They rummaged through his suitcase and found another.

"How many more?" the officers shouted. "How many more?"

My parents were held separately for hours. Every thirty minutes, a sneering man would come into my mother's cell and tell her that she would never see her husband again. They were only released after the American embassy got involved. My father accepted the job in Saudi Arabia despite her threats, but my mother never had the chance to make good on them.

During this time, the Soviet Union began experiencing seismic unrest. Like many of its other territories, Ukraine was agitating for independence. In 1990, the Soros Foundation offered my father a job as one of the directors of Ukraine's first national bank, and he took it instead of the job in Saudi Arabia. His plan, he told us, was to spend two years in the position. He'd come back to America for a few weeks every few months.

My father didn't tell me why he was working in Ukraine, and I didn't ask. He was gone, just like I'd always wished. There was much more space around me and in my head. The difference in my life was so great that I often thought about him dying; if that happened, I'd be rid of him forever. I imagined his funeral and how sad my mother would be. These fantasies made me feel guilty, but they were also thrilling.

I didn't consider how my mother felt, or how his departure changed her life. After twenty-three years of marriage, her husband was gone. He wasn't away on a business trip; he'd moved to a country where he could rarely make international calls, and where he couldn't be called, even though he lived in the nicest hotel in Kiev. My parents mostly communicated via fax. My dad's came in the middle of the night. The machine's screech and buzz reached me in my bedroom and snapped me awake. In the morning, I'd find a note for my mother so long that it reached the floor and curled into itself.

I was happy, or could have been happy if my life hadn't also suddenly gone in a new direction. The year my father left, I started middle school. I'd failed to test into Boston Latin, the city's best public school, and because my parents feared I'd "get lost" at another public school, I'd applied to a bunch of suburban private schools and was rejected by all but the worst two. My parents decided that I'd go to the one that was coed and that I'd repeat sixth grade instead of going into seventh. They told me I wasn't prepared to be a seventh grader at this new school, where I'd have science and foreign-language classes for the first time. They also said I was too small to go into seventh grade. I *was* small, but I didn't grasp why that mattered. I protested, indignant about the decision and that it had been made without me, and at my parents' dismissive response: "You'll be fine."

After commuting for forty minutes on the subway and then walking a mile, I entered my new school boiling with a mixture of defiance and insecurity. I wanted to be everyone's favorite friend, but I also wanted to shun my peers because I was older than they were. I wore my favorite jean jacket, which I'd covered in Guns N' Roses patches and pins, and was delighted when I heard the other girls talk about the New Kids on the Block. It gave me the perfect opportunity to roll my eyes and establish that I was the sophisticated one from the city.

The students were the first rich suburban kids I'd ever met. They went to expensive summer camps, had lots of clothes, cared about having boyfriends and girlfriends. I could ride the subway by myself, which none of them were allowed to do, but I was totally unequipped to survive in their world. I'd arrived with an attitude that I hoped would elevate and protect me, but they had a Machiavellian understanding of social dynamics and power cultivated in basement rec rooms. At my old school, where almost everyone in my twelve-person class had been together since first grade, there were no cliques; everyone, at least all the girls, were friends. At my new school, girls paired off instantly so they'd have a best friend, and no one chose me. I had thick glasses and hopeless hair, and was both too eager to be liked and too obnoxious. I looked and acted like everyone's least favorite little sister; I wouldn't have chosen me, either.

Sixth grade the second time around was full of rejection and judgment as bad as my father's. Previously, his voice had been the only one besides my own telling me I was terrible. School was the place where I could usually avoid it. But I quickly understood that home was now my refuge since he was gone, and school was the place to hide.

Other students gleefully told me that I was ugly and weird. They ganged up on me in all the ways kids do at that age, making fun of me for not having breasts and for loving heavy metal, and I became twitchy and apprehensive. Sometimes I'd have a friend for a week or two, but they'd always drop me and I'd again find myself alone. Every day when I arrived, I wondered if something had changed the night before, if a new alliance had been forged over a series of phone calls and given me a new fate. It usually had, and I'd wander between classes with what felt like a fatal case of the left-outs.

I hadn't ever fought back against my father because I was too afraid of him, and though I was often in trouble, it was rarely because I'd done something on purpose. I was getting yelled at enough; misbehaving wasn't worth it. Once he left and I began having so many problems at school, I felt I had to rebel against my enemies, new and old.

I didn't do my homework, picked fights, violated the dress code, failed tests, and received weekly detentions that turned into full-day Saturday detentions where I had to clean the cafeteria. When I finally got some friends and a little bit of power, I became just as cruel and conniving as the kids who'd terrorized me as our alliances continually shifted. I'd be swapped out when a cooler prospect had showed interest, or when someone's parents, having heard that I might be a bad influence, warned their child away from me. I'd try to insulate myself by recruiting anyone I could, and found boys to be the easiest gets. I flirted with them, hoping it would help. But some of them—particularly those who were similarly ostracized—wanted to be my friend anyway, so all that did was start rumors that I was a slut.

My mother begged, then yelled at me to do a better job on my homework, to get along with people, dress normal. I begged, and sometimes yelled, that I wanted to go to another school. I told her how mean the kids were. How miserable I was. But she was convinced that I was the source of all my problems. Every time I reported someone's cruel deed, she asked me what I did to cause it. What was I doing that made the kids not like me? Why couldn't I just dress and act like everyone else?

I couldn't be like them because I wasn't, and I didn't want to be. I liked different music. I wasn't rich. My mom didn't drive me to school or to the mall. I wanted to be myself, but I also wanted my classmates' acceptance as much as I had wanted my father's. They made me feel like a mutant. I tried to pretend that I didn't care and was mean when I thought it could help. But I walked the halls nauseated, knowing that at any moment someone would tease me and I'd have to force myself not to cry. I was sick with the expectation that girls wouldn't let me sit with them at lunch, or that they'd laugh when I spoke in class.

At the end of the year, I started seeing the school psychologist. I loved her because she let me talk endlessly about my problems with the other kids and didn't blame me for my problems. Talking to her was my favorite hour of the week, and I continued to see her for the next two years.

When seventh grade came, the majority of my classmates had their bar and bat mitzvahs. Suddenly, I had to be out in the suburbs on weekends for a service in the morning and a party in the evening. Even though my classmates had to invite everyone, I was excited to be included and to have the chance to redeem myself by showing I was likable. But my mom refused to drive to the suburbs twice in one day, so she only drove me to the evening celebrations. I didn't want to go to temple, but I knew it was wrong to only go to the party because my friends' parents always commented that I'd skipped the service. When I explained this to her and begged her to please, please get me to both, she told me the drive was too long, and added that it was ridiculous that my classmates' parents were throwing such extravagant parties for their children, with booths where you could record your own music videos, chocolate fountains you could dip Twizzlers in, and personalized cameras already loaded with film. I believed she was being selfish and making my life harder when I badly needed her to help make it easier.

I'd never owned a party dress, and since my mother refused to buy me one, I begged a friend in eighth grade to loan me hers. I knew I couldn't wear a dress more than once, and agreed with my mother that the ones I was loaned, or looked at in stores, were too shiny or covered with too many rhinestones. But I also wished she'd just buy me a stupid ugly pretty dress so I could fit in for once. When she refused, I used birthday money to buy a tight black Betsey Johnson dress, which I hoped would be more successful at telegraphing my coolness than my jean jacket. However, what it seemed to tell my peers was that I was officially and undoubtedly a slut.

The word stuck this time, though I didn't know why. Sure, I dressed kind of "slutty" and flirted with boys, but I wasn't doing anything beyond making out with them. In a way, I liked the word. It made me feel dangerous and exotic, more complicated than "weird." I'd been veering toward goth, and being a slut gave me the final push. I wore low-cut velour shirts, spray-painted my shoes, piled on the makeup no one else was allowed to wear. I dyed my hair red, then blond, then maroon. I was frightened of actual sex but interested in the power I could have over boys.

I liked pushing boundaries, but I wasn't good at dealing

with the name-calling and rumors that resulted. I wanted people to like me, and when they didn't, I became impulsive, then explosive. I'd had to swallow so much rage in front of my father; I couldn't hold it in anymore. And since he was gone, I felt free to express all of it, but I wasn't in control of what erupted. Anger at him, at my mother, anger at everyone and everything.

One weekend, I had a friend over. Chloe wasn't very cool, but I was happy to have a friend for a bit and liked that my mother didn't like her. I'd gotten some fireworks on a trip to New York, and I decided that we should light one and toss it out the window.

My mother heard the noise and started screaming my name from the kitchen. Chloe and I went downstairs and found my mother cooking. She yelled at me about how dangerous what I'd done was. I knew she was right. If I'd bothered thinking about it, I wouldn't have done it. But I hadn't. I apologized, but she wasn't done. She turned her anger on Chloe, who was standing silently next to me. "You always do something bad when she's around."

I was incensed that she'd attack my friend. "It was my idea," I said. "Not hers."

She didn't seem to hear me. Her eyes were fixed on Chloe, who was looking at the ground.

"It wasn't her fault. Apologize to her," I said.

My mother refused, and said that Chloe needed to call her parents and have them pick her up. Chloe looked at me nervously.

I felt protective of Chloe, who like me wasn't popular with

kids or their parents. I knew my mother was echoing things she'd heard before. "Say you're sorry."

My mother said no.

There was a long knife on the counter next to a stack of carrots. I picked it up and pointed it at my mom.

"Say it," I hissed. I held it firmly while my mother and Chloe stared at me. It made me feel powerful, as did the terror twisting my mother's face.

"Put that down," she said quietly.

Again, I told her to apologize. I needed her to make the situation right. "Do it."

She did. I placed the knife back on the counter. Chloe's parents picked her up, but my mother didn't talk to them. I spent the rest of the night in my room blasting Mötley Crüe and feeling satisfied. I'd gotten what I wanted. I could hear my mother talking on the phone in the quiet between songs and felt safe knowing that she wasn't talking to my father. She couldn't get in touch with him. We never spoke of that incident, and though I'm sure she told my dad about it, he never brought it up. Neither did the school psychologist. I took this to mean that I'd successfully asserted my power, and I thought I was done with being bullied. Years later, I learned from Aunt Arlene, my mother's sister, that my mother had told her, and many other people, about what I'd done, and that I'd terrified her.

When my father swept into town after weeks in Ukraine, he saw that our lives in Boston were continuing in a way he didn't like. Alexandra had started college in western Massachusetts, so it was only the three of us. He'd try to impose order, reinstate the rules and structure that my mother had abandoned. He didn't care that my hair was always a different color or that I wore pounds of dark makeup and combat boots, but he hated how bad my grades were and that my mother was obviously not doing enough about it. He'd tell me when I had to be home and when I could or couldn't go out, reminding me that I wasn't actually free of him. I raged to myself when I encountered his obstacles, but I suffered them because I knew they'd disappear when he did.

I still didn't know anything about his job. I didn't ask what he did; instead, I asked my mother when he was leaving. I also didn't ask about the strange things that appeared in our house, including enormous boxes of *kupon,* the interim currency that my father helped develop to replace the ruble. Inflation in Ukraine was so rapid that the *kupon* was near-worthless upon printing. It looked like Monopoly money and was barely more valuable. My sister and I would throw fistfuls of it in the air and at each other when she was home on break, fill our claw-foot tub with them so we could bathe in money and pretend we were the richest kids in the world, and try to pay with them at the 7-Eleven down the block.

That year, my father left his position at the National Bank of Ukraine after a year and a half. When I asked my mother why, she simply said, "Corruption." Instead of returning to Boston as he'd promised, he established the first venture capital fund in Ukraine with the help of one of our neighbors, David, who ran such funds in China. My father promised my mother it would only be a few more years of back and forth. His plan was to make the fund successful enough that he could manage it from Boston.

In eighth grade, life at school became particularly bad after a new friend I'd had for almost a year turned against me and went after me ruthlessly. She and another girl took markers to the bathroom and wrote all over its walls and stalls that I was a slut; the school had to close the bathroom for a week so it could be cleaned. The following month, she stole my copy of the script for a play I was in and wrote the same thing on its pages. Teachers I spoke to said they couldn't prove who did it, and I knew better than to tell my mother what was happening, so I walked around feeling the way I had as a kid—like an open target. It didn't matter that I had some friends. Nothing made me feel safe. I assumed this was what life would always be like for me.

At the time, I had an obsessive crush on Josh, a boy in the ninth grade. Lots of girls had crushes on him, but mine was the most obvious because I followed him around and giggled whenever he spoke. One day, I noticed that people were staring at me more than they usually did as I walked between classes, and that the high-school girls laughed whenever I passed them. I grabbed a friend and demanded she tell me what was happening. "People are saying you gave Josh a blow job in the library," she said quietly. I was more shocked than hurt by the rumor. I'd never even seen a penis in real life, and I didn't want to. I'd given my summer boyfriend access to my whole body, and he'd used it happily, but even when I was naked, his jeans stayed on. Unlike the many others I'd endured, this rumor had traction, and by the end of the day, I was summoned to the principal's office.

The principal and I were already enemies. British and in her sixties, she'd come to the school that year. She'd tried to be nice to me, but I refused to be nice back. I sat on her long floral couch as she pulled her chair out from behind her desk and sat down across from me.

Finally, she said, "I suppose you've heard the terrible rumor going around."

I burst into tears. I was mad that I was crying in front of her, but it probably helped her believe me. "I didn't do it!" I said.

She asked if I knew who started the rumor. I told her I figured it was the high-school girls who always made snide comments about my clothing.

When I was finally calm, she told me that she was going to call my mother. "Please don't," I begged. "It's stupid. She doesn't need to know."

She told me she had to.

After school, I walked into the living room and threw down my backpack. When my mother spoke my name from the couch, I groaned. I dragged myself over and sat as far away from her as I could. "Your principal called." When I didn't speak, she continued. "She was so upset. She told me, 'I can't even say the word.'" She started to laugh, but caught herself.

I crammed my face into a pillow. "I didn't *do* it."

My mother nodded. There was nothing either of us could say that we hadn't said before.

I didn't understand how alone my mother was, or how she'd come to resent my father's absence during this period until months later, when she mentioned that she'd once called him to vent about my behavior, though she didn't say what I'd done to prompt the call. She was excited that she'd actually been able to reach him, but he'd interrupted her rant and said that he had tickets to a concert and didn't want to be late. "He has a life there now," she told me sadly. He'd created a world for himself that didn't include her. She was solely responsible for dealing with me and all of my problems.

I understood the extent of the distance between them when I found a fax he sent her for Mother's Day in 1993.

Hi! We don't have any real contact with the U.S. calendar here so it was only this morning when several U.S. types got together that someone mentioned that yesterday may have been Mother's Day. If that is the case, please accept deep and humble apologies for not having properly noted this important day!

Be it hereby duly noted and proclaimed that the finest, sexiest, and generally kinkiest mother in the world is one said Anita Kieras Yurchyshyn. A pillar of strength and inspiration to her daughters, an awesome source of love, support, and erotic dreams to her husband and a general source of liveliness and linguistic communications to the community.

We all respect her deeply and love her intensely. Happy Mother's Day!

Love, George

When I read it, I was annoyed at my dad for forgetting a holiday that may have been important to her, but I couldn't comprehend how hurt and invisible she may have felt.

Since I was still struggling with my schoolwork, my teachers and my therapist recommended I be evaluated yet again. The report, which is covered in my mother's illegible notes, stated that I was there for issues with "spelling, behavior, fine motor difficulties, and peer relationships." My school had told the doctors that I was

> extremely hyperactive and impulsive, demanding of attention and sulking if deprived . . . explosive behaviorally, and appeared to have difficultly separating her personal preoccupations from class activities. Her teachers have hypothesized that attentional and emotional issues are combining to make it difficult for Anya to learn and function at age-appropriate levels.

The report stated that I had

> mild to moderate levels of depression. She indicated she felt sad and discouraged about the future. She indicated she does not enjoy things the way she used to, expects to be punished, and has thoughts of self-harm but she would not carry them out.

After a day of tests, doctors determined that I had ADHD, and I was put on Ritalin. Because I often didn't eat breakfast, the medication made me nervous. My schoolwork didn't improve, but my behavior did because I was too anxious to interact with anyone.

My mother and sister visited my father in Ukraine for a few weeks that winter while I stayed with friends so I wouldn't miss school. They returned with stories of empty supermarkets and department stores, and brown tap water. They'd seen churches, gone to the ballet, and visited artists in shared apartments or storefront galleries, but they hadn't liked it. My mother said it was a terrible, depressing place and swore she'd never move there. I hadn't known that was an option, and was glad that although it could be, it still wasn't.

She returned to Ukraine a year later and took me with her. I was fourteen and had just dyed my hair black, and was living in overalls and men's T-shirts. I had zero knowledge of or interest in the political and economic changes that were sweeping the region. The trip was a chore. I was annoyed to have to see my father and abandon my friends and free summer days for even a few weeks.

We arrived at the hotel where my father had lived for three years, having chosen, like most foreigners, a place that usually had heat and hot water, unlike even the nicest apartments in Kiev. The nodding staff said hello to my mother, then looked at me with shock before forcing smiles onto their faces. They said something to my father in Ukrainian. He laughed, said something to them, and then they all laughed together.

He saw me looking at him with suspicion. "They said they didn't know that my daughter was a mechanic."

"What did you say?" I asked.

"I said you'd be here for three weeks and could look at their cars anytime."

I rolled my eyes and stomped to the elevator.

My father's room was a suite. He used the large living room as his office. Towers of papers stood on his desk and on the brown carpet, and modern paintings, which he'd been collecting, leaned against the wall because he'd already hung the others he'd bought and there was no room left. He had a small TV and a VCR and three videos: *Dick Tracy*, *Raiders of the Lost Ark*, and Madonna's *Truth or Dare*. My father was a huge Madonna fan—he even bought her controversial book, *Sex*.

When I asked why he liked her so much, he told me that she was a very smart businesswoman. I watched the videos at least a dozen times, and when I got bored, I watched American and European movies on one of the television's few channels. All dialogue seemed to be dubbed by the same Ukrainian man, regardless of the age or gender of the person speaking the lines.

My mother and I trailed my father out of his room for meals in the hotel's staid restaurant. Every time we sat down we were handed a menu, but after the first morning, we understood not to bother reading it. The waitress would tell my father the one or two dishes they were serving that day: usually boiled noodles and kashi for lunch; boiled noodles and kashi with an unidentifiable meat cutlet for dinner.

Kiev seemed overcast even when it was sunny. No one smiled. The roads outside the city were littered with cars. Some were wrecks that had been stripped. Some had been abandoned when the driver ran out of gas, and those, too, were missing tires, bumpers, even doors. We visited old wooden churches and spent a few nights in a resort that wasn't yet open in the Carpathian Mountains, where there were only a few other guests. We went to Lviv, which I grudgingly agreed was interesting and pretty. Somehow I ended up hanging out with a group of local girls my age—perhaps they were distant cousins, or friends of some distant cousin—and we went to a decaying amusement park where I bought us all tickets and Popsicles, as I'd been instructed. My parents didn't bother taking many pictures of me during the trip, and in the few they did, I'm scowling.

When other Westerners asked about my impressions of

Ukraine, I'd say, "Ukraine's awful!" I'd get them laughing with stories of choking on the random chunks of bone in a gray pork patty, or how once, when my father's driver Igor was cut off on the road while he was taking my mother and me to a church, he sped up so he could cut off the other driver and forced him to stop. Igor grabbed a crowbar from underneath his seat and leaped out of the car as the other driver approached with a pipe. Igor forgot to put the car in park, so we started rolling backward and screaming until Igor abandoned the fight and ran after us. I couldn't imagine why my father—why anyone—would choose to be there. Most of the Ukrainians I saw looked like they'd be thrilled if they could leave. But my father seemed happy. He looked like the people I saw on the street and spoke their language.

I was able to leave my school for a public high school when I reached ninth grade. My first semester, I received D's in a number of classes and got suspended for skipping, but found there were a few things I cared about. I became a sex educator for a nonprofit, and began giving talks at schools and community groups, and also got very involved with my school's drama program. I was as committed to ignoring my academic responsibilities as I was to ignoring any demand my mother made. I no longer asked to do things; I either told my mom I was doing them or just did them and dealt with the consequences, which were rare. She let me smoke pot and have my boyfriend in my room with the door closed. She'd never been strict, and I didn't question why she'd become increasingly lax. Whenever she tried to corral my behavior, I lashed out like she was trying to leash me.

One morning, I encountered her while I was about to

leave for school in a velvet blue crop top. I was surprised to see her; she still slept through the mornings like she had when I was a child.

She grabbed my shoulder. "You can't wear that shirt to school. It's barely a shirt! Go change." Her voice was firm, but she was calm.

I told her that I wouldn't.

She said that I would.

I'd grown so accustomed to an absence of rules that being told what to do seemed like an outrageous injustice. I brought my face to hers and snarled, "Fuck you."

Her smack was hard and fast, and the one I retaliated with equaled its force.

We glared at each other. I was appalled by my behavior, not hers. I mumbled "I'm sorry," ran to my room to switch shirts, and stuffed the one I'd wanted to wear in my backpack so I could change into it at school. As I ran to the subway, I kept seeing my mother's stunned face. She'd looked so tiny and vulnerable when I'd hit her. I knew I was responsible for the awful thing I'd done, but I tried to find a way to blame her for it.

When I came home late that afternoon, my mother was on the phone. She chased me down and handed it to me. I found myself listening to my father telling me how terrible I was for hitting her. Surprisingly, he wasn't yelling; he was just trying to explain how wrong it was. I handed the phone back to my mother, then "ran away" to my friend's house. Her mother, who knew mine, rolled her eyes when I told her not to tell my mother I was there. Later that evening, she found me and said, "Your mom says you can come home whenever you want tomorrow." I understood this to mean that my mom wanted time away from me—not that I'd bullied her into giving me more space—and that made me feel even worse. I didn't care that she'd hit me. I thought I deserved it. As angry as I was with her in that moment, and had been for years, I believed I'd made an unforgivable transgression. Smacking her felt worse than raising a knife to her. I hadn't bothered regretting that. Seeing how sad and weak she'd looked when I'd hit her made me feel sorry for her.

When I came home the next day, both of us pretended the previous morning never happened. I was still sick about what I'd done, but I couldn't make myself apologize again.

The following summer, we took a family vacation to Italy. My mother, sister, and I flew from America while my father flew from Ukraine. My parents had rented a villa in Tuscany with their old friends from England, Sue and Martin, whom I'd met in London a few times on family vacations and adored. My father was in a good mood. He never yelled, helped Sue with the cooking, and took long walks with Martin. But my mother's energy was sour, and she picked fights with my father whenever she could.

Over dinner, Sue asked about their home in Boston. My mother turned to my father. "Is that still your home?"

He looked at the table. "Of course."

"Is it? Are you returning there with me and your daughters when this wonderful vacation is over?"

"Anita."

She glanced at Sue and Martin. "Ask him about Anya's last report card. Ask him how Alexandra's sailing team is doing—"

Sue interrupted. "How about some dessert?" She brought

gelato from the kitchen and a stack of bowls. My mother poured herself more wine.

When we got home, my mother began spending most weekends at our New Hampshire cabin, and my friends and I, including my new boyfriend Eli, quickly got used to reigning over the empty house and its many bottles of vodka, which my father inadvertently supplied when he returned to Boston from Ukraine. We called it "Ukrainian Death" because even when there wasn't a drawing of a pepper on the label, even when we mixed it into extra-large cherry Slurpees, it seared our lungs and made us howl. I'd toss a Duraflame log into the fireplace, fill coffee mugs or paper cups with vodka, let people smoke packs of my mom's cigarettes, and watch my friends make out or mug with our statues. I fed them and made sure they puked in appropriate places, and they did the same for me. If the Duraflame was still burning when we needed to pass out, we'd throw water on it. When that didn't work, we brought it out to the sidewalk and beat it with a shovel.

Christmas that year was stiff with tension. My father flew back from Ukraine, but nobody wanted to be there. Alexandra and I went to our rooms early on Christmas Eve because we couldn't stand to watch our parents not fight when they so clearly wanted to.

Early next summer, when I was sixteen, my father came home again for a few weeks. One Sunday morning, I wandered into the living room and announced that I was going out with Eli. School was almost over, and Eli was going to Ecuador for a community-service program. We wanted to spend the day together.

My father casually declared that I wasn't going out, and

said I should be doing homework. When I explained that I didn't have any, he said I should be studying because my grades were bad. My grades *were* bad, but I didn't care. I sputtered out excuses and pleas until I shattered and screamed "I hate you!" at adolescent level ten. "You can't stop me!" I ran to the bathroom and got into the shower.

He followed and yelled at me from the other side of the bathroom door, telling me that I wasn't going out. With shampoo streaming down my face and shoulders, I told him that I could do whatever I wanted, that he didn't live with us anymore. After repeating ourselves at an increasingly loud pitch, my father charged in.

The room was filled with steam, but the shower door was clear. Terrified, I retreated into the corner and tried to cover myself. My father seemed almost as shocked as I was to find himself there. He tried yelling some more, but my voice prevailed as I told him to get out get out *get out* until he did.

I finished my shower as quickly as I could and ran to my room, where knee-high piles of clothing spilled into each other. I was crying when my mother found me and was embarrassed to be caught. I didn't know if she'd heard what happened in the bathroom. I didn't want to tell her. I didn't want to *have* to tell her.

She sat down on my bed, a thin futon on a piece of plywood propped up by cement blocks. It wasn't comfortable, but I thought it was cool, the kind of bed I'd have if I were a junkie or didn't live at home.

"You can't tell your father that you hate him," she said gently. Her skin was shiny and her pores were large. I looked at the few patches of gray carpet that were free from clothing, which were dotted with black and maroon hair-dye stains. "You need to apologize."

I told her that *he* needed to apologize, and said that she should have interfered with our fight. "Why don't you ever help me?" I asked. "You never did when I was little. You just let him yell and yell, even though you knew I was miserable. You should have protected me." It was the first time I'd voiced the thought that had been bothering me since childhood.

My mother was quick to correct me. "I did protect you," she said. "Don't you remember the time I took you and Alexandra out of the house after your father came down particularly hard on you? We stayed with my friend Lili for a few days." I didn't. Like so many of her other stories, this one didn't produce the reaction she wanted. Instead of concluding that she was a good mother, I was left thinking, "Yeah, but you brought us back."

Sensing that her story hadn't done what she'd hoped, she abandoned it. "I talked to your father. He'll let you go out with Eli, but only if you apologize."

I couldn't tell if that was her requirement or his. I weighed my desire to have him apologize against my desire to go out, and went down to the living room.

My father had taken his place at the table. His shoulders tensed when I came in. I said, "I'm sorry I said I hate you." I got ready and left.

Eli and I had a great time, and when we were together I tried to forget about everything that had happened with my father. But when I was back home, I was overcome with anger. I couldn't get rid of the wild fear I'd felt when he'd burst into the bathroom. He was my father, and a stranger, and someone I hated. A person who respected me and what I wanted so little that he would come in while I was naked because he needed to keep yelling at me. I was certain I'd only be safe when he was gone.

On his last day in Boston, my father, my mother, and I stood in front of the house and waited for the cab that would take him to the airport. My mother smiled and wished my father a good trip. He thanked her, and their faces met for a quick kiss.

I wanted my father to leave, but I didn't want to have to hug him goodbye, although I knew I had to. It was one of the things that had to happen before he left, a step that had to be taken. It was what was done.

It was easy to get my arms around him, but it was difficult to touch him. The hug I gave him was quick and cursory, a light squeeze and my cheek against the stiff wool of his thick, black coat.

That's what I remember, but it couldn't have actually happened—the part about my cheek against his coat. It was summer, so he wouldn't have been wearing that coat. That's the one I always saw him in; it's who he was. But that day, he was probably wearing a thin navy suit or a blue short- or long-sleeved shirt. So my face didn't touch his coat; it touched something else or was scratched by his gray beard.

I hugged him because I had to, but then I did something I didn't: I told him I loved him. I was horrified to hear the words and see them floating over his shoulder. I wanted to stuff them back into my mouth, to return them to whatever place they came from, a place I didn't even know I owned. I felt dirty and confused, like he had something on me. I'd lied, and I didn't even have to. He didn't respond. He just got into the cab and left.

I settled back into my life of smoking weed, hanging out with my friends, and working at the drugstore down the block. I didn't think about his coming back. What I thought about was losing my virginity.

Eli was everything I wanted in a boyfriend. He had dark hair, blue eyes, a scar on his cheek, and a devious grin, and was desired by all the other girls but was somehow mine. He was enough trouble to be exciting but loving enough to be safe, a guy who was so ultimately good that his bad was merely fun. He'd skip class sometimes, but it was usually because I had a free period and we wanted to make out in the grass of the nearby nature preserve.

We decided to do it on the Fourth of July, two days before he flew to South America. My bedroom was too chaotic to be romantic, so we opted for my sister's, which she'd mostly emptied before going to college. It was on the top floor, where the air was thick and still. The room was dominated by a single piece of furniture—a rickety white particleboard twin bed that was attached to an empty bookshelf unit.

Our house was near the Esplanade, the center of Boston's Fourth of July festivities. A stream of people was making its way to the celebration down the street, and their voices reached us through the open window as we readied ourselves with Slurpees mixed with Ukrainian Death. The noise outside and the creaking quietness of the room made us feel far away and invincible.

Our skin was sticky, faces pink, tongues red. I lay on my back and looked at the spires of the enormous Gothic church across the street, where'd I'd spent mass every Wednesday in grade school and every Christmas. I wasn't thinking about God or guilt. I was just thinking it was pretty, that it had always been there, and that I was finally going to have sex.

We fumbled with a condom, then another, and another, but between our nervousness and the Ukrainian Death, we just couldn't do it. We gave up and went onto the roof and watched what we could see of the fireworks while swearing we'd get it done tomorrow.

We did, on a waterbed that belonged to some lady naïve enough to let one of Eli's friends house-sit for her. It was brief. It didn't hurt. He told me I was an angel.

Afterward, Eli and I giggled in the dark, wiped the sweat off each other, and looked at our arms in the thin orange light thrown by the streetlamps. When he dropped me off at the end of the night, we said goodbye and held each other. I went into my quiet house and jumped into bed, thrilled with myself and what I had done, and ready to wake up to a new world.

CHAPTER THREE
Ukrainian Death

On July 9, 1994, I woke to loud knocking on the front door. It was early Saturday morning, and I assumed some of my friends needed to crash after clubbing. My house was open to my friends and their friends when my mother was away, but she was home that weekend, and I didn't want her to discover what I got up to while she was gone.

I flew downstairs, wearing only the T-shirt I'd slept in, hoping to reach the door before she did.

I opened it to find my father's boss, David, stricken and pale. As I blinked into the sun and my mother hovered in the shadows at the top of the stairs, he announced that my father had been killed in a car accident.

My mother went back into her bedroom. I stood dumbly in the entryway until David said, "Let me in, let me in!" When I didn't move, he pushed past me.

The phone rang. It kept ringing. When I answered, I heard Alexandra's voice, fogged with distance. She was interning in Ukraine that summer and had just returned from identifying our father's body.

My mother picked up the phone from her room. "Please tell me it's not true," she whispered.

Alexandra couldn't. I listened as she told our mother what had happened. My father and two of his Ukrainian coworkers, Yelena and Serhiy, had been visiting a factory they'd recently funded in Cherkasy, a city three hours south of the capital. They'd traveled by car, driven by my father's driver of a few years, Vitaliy. They were supposed to spend the night there, but my father insisted they return to Kiev that evening so he could get to work immediately the next day. As they approached the city, a van coming from the other direction drove into their lane. Vitaliy swerved left to avoid it, but the cars collided. My father was killed on impact; Serhiy and Yelena died at a hospital a few hours later. Vitaliy, and everyone in the van that hit their car, only sustained minor injuries.

This was the story I whispered to people as they filled the house. News spread quickly through the neighborhood, and my mother's friends descended fast. They found her on the couch, the floor, wordless or wailing that she'd lost both of her men, first her son and now her husband. Someone took her to the kitchen so she could have privacy. As my mother's screams filled the kitchen and the house, a woman I'd known from birth looked at me and said, "You know there's a chance your dad was murdered, don't you?"

I was still getting used to the story I'd woken up to; I hadn't had time to doubt or complicate it. I said, "I guess," because I had to say something, and sure, it was *possible*.

But the idea seemed ridiculous. Why would anyone murder my father? I decided she was being tacky, trying to turn a bad situation into an interesting one.

That summer, I was working at the drugstore down the block, and I was due there at eight that morning. I asked a neighbor to give the pharmacist the news and tell him that I wouldn't be in for a few days. The neighbor returned with condolences—the whole staff knew my family well—and two Valium for my mother. When the pills landed in her palm, she looked up and said, "That's it?"

I took advantage of the commotion and walked to Starbucks. I didn't drink coffee, but I needed something to do. I took my time getting back, saying "My father is dead" out loud to see how it sounded.

At home, my mother was moving in hobbled shock. It was as though the car that had hit my father's had crashed into our house as well. We all had to sway for a bit longer before we could assess the damage, glancing at our bodies and touching our faces before we tried to stand. I pressed my fingers to my chest and cheek, but found no injuries.

As the day stretched out, I performed the tasks expected of a daughter who'd lost her father. I accepted flowers and muffins, shook hands, received hugs, and tried to look sad. But I wasn't. I didn't *want* to feel sad. To feel anything other than relief over my father's death meant being generous to a man who had never been generous to me. The weight that had been crushing me for my entire life was gone. There was so much grief around me, but to me, the world looked friendlier than ever.

The freedom I'd enjoyed when he was in Ukraine was now permanent; he was never coming home. But I couldn't begin my life without him that day, or even that week. There was too much to do: streams of papers to sign, meetings with florists and priests, formalities and calls and waiting. A fax arrived from the American embassy in Ukraine, explaining what we needed to do to get my father's body and personal effects back. We needed to plan a funeral in Boston, a burial, and we had to decide if we would be flying to Kiev in a couple of weeks to attend another service honoring my father and his coworkers.

My mother was fixated on my father's body. She wanted it back in Boston immediately, but the process was complicated. We needed the death certificate. We needed the death certificate translated into English. We needed the body shipped, which required a zinc container, and a funeral parlor to receive it. What companies shipped dead bodies from Ukraine? Why was it so hard to find a translator? Why did we have to get an autopsy if he was killed in a car accident? My mother called someone every hour: the Ukrainian embassy in Washington, the American embassy in Ukraine, David, Aunt Lana, anyone she thought should help. No one was doing enough.

Two days later, Alexandra called crying from Ukraine. She'd been staying at the apartment my father had recently bought so she could organize his things but had been kicked out by David and another coworker when they arrived from Boston. They told her that the company owned the apartment, not our father—he had purchased it on behalf of the company and kept it in his name, to simplify what was usually a complicated process for foreigners—and that she needed to find somewhere else to stay. The only personal items they allowed her to take were his passport and briefcase, where, she discovered, he'd kept nude photos of our mother that he'd taken on our recent trip to Italy. Alexandra had her own apartment, but she'd felt my father's bosses had been needlessly cruel and was worried they were doing something shady. She'd asked for more time to go through his files, but they'd told her those belonged to the company, too.

Alexandra was back in Boston by the end of the week. She was quiet and detached, constantly ducking the net of our mother's hugs.

She and I at that age—twenty-one and sixteen—knew little about each other or each other's lives. The first time we were alone, I asked what it had been like to identify our father's body. She described the experience like she was reading a dishwasher manual. The morgue didn't have storage or refrigeration, so she arrived to find bodies piled everywhere and bloated from the heat. Our father's corpse, still wearing his bloody clothing, was laid out in the bed of a pickup truck because it was about to be transported to a morgue in the capital, and was partially covered by a sheet. His skull was smashed, his nose was broken, and his eyes were open. She held his hand, took his watch off of his wrist, and placed it on her own, then kissed his bruised forehead.

The scene was so vivid and appalling that it played like

something from a low-budget movie. Because she didn't seem upset, I didn't become upset, either.

Our mother alternated between bouts of grief that kept her in her room and a state of lifeless composure that allowed her to handle practical matters like the wake. But as the practical matters got more complicated, she became increasingly unhinged.

My father's mother inserted herself and her wishes into the planning process, and they differed greatly from my mom's. Babtsia insisted on having a wake, funeral, and burial that were "appropriate" and Ukrainian. She wanted to hold the wake at a fancy funeral home in Boston, the funeral at a Ukrainian church, the burial in her family's plot at a Ukrainian cemetery in Connecticut. My mother agreed to Babtsia's first two demands, though this meant the funeral would be in Ukrainian, so no one in our immediate family would understand the service, and neither would most of my father's peers. She wasn't capitulating; having a Ukrainian funeral supported the story she was telling to comfort herself: Her husband had been so dedicated to helping Ukraine and its people that he sacrificed himself for its eventual glory. My mother, of course, had also made sacrifices, and she'd made them happily, because she had been the good wife of a great man.

However, she was livid that Babtsia wanted my father buried in a cemetery that was close to our grandmother but an almost two-hour drive for us. Not only was it far but Babtsia knew that my mother wouldn't want to be buried there. She wasn't Ukrainian, and she didn't want to be near the in-laws who'd rejected her. There was another problem as well. My father had told my mother that he wanted to be cremated and she was determined to do it, but she knew Babtsia would object.

My mom confessed her concerns to my father's sister, Lana, and was relieved when Lana understood why my father needed to be cremated and agreed to help find a solution that would work for everyone.

Lana consulted the director of the Ukrainian cemetery, and after some pleading, he agreed to bury an empty coffin. My mother purchased a fancy wooden casket and had my father cremated, sprinkling some of his ashes over the photographs and bricks that were entombed instead of his body. The rest were spread by her under an apple tree on our New Hampshire property, and scattered in India when Alexandra traveled there the following year.

The day of the funeral, my mother insisted that Alexandra and I act as pallbearers with her, instructing us to raise our chins so we looked proud and strong as we accompanied the casket to the front of the church. When we entered, I saw it was so full that rows of people were standing in the back and along the sides. It was a formal Ukrainian service, but my godfather gave a eulogy in English as well as Ukrainian. I tried to force myself to pay attention, telling myself that this was a huge moment in my life whether I was sad or not, but I kept staring at the Byzantine-style art that hung on the walls and zoning out. When it was over, my mother ran to the casket, flung herself on it, and sobbed while guests silently made their way to the exit.

We were driven to the Ukrainian cemetery in black town cars. I'd been there a decade before, when my grandfather was buried in a double plot that would later also accommodate my grandmother, whose name was not yet inscribed on the pink headstone.

A space next to my grandparents' had been dug. The casket had beat us there and hovered above it. The priest at the cemetery was Ukrainian as well, so he only said one word that my mother, sister, and I understood: Amen. My sister and I glanced at each other as Babtsia wept silently. We knew she wouldn't do anything dramatic like open the coffin, but what if something else happened? What if the coffin somehow flipped over and revealed its true contents? Did the priest know what was happening? Had anyone been bribed? What if the director of the cemetery was suddenly overtaken with guilt and confessed?

My mother wept as well. I wanted to remind her that the burial wasn't real; it was a performance. It didn't occur to me that it didn't have to be real for her to feel sad. The burial was fake, but her husband was really dead.

Alexandra returned to Kiev to attend the service honoring my father and his coworkers and to finish her internship. My mother said she was too bereft to attend, but sent along a short letter to be read to the crowd and toys for the children of the other victims.

My mother spent the rest of the summer sitting at the dining-room table, the spot that had been my father's, reading stacks of papers and legal documents, and agonizing over what they did and didn't say. Before he'd died, my father had told her he'd been made partner, but his company claimed that he hadn't and there was no document that proved otherwise. She believed he'd been given a partnership agreement and had held off on signing it until he next returned to America, and that the coworkers who'd told my sister to leave his apartment had stolen it. My father's status at the time of his death affected whatever payment she might receive if the investments he'd made were successful. This money, worker's compensation, and whatever she earned from teaching part-time would be our only income. My father had a retirement account with a decent amount of money, but she wouldn't be able to access it until she was sixty-five. There were other issues as well. His boss said that money was missing from the petty-cash fund and claimed that my father had used it to purchase art for himself. My mother disagreed, explaining that my father had told her he often had to use that money to pay their workers because it was so difficult to get dollars. They also fought about the apartment that my father had been living in. Since it was in my father's name, my mother believed he was the owner and she wanted to sell it for cash, but the firm insisted that the apartment belonged to them, telling her what they'd told my sister: It was a company investment that was in my father's name only to make the purchase easier. My mother was overwhelmed and exhausted, and didn't understand what she was being asked to read or sign.

She hired a lawyer who said the company was making things unnecessarily difficult, while my father's company accused her of slowing down the process. When I listened to our answering machine, I often heard my father's boss tersely telling my mother that she needed to sign something or hand over a document. As he lived on our block, I occasionally ran into him, and he'd tell me that my mother needed to "pick up her pace." I didn't report these interactions to my mother; she'd told me many times that my father's company was harassing her when she should be given time to grieve. I agreed, and when Halloween came around a few months later, I had Eli unload two dozen eggs on his house.

I was on her side for that battle, but I didn't want to be near her pain. My reactions to her grief ranged from uncomfortable to disgusted. I was happy, and I thought she should be, too. Every time I came home from work or hanging out with friends, she'd put on a plastic smile and ask me how I was. I'd go to her, but since I felt fine, I didn't have much to report, so instead she'd tell me how *she* was feeling. She'd whimper and say that she felt alone, that she missed my father's touch, that all the men in her life had left her, and I'd slowly recoil. Once I realized how these conversations would go, I avoided them, and her. When I came home, I ran straight up to my room. "Your marriage wasn't even that great," I fumed silently. "This is a second chance!" I thought she was choosing to wallow.

One day, when we'd ended up in the kitchen at the same time, she told me about a nightmare she'd had the previous evening. She spoke quietly as her hands shook. My father had come to her, covered in cobwebs, and said that he'd been murdered. She'd asked and then begged him to tell her who'd done it, but he couldn't answer.

"Do you really think he could have been murdered?" I asked. I hadn't considered the possibility since the day he'd died.

She nodded.

When I asked why, she just shook her head. I took that to mean that her nightmare was her only evidence, and thought she was being paranoid or was turning her fight with my father's company into something bigger than it was. From what I knew, there was no reason to think the crash had been anything but an accident.

My father's death upended the house. My mother emptied drawers looking for his life insurance policy, put his clothing in piles, stacked the paintings he'd collected in Ukraine wherever there was space. One night, when she was out to dinner, I failed to close the front door properly after leaving. A neighbor saw the open door and called the police. After seeing the state of the living room, they determined our home had been ransacked. The police were still there when my mother returned. After an initial panic, she explained that we hadn't been robbed; she was newly widowed and struggling to keep the house clean. "Thanks a lot, Anya," she said when I got back. "Now everyone thinks we live in chaos."

We did. Melancholy had seeped into the walls. Our home was rotting, and I retreated as I had when I was a child, trying to avoid its decay by insulating myself, or better, by not being there at all. I took extra shifts at the drugstore and camped out at Eli's.

One morning I woke up and found myself covered in small bites. I'd been itchy for a while, but couldn't figure out why. I looked at our cats, Mischa and Topsider, and saw them scratching themselves furiously. I inspected them both; they were covered in fleas.

I showed my spotted arms and legs to my mother. "We have fleas," I told her. "We have to do something."

She rolled her eyes. "Oh, Anya."

I pushed up her sleeve and found she was covered in bites as well. "See! Aren't you itchy?"

She pulled her shirt back to her wrist. "Those are mosquito bites."

"Look," I said, and revealed the bumps I had on my ankles. "These aren't mosquito bites."

She sighed and said, "How could we have fleas?" to an audience who wasn't there.

I pointed at the cats. Mischa was scratching himself feverishly, while Topsider was rolling spastically on the carpet. "They go outside."

"There aren't fleas in Boston," she said, and then floated out of the room like she was in a trance.

That afternoon, Eli came over wearing white socks. Within a minute, they were covered with trembling bugs. He kissed me and said, "You know I have to leave, right?" I nodded. He told me he'd try to get his mom to talk to mine. She called, but my mom refused to talk to her. "I'm sorry I can't help," his mother told me. "Ask one of your mother's friends. And hon, please understand, we adore you, but we can't have you over until we know you won't come with fleas."

I showed my mother my bites again, told her I was too itchy to sleep, didn't know what to wear, that *Eli's mom said I couldn't come over*, but she turned away. When I got hysterical, she waved me off. "Mom," I cried, "what is going on?" Instead of answering, she went to her bedroom.

Sylvia, my mother's best friend since grade school, arrived the next day. She'd been at the funeral and had come back to help my mother organize and get rid of my father's things. When she rang the bell, I ran to the door and announced we had fleas.

She grimaced. "Fleas?"

"I've been trying to get Mom to do something about it, but she won't listen. You have to help me."

My mother came down the stairs and threw her arms open for an embrace. Sylvia held up her hand and my mother froze. "What's this about you having fleas?"

My mother laughed. "Anya's being dramatic. Come in!"

We all went to the couch. By that point, the fleas in our house were acting like cartoon characters, somersaulting in top hats from human to cat to rug. I told my mother again that we, our four-story house crammed full of shit, and our two cats had fleas. Once again, she denied it. Sylvia moved her hand toward a lamp so my mother could see the flea that had already jumped into her palm. "Anita, you do."

My mother nodded. I cheered and tried to hug Sylvia, but she wouldn't let me.

Sylvia arranged for an exterminator to come two days later. Before the house was bombed and we had to wash everything we owned, I had to give the cats a flea bath. They were going to be temporarily boarded at the vet, and they had to be as flea-free as possible.

I bathed them in the claw-foot tub I'd once filled with *kupon* and stained with hair dye. Topsider was almost impossible to wash, scratching my arms bloody and biting my neck. When I was finally able to submerge him, pools of red appeared and pulsed away from his body.

Mischa was next. He was old and already a bit weak from leukemia. He did not have Topsider's size or ability to fight, so he just wailed in the tub as I scrubbed his thin frame and fleas abandoned his body. As the water got darker and darker, his wails turned into moans. Over and over, I apologized to him.

"I'm sorry, Mischa. I'm sorry, baby." I rinsed him, wrapped him in a towel, cradled him to me, and for the first time that summer cried on his bony, wet head.

The extermination was successful, and we stopped letting the cats outside. The house stayed messy, but I didn't care. I was relieved to be flea-free, and hopeful that my mother's alarming denial of that problem was a blip in her sanity that would pass when she stopped grieving, which I assumed would happen soon.

When school started, I learned that over the summer, I'd become the girl whose father died. My friends who'd come to my father's wake had spread the news of his death, and as I walked the halls, people stared at me for a moment too long. In their faces, I saw a respect that I liked. I didn't want sympathy, but I liked being marked by tragedy because I could show everyone how little it affected me.

The night before my birthday in September, my mother crawled into my bed and wrapped herself tightly around me. "It's your birthday," she said. Her voice was calm, but her breath was hot and sweet with alcohol. She was drunk.

"It's the first holiday since your father died. You're probably upset. You can tell me if you're upset." She tried to stroke my head, but slapped it instead. "Your father loved you so much."

I curled away from her and tightened my jaw. "Please let me sleep."

"It's okay," she said. "I know you're sad."

I pretended to pass out, staying still under my blanket even though its weight and the warmth of her sticky skin were making me sweat, and eventually she left.

When I woke up the next morning, I felt dirty. I tried to dump my mother's grime in the shower, but even soap and a scratchy sponge couldn't remove it. I put on a smile as I walked into school and accepted my friends' birthday hugs and Eli's kisses, but by the end of first period, I was tipsy with worry that something was very wrong. Instead of going to my next class, I sought out my guidance counselor and told her what had happened.

She pushed me into a chair and handed me a box of tissues. I took two and crumpled one in each hand, though I knew I wasn't going to cry. She softened her already soft eyes and said, "When your mother was in your bed, did she touch you in a sexual way?"

"What?" I yelped. "No!"

"Okay," she said, and continued. How often did this happen?

It was the first time.

How often was my mother drinking?

I had no idea.

Was it possible she was drinking often and hiding it from me?

Sure, I said. It was possible.

My mother never came into my bed again. She started spending more time in New Hampshire, and my life became the best it had ever been. I had more time with Eli and more time for parties. It was easy to conceal what I did on the weekends. My parties were small, so the house never got too trashed. My mom didn't keep track of her cigarettes, and she didn't drink my father's vodka, so she didn't notice when it disappeared. I could have been worse at hiding my activities than I thought; she could have adopted the strategy I used to deal with her: Ignore, ignore, ignore. Only once did she confront me with evidence of a party, when she'd found a beer cap under the couch. I told her that Eli's older brother bought us some beer, that we rarely drank, that it wasn't a big deal.

"Oh, you did more than drink beer." She ran a finger across a dusty Chinese chest and held it to my face. "What's this?"

"Dirt?" I said.

"It's cocaine, Anya. You can't fool me."

I laughed, but when I saw that she didn't believe me, I tried to explain that it definitely wasn't. I'd never done cocaine and neither had any of my friends. No one had ever done more than mushrooms at my house; we'd spent our childhoods watching *Miami Vice* and were terrified of hard drugs. Even if we'd wanted to do it, we wouldn't have known where to get it.

She told me that she expected me to experiment, and launched into a story about doing coke with my father and their friend Helmut on New Year's in 1980. "This was before anyone knew it was bad for you," she said. "It was so fun to do cocaine with your father because he was so quiet and reserved, but when he did coke, we would stay up all night talking." Her face brightened at the memory. "Your sister was in bed but you wouldn't go to sleep, so I had you on my lap. Everyone was talking and talking, but then I saw you grab the straw and try to put it up your nose. And then I knew . . ." She paused and put her hand on her heart. "It was time to put you to bed."

Like so many of her stories, she hadn't considered how this

one might sound. As usual, I didn't hear that she was a great mother. "*That's* when you knew?" I thought. It was okay to snort lines with me on your lap; your maternal instinct only kicked in when I reached for the straw.

"But it's a bad drug," she continued. "Helmut got into a lot of trouble. I don't know what happened to him. Last time we saw him, he borrowed a few hundred dollars from us and never paid us back."

"I know it's bad!" I cried. "I haven't done it!" She didn't seem to believe me, but I was never punished. Years later, once I finally had done it, I realized that she'd have easily been able to determine if the dust was coke or not, so maybe she just wanted to scare me.

That year I began trying to do well in school. I did most of my homework and studied for tests. When my father was alive, I didn't see the point of putting in the effort; nothing I did was good enough for him, and I didn't want to work hard and discover that everything he'd said about me was right. Before he died, I'd been determined to be an actress. I loved theater and had some proof that I was talented. My freshman and sophomore years, I'd been in plays that were a part of local competitions and had received awards for my performance in each. But my junior year, I was in a play that went to a state competition and lost badly. The experience exhausted me, and after a number of run-ins with my controlling acting teacher, who reminded me way too much of my dad, I gave it up as my main activity and decided I'd go to college for public policy instead of acting. My experience as a sex educator had brought me into so many different schools; I was stunned by the education inequalities I saw and wanted to fix them.

I pushed all my creative impulses aside and tried my hardest to get B pluses in everything but science and math.

In the spring of my senior year of high school, one Friday I came home to an empty house. I ran to the kitchen and saw that the answering machine was blinking. I put a tall glass under the fridge's water dispenser as the first message unfurled, but stopped the water when I heard the urgency in the caller's voice. "Anya, it's Sydney. You have nothing to worry about. Your mother is safe. She's in the hospital for the weekend because she needs some rest. I took her there this afternoon and helped her settle in. She said you'd be fine for the weekend, but you can call me if you need anything."

The fridge cooled my back as the next message played. It was another friend of my mother's. She said the same exact things, but she was calm and positive.

I thought it was strange that my mother needed a weekend of supervised rest because she slept so much already, but that thought didn't turn into concern or questions. I figured she must be really, really exhausted.

"Your mom in New Hampshire again?" my friend Josh asked as we got high on my couch later that night. I nodded. I didn't want to explain where she was, or actually think about why she was there.

I managed to get into New York University and happily abandoned Boston for New York, where Alexandra now lived and I already had lots of friends. When I started college, I turned into someone I didn't recognize. Most of the freshmen I met seemed only to be interested in partying, but I told myself I'd fucked around plenty in high school. I became fascinated by how cities functioned or didn't, and designed my own major out of urban studies, philosophy, and education, convincing myself that I would become the next Jane Jacobs.

I was obsessed with doing well in school, but since I didn't really know how to study, I was immediately overwhelmed by the workload and spent most of my time in the library or computer labs. I liked my classes, and I loved getting A's. My devotion was fueled as much by the thrill I got from doing well as by my persistent insecurity; my grades were good because I'd managed to trick my professors into thinking I was smart despite actually being dumb as shit. When I became too anxious and crazed, I got hammered with my friends on the Lower East Side or went to hip-hop shows. I decided I was going to be a New Yorker forever, and because I was so focused on my new life, I didn't notice how rarely I spoke to my mom.

As I was walking out of my dorm room to go back to Boston for Thanksgiving, my mother called for the first time in more than a month. "I want you to know," she slurred, "that I'm drunk. I don't want you to be surprised when you get home."

"What?" I let my bag fall from my shoulder. "Are you okay?"

She said, "I'm drunk," and hung up.

My roommates had already left for the holiday, and I stared at our dirty bedroom. It was thoughtful of my mother to warn me, but why the hell had she drunk to the point that she had? I wanted to go anywhere but home, but I didn't think I had a choice. I didn't know any of her friends' numbers so I couldn't call them for help, and my sister was spending the holiday with her boyfriend. My mom and I were supposed to drive to

Connecticut the next morning so we could have Thanksgiving with my father's family. I could recruit them, but as angry as I was with her, I still didn't want to rat her out. I spent the hot bus ride home with my knees and forehead against the seat in front of me.

My mother didn't respond when I opened the front door and called her name. After searching the top of the house, I found her in the kitchen. When I turned on the lights, I saw that she was passed out, naked, and falling out of a chair in the middle of the room. Her stained robe was on the floor next to her.

She smelled like wet trash. I patted her cheeks. "Hey!" I shouted. "Wake up." Her eyes fluttered and she began to mumble. I righted her in the chair, but when I let go, she collapsed like a puppet.

I didn't know what to do. I thought about dragging her up the stairs to her room, or making a bed for her in the kitchen so she could sleep it off. Maybe she'd be okay tomorrow. "I'm going to put you to bed," I yelled, but when she didn't respond, I began to panic. I told her we were going to the hospital, then I realized I wasn't sure how to get her there. I didn't have a driver's license, and I didn't want to call an ambulance and cause a commotion in our quiet neighborhood. I didn't want to call her friends the night before Thanksgiving. There was one person whom I knew I could call—Eli—but I hesitated. We'd had a bad breakup (or five) after he went to college a year ahead of me, and I'd been desperate to get back together with him. I was worried he'd think my call for help had an agenda; even if he didn't, I'd be humiliated. But when I heard my mother moan, I knew I didn't have a choice.

After exchanging pleasantries with his mother, I asked to speak to Eli and told him what was happening. "I'm really sorry," I said. "I don't have anyone else to call."

My mom kicked me when I tried to wrestle her into clothes. When Eli rang the doorbell, I tied the belt of her robe around her waist before realizing I'd also tied it to the chair.

Eli greeted me with a "Hey" and a limp, sad smile. He followed me to the kitchen and wordlessly scooped up my mother as she fought him. I tried covering her with her robe but she fought me, too. She didn't know she was naked or who was holding her, but she knew to resist, flailing and hitting our faces as we carried her into his double-parked car. I ran back into the house to grab her purse and bag the clothes I hadn't been able to get onto her body.

When the car started moving, she began to shout. I turned to Eli. "This was supposed to be easier. I couldn't get her to answer my questions or even look at me twenty minutes ago, I swear."

She pawed at the windows and tried to open the door. I turned on the radio. When we got to the emergency room entrance and I opened her door, she kicked me and cried, "No!"

I pulled her out of the car toward Eli. She thrashed in both directions; the terror in her voice didn't quiet until we got her through the automatic doors and a nurse ran up with a wheelchair and a blanket. Two male orderlies followed fast. "This is my mom," I told them. "Her name's Anita, and she's really drunk." My mother tried to slip out of the chair, so the orderlies grabbed her shoulders and held her still.

"Anita!" the nurse shouted cheerfully. "Your daughter brought you here because you need someone to look after you. You're not going anywhere, so relax. It's Thanksgiving, and it's already been a long night."

As my mother was wheeled away, I looked back at Eli, who was standing by the doors with his hand burrowed in his sweatshirt. We waved goodbye.

When I went into the intake office, my mother was wrapped tightly in a blanket.

"You like to drink, Anita?" the nurse asked as she copied information from her driver's license. Her voice was loud and flat. "Are you an alcoholic?"

When my mother shook her head, the nurse glanced at me. "Maybe?" I said. "She likes to drink, but this is new, at least to me."

An orderly walked in and handed her a file. She flipped through it and glanced at me again. "She's been here before for the same reason. You didn't know that?"

I told her I didn't. When she sighed, I added, "I live in New York."

She tried again with my mom. "Hey, Anita, stay with me, kiddo, we're almost done. How many drinks have you had today?"

My mother looked at the nurse for the first time. As her chin wobbled, she said, "Every man in my life left me."

"Mom! How many drinks? You have to tell her."

She closed her eyes and pretended to sleep.

I asked the nurse what would happen next.

As she scribbled notes in my mother's file, she said, "We'll stabilize her and send her to dry out for a few days. You can go."

I put my mother's purse and clothes on a chair. "This is her stuff." When the nurse didn't respond, I said, "Thanks. And happy Thanksgiving."

It had been three years since my father died. I didn't think my mother was still sad; I thought she just wanted to tell her stories again. I thought she wanted pity. I took a cab home and went to sleep. The next day, I called Aunt Lana to tell her what happened, and that neither my mother nor I would make it to dinner. She asked if there was anything she could do, and I told her there wasn't. My sister phoned about an hour later, after calling Lana and hearing that I wasn't there.

"Mom's in detox," I told her. "She was wasted yesterday. It was really scary. Has she been doing this a lot?"

My sister hesitated before she answered. "Not a lot," she told me, "but sometimes."

I spent my Thanksgiving at the tables of three different friends whose families were more concerned about my mother than I was. I returned to New York on Sunday, and a few days later, my mother called to apologize. "I get lonely around holidays," she explained, "but it won't happen again." I chose to believe her. But a few months later, she had to go to detox again. Alexandra told me that our mother's friends had taken her to the hospital and had called to say that they were really worried. They'd told our mom that she needed to go to rehab instead of detox before her drinking got worse, and she'd told them that their concern was unnecessary. She was giving up drinking for good. "So, you know, good news!" Alexandra said.

One weekend while she was in New Hampshire, my mother met Dave, who soon became her boyfriend, her first since my father's death. He hadn't gone to college, was thrice divorced, and was "as poor as a church mouse," but she liked his company. "He really loves me," she gushed. I was happy for her, but when I met Dave for the first time, he and my mother were drinking beer in the kitchen, and I started wondering if he was a bad influence on her. As their relationship continued, I understood I had it very wrong. She'd never stopped drinking like she said she would, and still regularly drank enough that she had to go to detox. She shamelessly took advantage of Dave, drinking as much around him as she wanted because she knew she had a ride to the emergency room. He'd stopped drinking around her, but if she got too drunk alone, she'd call him, and he'd drive from New Hampshire in the middle of the night, even when he had to be at work at six a.m., to take her to the hospital. She made him promise not to tell Alexandra or me what she was doing, but after months of shouldering the responsibility and worry alone, he told Alexandra what had been happening and broke up with my mom. She'd stop drinking for a few weeks and ask him for another chance, but she'd slip up soon after they reunited.

I saw my mother as little as I could over the next few years. Every time I did, mostly around Thanksgiving or Christmas, I'd beg her to stop drinking and get serious help. She often missed the holiday celebrations because she was too drunk to attend, but I'd see her before or after. Her presence was more frustrating than her absence; she'd have tried to sober up but would still be drunk. She usually hadn't showered, had trouble following conversations, and was unsteady on her feet.

Most of my visits included some sort of disaster. One time I came home for Christmas to find that my mother was in detox. My friend Hillary and I took advantage of the empty house to smoke weed in the living room. While we were laughing, the phone rang. I picked it up to hear Dave in hysterics. He'd been living in our cabin in New Hampshire and had woken up the night before to find the house on fire. By the time the fire department arrived, the cabin was gone.

My brain was clouded by pot. "Mom's in the hospital," I mumbled. "I'm glad you're okay. I'll tell her when I see her tomorrow." When I hung up, I rested my head on Hillary's shoulder. "You've got to be fucking kidding me," I said, and told her what had happened. She'd been to the cabin and knew that my parents had filled it with Native American antiques, that my father's ashes were spread on the property, that it was my mother's refuge. I knew this catastrophe would be punishing. I felt worse for her in that moment than I did when my father died—another loss seemed so unfair. I was relieved that I'd be giving her the news while she was in detox so she couldn't immediately get bombed, though I imagined that once she'd heard what had occurred, she'd begin counting down the minutes until she could. I pictured her sober, shaking with pain and desperate to douse it with gin.

When I went to visit my mother the next day, she was chirpy and alert. She complained that the other people in with her were all "drug addicts and junkies," which was what she always said. She didn't have problems like they did. "It's not like *I'm* an alcoholic."

I asked her to sit down and told her about the cabin. "Dave's okay," I said, "but the house is gone. Apparently, squirrels got to the wires." Her face went gray. "Mom, I'm so sorry."

She nodded and told me to leave. I didn't see her again that break.

Although Alexandra and I were both in New York, it was Alexandra whom Dave or my mother's friends called when they were worried about her. Alex went to Boston often to take care of my mom or get her to detox.

Every time I got a call from my sister, or from any 617 number I didn't recognize, I feared it was someone calling to tell me my mother had died—a hospital or morgue who'd taken away my mother's body after she'd been found in a heap at the bottom of the stairs. I channeled my growing anxiety about her drinking into my classes, which made me anxious anyway but were a welcome distraction. My efforts surpassed even my own expectations, and I spent my junior year at Oxford.

That spring, I took a six-week trip to Turkey, Israel, Jordan, and Egypt, eager to see the places I'd heard about for so long. My parents had set a high bar for travel, which I wanted to meet and, eventually, exceed. Until I landed in Turkey, I'd understood their adventures only through the interesting things that they brought home. When I became a teenager, the items that interested me were the ones I could steal or show off: a pair of bespoke suede bell-bottoms that my mother'd had made in India, whose ass I'd split when I zipped them up because she'd been even skinnier than I was; a white brocade dashiki I repurposed as a beach cover-up; masks that elicited screams when I answered the door in them. Travel to me seemed to be about objects, not experience, and I didn't grasp the extent of all that my parents had seen or done. My sophomore year of high school, I'd shoplifted a copy of Bob Marley's album *Legend* and told my mother I thought she'd be into it, figuring she'd be grateful that I'd bothered to share something so cool with her. She snickered and said thanks, she was already aware of his music—was *I* aware that she and my father had attended Marley's famous Independence Day concert in Harare in 1980? I was not.

As I bounced around Istanbul, camped in Wadi Rum with Bedouins, and spent nights drinking on a felucca that lazed down the Nile, I wondered if I was doing it right, doing it as well as my parents had. I was as in awe of the world as they had been but desperate to have only "authentic" experiences. I sneered at travelers who seemed too impressed or green, though I was stumbling to ensure I wasn't being rude or had gotten on the wrong bus. I usually had, but rarely recognized my mistake until it had become deeply inconvenient for me. My parents hadn't taught me how to travel because they'd never brought me on any of their trips, but they'd shown me that travel was something you did. It wasn't a big deal; you got your ticket, got your shots, got on a plane. Once I realized how lucky I was to feel that way, I begrudgingly admitted they'd done at least one thing right.

When I graduated magna cum laude and scored a prestigious fellowship with the New York City government, my mother said she'd buy me a ticket to wherever I wanted to go that summer, as long as I paid the rest of my way. She'd given the same graduation gift to Alexandra, who chose India. I chose Indonesia. I spent close to three months island-hopping, tripping on mushrooms, and clubbing in Hong Kong—where I extended a ten-hour layover to five days—with the son of one of the city's most infamous triad operatives.

After returning to New York and realizing that I didn't actually want to work in government, I sent emails to all of my friends asking if they had any leads on jobs abroad. The one that came back was about a position on Zanzibar. I agreed to go for a year, booked my ticket for three weeks later, and told my mother what I'd decided to do only ten days before my departure.

"Zanzibar?" she said in shock.

"Yup," I said. "I'll be handling a hotelier's philanthropic projects."

In the long pause that followed, I imagined her arguing with herself. She wanted to tell me not to go but knew that she couldn't. I'd grown up watching her and my father in what felt like a constant state of departure. How could she tell me not to do what she herself had done?

The first time I ever missed my father was that year, when I was twenty-three and pressed against the window of a crowded bus that had just crossed the border from Malawi to Zambia on my way to Zimbabwe. I hadn't missed my father when I'd been in the Middle East, although I associated him with that region as much as with East and West Africa.

Next to me was a woman with two children in her lap; the three of them were being shoved into me by the people sitting on bags of maize in the aisle. I was breathing through my mouth to avoid the smells: breast milk, dirt, chickens, and chicken shit. The bus had been twelve hours late, and the ride itself felt interminable. Every time I thought we might tip over or pop a tire—and there were plenty of overturned buses along the road, some abandoned, some surrounded by passengers and their luggage, to show me how possible this was—we pulled over and picked up someone else. Aches burned in my hips and neck, and I couldn't feel my feet. When we hit a bump, bags and limbs flew into my head and knocked it against the scuzzy glass.

I was ecstatic anyway. *Zimbabwe.* I couldn't believe I'd finally gotten there. It was the place I most associated with the *far away* I'd fantasized about as a kid. My parents spoke of Zimbabwe often and showed me pictures of its cities and the people they'd met there. I'd worn the word across my puffy teenage breasts after I'd found a T-shirt of my father's commemorating the opening of the bank's Harare branch, which I'd paired with a flannel shirt, hot pants, fishnets, and Docs.

As I tried unsuccessfully to shift my weight to get a better view out the window, I suddenly thought, "I'd really love to have dinner with my father." I hadn't spoken the words; I corrected myself as if I had. "But only if he wasn't my father."

We'd meet at a dinner party. He'd tell me about his time in Zimbabwe, and I'd tell him about mine. He'd be impressed by me. Not only with my interest in the world but with what I'd managed to achieve since he'd died. I still believed I'd only accomplished what I had because his death granted me the space to try hard and occasionally to fail. So we couldn't be related. If we were, I wouldn't be whoever I was slowly becoming. We'd have to be strangers, some sort of equals.

After returning from Africa and going to Burning Man and being seduced by its freedom and its all-is-good-ness, I moved to Los Angeles in 2003. I wanted to escape my mother and to pursue writing. I settled in Venice Beach and into a life where I could walk to the beach in my bikini even though I lived nine blocks away, make a ton of money cocktailing so I could write during the day, and wear crop tops and flip-flops.

ANYA YURCHYSHYN

Within three months, I went from being a hard-core East Coast skeptic who couldn't watch a game of hacky sack, to someone who believed that the reason I wasn't motivated or talented enough was because there were holes in my aura. It seemed like a miracle that I could pay someone—usually the person who'd pointed out the holes—to sew those things up. In California, I learned there were chakras to clear, past lives to investigate, mantras to chant, and evil entities to be removed. I was sure that a combination of these things would finally provide the solution to the problem of myself.

I was sick of the therapists I'd seen on and off since childhood. I knew myself and my story way too well. Mean dad, dead dad, drunk mom. It was *boring*, and when I had to recite it to someone new, I heard my mother's voice instead of my own. I didn't want to be like her, waving my narratives in people's faces. When I reduced myself to those plot points and antagonists, I was doing what she did: asking for sympathy and making excuses. I didn't want to talk about my childhood anymore. I'd done it so many times, and my feelings and behavior hadn't changed. I still believed that what was wrong with me was my innate me-ness, which was beyond my control. I doubted that I could be cured, but if it was possible, I thought it would be at the hand of someone who had superpowers.

I wasn't just looking to fix myself. I was looking for comfort. The people I paid to help me felt like surrogate parents during the hour I spent with them. My mother wasn't a mother who could be called during an emergency, or who would ever call to see how I was doing; that person was my sister. And even though I was an adult and was, in some ways, more responsible than many of my friends because I'd been emotionally and financially independent for a while, I really needed, and wanted, to be told that I would be okay. That I *was* okay. I wandered from Reiki master to monk to meditation circle, searching for reassurance, direction, and antidotes.

I befriended a massage therapist who also did energy work, and we meditated together weekly. I talked to her about my father and my writing, and told her how I was convinced that I was a failure who would only keep failing because I was put on the earth to fail. One day, she asked who had decided this was how it would be. Was it God?

I told her I didn't believe in God, but that yeah, whatever was out there had put me on the planet knowing that I'd never be able to succeed, no matter how hard I tried.

She told me that whatever was out there—the universe, the divine—didn't loathe me the way I felt my father had. The universe wasn't my dad, and it wasn't an asshole. She was smiling so beautifully as she spoke, lit from within as well as from above. I suddenly felt what she called "divine love" in the room and in my body, a disorienting flood of acceptance and lack of judgment. I started crying and asked if she'd put something in my water when I wasn't looking. She laughed and said nope, this is all you, and told me that whenever I felt alone, fruitlessly fighting against my fate, to remember how I was feeling at this moment.

As I walked home under the shadows of palm trees, I thought about how I could dismantle the power my father still had over me. What if *I* was the person who decided my value, not him? Was such a seismic shift in perspective possible? He'd been dead for more than a decade, but his voice was tightly intertwined with my own; my loud self-criticism was an echo of his. Taking him on meant taking on myself as well.

While I was trying to project myself to other dimensions, Alexandra got married and moved to Boston with her husband, Raj, and lived with our mother while they looked for a house of their own. Alex hoped their presence might help my mom, but it seemed to make things even worse. Alex and Raj would often have to step around her pale, naked body as they left for work because she'd passed out in the hallway on the way to the bathroom. When they went by her bedroom at night, or checked on her, they'd often find her in the dark, mumbling to herself. As she had with Dave, my mother seemed to think that Alex living with her meant she could drink as much as she wanted because someone was there to rescue her.

"I thought being there might be good for her," Alex told me when they moved out a year later. "If she saw people getting up, going to work, and eating real meals, maybe she'd want to do the same. I don't know what I was thinking." Even after my sister moved out, our mom, and her friends, treated Alex like a nurse. That continued even after Alex had her own children, Toshi and Naveen.

Neighbors called her when they hadn't seen our mother for a while or when they found her wandering home from the liquor store looking more haggard than usual. I received dispatches from Alex about having to clean up my mother's shit, finding her on the floor and checking her pulse. She'd tell me about my mom's crazed antics, how she'd recently visited an old professor friend at Tufts and gotten so drunk and wild that he'd had to call the campus police to get rid of her. To get back at him, she stripped naked so the police would "really have something to see."

"I hate telling people that my mother lives in Boston," Alex told me. "They always say, 'Oh how nice that you have help nearby.' I can't tell them that I'd never let her babysit, or that I'm always helping *her*, leaving work in the middle of the day to figure out if she's dead or needs to go to the hospital."

I asked Alex again and again if there was anything I could do, if I could help in some way, but she told me no. She could handle it herself. So all I did was call my mother every few weeks and leave messages. When she called back, she made sure she was sober. I'd ask her if she'd been drinking, and she'd say, "No." I'd recite whatever story Alex had shared with me most recently, and my mom would deny it. I called, and I worried—worried that she'd fall down the stairs, starve, or get hit by a car. The hopelessness she felt found me on the other side of the country. I shrank when I thought of how helpless I was, how miserable she must have been to drink the way she did, of her skill for self-destruction. I wondered if it was contagious.

My mother had periods of sobriety that were usually short, just a month or two, but one lasted as long as a year. Alex and I cheered her on as she went back to teaching and later took a job at a nonprofit. Even though she was working, her income was low because she could only earn a certain amount before she lost the little workers' compensation she still received from my dad's employers. She worried about money, and that, or something else, seemed to cause her to start drinking again, which led her to lose her job. After not hearing from her for a while, I called the company I thought she was working for.

When I asked for her, the receptionist laughed and said, "She hasn't worked here for a while."

My mom decided to visit me in California toward the end of my four years there. The visit was ambitious; our itinerary included going to Big Sur, as well as visiting her sister, Arlene, in San Diego. I spent the week before she arrived snapping at my roommate and coworkers, and worrying that I'd have to search her purse and coat for bottles. Two days before she arrived, she called to tell me that she'd hit her head on the corner of our kitchen counter, not because she was hammered but because she was *dizzy*. She'd been to the doctor and didn't have a concussion, but she was badly bruised.

I shuddered when I spied her at LAX. Her face was no longer swollen, but it was every color in a rainbow of sea glass—green, yellow, light and dark blue, and a purple that veered toward black. She looked like she'd sprinted into a brick wall.

When I hugged her, she winced. "Don't worry," she told me, "it looks worse than it feels. I just hate having these dizzy spells."

I grabbed her bag and said, "Funny, I get dizzy when I'm plastered, too."

We drove to Big Sur, and she was silent for most of the six hours we spent winding up the rocky, gray coast. No topic I introduced interested her. When I told her about my writing projects—the reason her magna cum laude daughter was waitressing—she asked if I'd given myself a deadline for "making it."

"I haven't," I said, and sighed, "but I appreciate your encouragement."

She nodded, and I couldn't tell if she'd heard the sarcasm and hurt in my voice.

We stopped at a lonely gas station tucked against tall, dark trees. After dropping our provisions on the counter, the cashier asked my mother if she'd had brain surgery. "My own mother just did," the cashier said. She waved her hand in front of her face and grimaced. "She looks like . . . that."

"I had a bad fall," my mother curtly replied.

When I handed over my credit card, the woman glanced at it. "Anya! What a lovely and unusual name."

My mother perked up and said, "Thank you, I made it up."

On the way back to the car, a cool wind was tousling our hair and jackets. I turned to my mother and yelled, "You did not make up my fucking name!"

"Yes, I did," she said, still walking.

"Give it up. It's a character in a Chekhov play!"

My mother shot me a withering look as she struggled to light a cigarette. "These people don't read Chekhov."

Everywhere we went, people asked my mother if she'd had brain surgery. Some of the people inquiring had had surgery themselves, and they wanted to tell my mother all the details of their recovery in slow, stilted voices. My mother grew so tired of being accosted that she stopped accompanying me into stores and museums, and refused to eat in public.

She was sober the whole time. I told her repeatedly that I was proud of her for not drinking, and that I was worried she'd start up again once she left. "Look what just happened," I said as we were driving to San Diego. "Next time, you might hurt yourself even worse." She insisted that she hadn't been drunk when she fell. "Fine," I said. "You weren't drunk. But what if you were?" She nodded and agreed that, occasionally, she drank more than she needed to but said that I didn't have to worry.

I smacked the steering wheel. "But I do," I told her. "I worry all the time. I am always scared. And I think that's the right reaction. I hate what you're doing to yourself, and I want you to get help."

"Thank you, sweetie." She squeezed my arm. "I feel like I was destined to be your mother."

"Destined to be my mother?" Where had she gotten that absurd phrase? And what did it mean to her? Was she suggesting that we had a good relationship or that she was proud of me? Did she know what a burden she was? What had I done in a previous life to end up with her as my destiny?

After another year with bouts of sobriety, long binges, and multiple accidents, my mother decided to go to the Betty Ford Center for a month. My sister and I didn't know what had caused her to finally seek long-term treatment, and we didn't care. We were elated and agreed to attend the clinic's family week along with Aunt Arlene. My mother flew to San Diego, and I drove down to see her off. We had dinner at a Mexican restaurant and talked about how proud we were of her, how brave she was being, how great the clinic would be, while she dejectedly sipped Coke.

When Alex, Aunt Arlene, and I showed up at the Betty Ford Center a few weeks later, we were wary but optimistic. Our thin hopes were crushed when we saw that she was treating the experience like summer camp. She paraded us around and bragged about us, telling other patients, "Alexandra has beautiful sons! Anya went to Oxford!" They responded with heavy nods. The toll of their substance abuse, of being sober, and of the knowledge of the fight that was waiting for them when they left made them somber. The sunshine and the tennis courts were a nice backdrop but couldn't distract them from the pain of their past and the worry about their future. My mother's use of that particular group of people as an audience made her charade look scarier than ever and her appear more delusional than ever.

That first afternoon, Alex and I attended a lecture on addiction for the visiting family members. As we left, we encountered a group of patients who seemed just like our mother: smart women in their fifties with short hair who could be on their way to bridge club. They pounced on us and said how annoying everyone found our mother, who was always asking therapists philosophical questions like, "But what does addiction mean on a *soul level*?" They believed she was trying to show that she was an intellectual, and her act was ridiculous and transparent. After all, the clinic was a place for professionals, women with PhDs, which, they pointed out, our mother didn't have. And, they added, whenever she spoke and called herself an alcoholic, which was standard practice for everyone in all therapeutic sessions, she rolled her eyes after saying "alcoholic." They gossiped like high schoolers. "Poor kids," one of them said. "Your mom just doesn't get it." As they walked away, someone else wished us good luck and said we'd need it.

This run-in confirmed our biggest fear. Though she'd gotten herself to the Betty Ford Center, our mother wasn't committed to working on her sobriety because she still didn't think that she had a problem or understood that she was on her way to killing herself.

Alex, Arlene, and I were put into separate groups comprised of the family members of other addicts. In my group, there was a quiet twelve-year-old boy whose father was a patient who'd lost his job at a nuclear reactor when he was caught guzzling tequila at his desk. Each day included group-therapy sessions, lectures, and presentations about addiction. We learned about the various codependent roles we might have adopted, such as caretaker, hero, or the lost child who withdraws and becomes self-reliant. I'd been each.

This was the first time I'd encountered the ideas of Alcoholics Anonymous and Al-Anon outside of a brochure. The staff constantly spoke of the three C's: cause, control, and cure. We didn't cause our family member's addiction; we couldn't control it; and families had to understand that no one could "cure" chemical dependence because it couldn't be cured, only managed. Addiction, we were informed, was a "no-fault disease." Addicts didn't want to become addicts. They'd chosen to abuse substances, but hadn't chosen the noose of addiction. However, they still needed to take responsibility for their actions.

I spent much of the week in my head, arguing with what I was being taught because I didn't want to feel sympathy for my mother. I was out of what little I'd ever had. It seemed like she'd spent her entire life waiting for the opportunity to abandon herself to addiction. When my father's death presented one, she grabbed it and refused to let go. Even if she hadn't wanted to become who she now was, she'd let herself. She blamed others and the traumas of her life for her situation, and I blamed her for not getting enough help and for not taking the help she'd gotten seriously. I realized I was fixated on blaming her, on making her accountable for what she'd done to herself and our family. And what I was learning worried me. I was told patients would only succeed if they were honest about their problems and committed to doing whatever they needed to do to live sober. If my mother was rolling her eyes when she had to identify as an alcoholic, and was treating the clinic like a vacation, she was still in denial. She wasn't preparing herself for the hard work she'd face if she actually wanted to stop drinking. Meeting people who'd been sober for decades, such as the therapists and other professionals, showed me that the end was achievable if your desire was strong enough to motivate you through phases of desperation. I didn't think hers was.

We were encouraged to lovingly detach from our addict and focus on ourselves. I thought I'd detached a bit—I'd moved across the country and cared for myself by going on New Age adventures—but I couldn't be with my mother for more than five minutes before I slipped into one role or another, or wanted to screech at her like I was thirteen. I didn't like the idea that I couldn't help her recovery, that getting better had to be only her responsibility, one undertaken because she truly wanted to stop drinking. But I hoped that attending family week would show her that I believed in her, even though I was no longer sure that I did. I also hoped it would help me own my complicated and contradictory feelings.

As bad as my experience with my mother had been, being in this group showed me I could have been subjected to situations far worse. Other people were speaking about drained banks accounts, STDs, guns held to their heads, bailing someone out of jail who didn't know why they were there. I kept quiet for the first few days because I worried I'd come off like a whiner, offering only an occasional joke when I felt the mood got too heavy, which got me strange looks instead of laughs. With some prodding, I finally began to talk. I said that it sucked that my mother was an alcoholic. I felt helpless whenever I thought of her. And scared that she didn't want to get better and would only get worse. I blamed my mother for her state, as well as for not taking care of me the way she should have when I was a child. My body relaxed once I finally began participating.

The final day of family week was the only time addicts and their families were together. If patients had multiple people visiting, as my mother did, they had to attend each of the separate groups. That morning, my mother orchestrated an elaborate photo shoot of herself meditating alone in the Serenity Room. She sat in the lotus position with a humble smile and her chin tilted toward her higher power as Arlene snapped pictures and patients who actually wanted to meditate paced outside.

My group convened with our family members soon after, and we were told that we each had to sit in the middle of the circle with our addict and relate what we'd learned that week. Everyone sat down, said what they were supposed to while the rest of us nodded compassionately, and then returned to their chairs.

When it was our turn, I stood up and moved to my chair in the middle. Instead of going to her chair, my mother stood behind me and said, "I just want to say how happy I am to see my daughter."

The week had been full of shocks, but when my mother went on to announce that her daughter went to *Oxford*, everyone gasped. She was deviating from the script after no one else had, and doing it with the gusto of someone giving a wedding toast.

The therapist cleared his throat. "Sit down, Anita."

"Can I give my daughter a hug?" she asked. As he was saying no, she bent over and squeezed me as I tried to squirm away.

"Anita." The therapist's voice was firm. My mother sat across from me and smiled. Her smile quickly transformed into her "I'm listening" expression, which I knew meant she wasn't actually going to listen to me. This ignited the anger I'd discovered that week. People gasped again when I began to speak. My body expanded, and a voice I didn't recognize as my own, or even as human, flowed up from my stomach. I wasn't following the script, either, though I'd planned to.

"My ex-boyfriend drove you to the emergency room," I spat out. "You shit on the floor. Every time Alex calls me, I think she's going to tell me you're dead." I listed more of her most upsetting behaviors, hurled my hurt and blame, and screeched about how alone she'd made me feel.

My mother's mask of empathy turned to a look of animal terror. She watched me like I was a shadow that might turn into a demon.

I stopped speaking because I got dizzy. I'd forgotten to breathe. My mother and I were still staring at each other when the therapist quietly thanked me for sharing and dismissed the group for lunch.

I turned away and hurried out of the room. I was disoriented but also a little excited. Whatever had happened, it seemed like it managed to shake her.

I found Alex in the cafeteria. She asked how my session went. I told her about my mom's comment about me going to Oxford, and how she'd insisted on hugging me.

"You let her?" Alexandra said as she speared a piece of lettuce. "She tried to hug me, but I wouldn't let her."

Arlene plopped down next to us excitedly. "Ooooh, I heard about what happened," she said.

I bristled. I didn't want my sister to know what had happened in my session. I couldn't imagine what my mother would say about it.

Arlene patted Alex's arm and continued. "I just saw your mom. She said she tried to hug you during your talk, but you wouldn't let her. She claims everyone is gossiping about it and people keep coming up to her, asking if it's true."

My sister and I just looked at our food.

I never told Alex what happened, and my mom and I never spoke about it. That night, and many times in the years that followed, I burned with shame as I remembered attacking my mom for her behavior in front of people who'd experienced much worse. My pain was so wild and my sense of having been wronged was so much bigger than that of the people who'd stayed in control of themselves. I hadn't been trying to blame her for both of our problems; that wasn't enough. I wanted to punish and shame her for them. At Betty Ford, I'd discovered that I was really, really angry, but I didn't yet know how to curb it. I wasn't in control, and I definitely wasn't detached.

Before we left, we spoke with our mother's therapist. We

told him that we were worried that she wasn't taking her time at the clinic seriously. She didn't seem interested in recovery, let alone committed to it. Was there anything we could do? He said he'd speak to her about staying for another week. After we left, we found out that she agreed.

My mom never framed the picture of her meditating in the Serenity Room. She started drinking the day she got home and didn't stop for two months. I was livid, but I told myself it was *okay* that I was angry. She didn't intend to hurt me; her behavior wasn't personal. I'd created expectations knowing they probably wouldn't be met. I knew I had to lower them, but I didn't know how much lower they could get. I didn't want to give up on her. Maybe she had tried. Maybe she'd tried really hard but hadn't been able to last a day and felt disgusting and guilty as she drank.

Her friends, loyal for so long, stopped calling. They'd spent years driving her to detox, listening to her cry. They were so depressed by what happened to their friend Anita, who'd made them laugh with her jokes, excited them with her wild travel stories, and inspired them with her tirades about the environment. Like me, they were mad. They didn't think she was trying to get better and worried that their continued help would only enable her. And they had their own problems—cancer, parents with Alzheimer's.

The following year, in 2004, Grandma Helen died. She was the one person my mother consistently spoke to, aside from Sylvia. Like Sylvia, Helen never told my mother to stop crying, and she never interrupted my mother's stories even though she could recite them herself.

My mom flew to Chicago to help Arlene clean out their

mother's small apartment. On the first day, Arlene left to run an errand, and my mother ran her own. She stashed vodka and wine in her purse, under the sink in my grandmother's bathroom, and beneath the couch. When Arlene returned, my mom was already drunk but tried to deny it. Arlene went to work boxing up dishes and throwing away old sheets and towels. My mom tried to help, but Arlene exiled her to the bedroom because she kept dropping things. Arlene slept beside her that night, and when she woke early the next day, my mom's side was empty and wet with urine. Arlene found her crouched against the tub in the bathroom. She'd peed on the floor, and was growling and mumbling gibberish.

Arlene called Sylvia and asked for help. Sylvia went to my grandmother's apartment, gave my mom water and food, and listened as she cried that "Mommy was gone." There was another person on the list she recited: son, husband, mother.

I moved back to New York for graduate school in 2006. I'd gotten into the Columbia University MFA Writing Program after applying in secret. I was back on the East Coast and went to Boston every two months, but Alex was still in charge of our mom. I'd call her for updates and ask if she needed help, but she never said that she did. I felt like a flaky little sister, the dippy creative one who couldn't be the adult Alex needed me to be.

My first Thanksgiving back on the East Coast, I arrived at our mom's house to find her passed out and breathing heavily in her room. I flipped on the light and waited to see if she would wake, but she didn't. A large bottle of white wine was on her nightstand. I looked under the bed and found seventeen empties. "Oh Mom," I said. As I moved them into trash bags, I thought of how she was continually hurting herself. Drinking until she blacked out must have felt too good to stop, far better than being sober, so good that the consequences didn't matter. I placed a large glass of water on the nightstand next to the wine and went to my sister's. I couldn't stay. I felt guilty because I figured she'd want company if and when she woke up, but I was terrified by how she was living.

Seeing the person she'd become made me fear that the same thing could happen to me. I was so focused on achieving success that I couldn't imagine developing a problem as extreme as hers—one that would prevent me from at least trying to accomplish the things that I wanted—but I knew that addiction had a genetic component. And although I never felt that I *needed* to drink, I loved doing it. When I was out with friends and had already had a few, I didn't want to stop. I'd get more drunk than I already was because it felt so good; I ordered more drinks, accepted free ones from bartenders, and finished other people's when they'd had enough. When I made it home, either by luck or with the help of friends, I fell climbing the stairs to my apartment, crashed into my dresser, and woke up covered in bruises. Multiple friends told me that they were worried about my drinking. I knew they weren't being judgmental or hysterical. They'd seen me reach for drink after drink and pour booze into my body, and they knew my family. I listened, but I didn't know how to change. A life without wine or hyperactive bar antics seemed miserable. It was hard to accept that I didn't need to be drinking every day to be out of control or have problem behavior, and

I didn't want to give up alcohol completely. But I was a potential version of my mother if I didn't learn to control my occasional need to be out of control.

When my mom sobered up a few days later, I sat with her in her bedroom and told her that I was scared she was going to die. I asked her to see a therapist, to go to meetings, to volunteer, to go into treatment again, this time for three months. When she said that she didn't have the money, that she was poor, I told her, "Take money from Dad's retirement account early. Use it to take cooking classes in Italy! Visit your friend in France. Do something for the environment. Remember how much you used to care about the environment?" I was the cheerleader Betty Ford warned me about even though I knew that my eagerness and optimism wouldn't help.

My mom sucked on a cigarette and gave me a look that said I was the one who needed pity. She just wanted to be left alone. Her world had been bigger than most people's, and then it shrank to the size of her bed. It was becoming increasingly difficult for her to walk. She could only get down the stairs if she went down on her butt like a child, and she couldn't stand for more than a few seconds without the support of a wall or another person.

I was relentlessly happy to her face but haunted by her misery when I was alone. I'd call her and leave messages, and she'd call me back weeks later. When she did pick up the phone, she'd ask why I was calling at two in the morning and I'd tell her it was two in the afternoon. I asked what she was doing, and she'd say she was paying bills or doing her taxes. She was always paying bills and doing her taxes. The only other thing she ever said she was doing was watching TV.

She'd tell me about *Grey's Anatomy, Dateline,* sometimes mixing up shows and characters, but I'd listen. I wanted to tell her to cut the shit, but I stopped myself. Shame or accusations would only make her drink more.

In New York, I was writing and going to classes at Columbia, working part-time at a magazine. I began dating a photographer named Marko. He was fun and talented, supportive and sweet. He was the opposite of my father and of many of the men I'd dated. We fell in love quickly. I received a two-year fellowship to teach writing, and together we moved to Red Hook, Brooklyn. We adopted a feral cat from the neighborhood, whom we named Dolores, and I marveled at how adult and mostly interesting my life was. My only problem was my mother.

I began having nightmares about her committing suicide. She seemed to be drinking herself to death, but if she purposely killed herself, it would prove how miserable she was, how desperate not to be alive. I could handle the duller, drawn-out version of this truth, but the thought of seeing such clear evidence of her pain made me feel miserable, too, and scared that I might one day confront it.

Arlene and my mother's cousin Chrissy visited her the year I began teaching. They called me the day they arrived and demanded I come to Boston.

"Do you know the state your mother is living in?" they asked.

"Yes?" I said. "No?"

"You don't," Chrissy said. "She had a gash on her arm that she couldn't explain. We took her to the doctor, and they said her insurance had been canceled months ago because she hadn't paid it. We got it reinstated, and they took care of her, but when we got back we went through her mail—months of it. Her heat's about to be turned off!"

I explained that whenever I spoke to my mother, she seemed okay, or what okay had become for her. "She says she's paying her bills, every time I talk to her!" I said.

"Well, she's not," Chrissy said.

The next day, Chrissy, Arlene, Alex, and I sat in my mom's living room and talked through different plans: getting her an apartment, getting her into assisted living, trying another stay at Betty Ford.

When I heard my mom stirring, I went to rouse her. She was surprised to see me. "Hi," I said. "I'm here with Alexandra because Arlene and Chrissy asked us to come to Boston. Come downstairs so we can talk." I helped her out of the bedroom, then stood behind her as she slowly moved down the stairs. When she reached the bottom, I hoisted her up and brought her to the couch. She scanned our faces, trying to figure out what was happening.

We tried to tell her how concerned we were about her, but she kept interrupting.

"Why are we sitting here talking about depressing things?" she asked. "Chrissy, Arlene, it's your vacation! We should be celebrating. Who wants a glass of wine?"

"We thought we were coming for a vacation," Arlene said, "but then when we came, we realized that your life is a mess."

My mother turned to me. "How's graduate school, sweetheart?"

She would not agree that the house was too big for her, that it was dangerous with its steep staircases and inconvenient with a kitchen that was two floors below her bedroom. She refused to look at apartment listings. She disagreed with us about everything, but she had a hard time following conversations. She'd interrupt herself to ask what she'd been saying, or interrupt us with an unrelated topic.

When we were away from her, we wondered if she had Alzheimer's and discussed having her rights taken away. Then we could force her to move, or have her involuntarily committed. But, we decided, that was the last resort. We knew that if we tried, she would clean up and charm the judge, and if she succeeded, she'd refuse to speak to any of us again, and we wouldn't be able to help her at all. The idea of taking away anyone's rights, particularly my mother's, felt too dictatorial and final to me. Freedom had always been important to her. I'd seen how having alcohol withheld reduced her to a primal state. Having a judge say that I was no longer in control of my life would produce that reaction in me.

Alex took charge as she always did. She convinced our mom to make her coexecutor of her estate so all the bills could be in Alex's name, and she arranged for home health care a few times a week. Since our mother wasn't willing to move, Alex had the house safety-proofed. Rails and handles were installed in the bathroom and shower. Since reaching the kitchen, or even the front door to receive a food delivery, was so dangerous for her, a mini-fridge and microwave were placed outside her bedroom. As I listened to everything Alex was doing while also working full-time and raising kids, I felt more useless than ever.

We told her aides that it was okay to buy her alcohol when she asked for it. We didn't want her trying to go to the store herself or falling down the stairs when she had it delivered. We wanted her to be as safe as she could be.

Her first two aides quit because taking care of her was too upsetting for them. The third stayed. Nora loved my mother despite everything she put her through, and my mother adored her in return. She would sit on my mom's bed and listen to her talk about my father and Yuri, or Nora would share stories about her own family in Ireland. She promised to take my mother there with her if she got better. When I spoke to my mom, she'd tell me how happy she was to have a new friend, how they gabbed like schoolgirls and were planning a pizza night. But Nora's weekly email reports were grim—some weeks my mother would only stay awake long enough to eat a bit of food. I felt guilty for outsourcing these responsibilities to a stranger, but I knew I couldn't handle them myself.

My mom's memory and cognitive skills continued to decline, and her mobility became increasingly worse. "I used to be a dancer!" she cried to me, to Nora, to her doctors when she was sober enough to show up to her appointments.

"How often do you drink, Anita?" her doctors asked.

She'd pretend to be insulted. "I haven't had a drink in weeks!"

During one of my visits, I took my mom to see a psychiatrist, and she begged him to give her Antabuse, a drug that made you sick if you drank. He refused, explaining that he couldn't give her a drug like that if she wasn't also seeking treatment and actively trying not to drink. I didn't normally speak to my mother's doctors beyond informing them that she'd lied and had been drinking a lot. But now I asked,

"You're sure you can't give her that drug? What about something else?" He shook his head.

Asking for the drug was the biggest effort my mother had made to stop drinking in a while, even if it was only verbal. I understood what she was hoping for: something outside of herself that would cure her problems.

The doctor told her she was having mobility problems because of her drinking. My mom told him she was only drinking *because* of her mobility problems, that she used to be a dancer. If you keep drinking, he said, you're going to lose the ability to walk permanently. If you don't kill yourself first.

My mother nodded somberly, then took my arm so I could help her out of the office. As she shuffled toward the elevator, she whispered, "He's so condescending. What does he know about what I've been through?"

CHAPTER FOUR

My Mother's Waltz

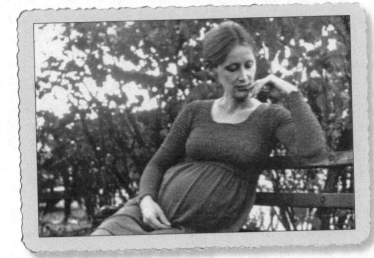

*I*n December 2009, Alex asked me to spend Christmas Eve with our mother so she could have the night with her husband and sons. I agreed, happy to have the chance to do something for her and for my mother as well, whose steady decline had turned into a rapid decay.

I decided to replicate the Christmas Eves from my childhood. We'd attend mass at the church across the street, where we'd donate toys that would later be delivered to families in need; sing carols up the block; eat a nice dinner (though not a Ukrainian one), and I'd give an enthusiastic reading of "'Twas the Night Before Christmas." Though this and other holidays had become increasingly depressing, I still felt there was magic in it and hoped I could harness some.

When I arrived the afternoon of Christmas Eve, the house was chilly and there was little to indicate that it was Christmas. I shouted for my mother, but she didn't respond, though I could hear the TV blaring in her room. I turned up the heat, then looked at the stack of unopened cards on the table. I shouldn't have been surprised by the lack of holiday cheer, but I was. My mother hadn't had a tree for more than a decade or done more than put Santa Claus candleholders on the mantel. I berated myself for not calling her aides and asking them to decorate. "Of course, *you* could have come a few days ago and bought a small tree," I thought, "but you didn't." I didn't want to spend more time with her than I had to. As I assessed the situation, I realized that the only planning I'd done was to buy teddy bears for us to leave at the church. I'd told myself that I wanted, and would, give my mother a nice Christmas, while worrying that she'd sleep through the whole thing and I'd be stuck sitting on the couch and reading the same old magazines that I'd read before, annoyed at both of us for thinking it could have been different.

"Anya!" my mother exclaimed when I finally peeked into her bedroom. "I didn't hear you come in."

Her hair was frizzy and unwashed, her skin waxy and loose. Slabs of atrophied muscle weighed down her once-small frame. The air was saturated with her smells, a half-eaten pizza was on the floor, and crunchy-looking tissues were scattered across her bed. But none of that mattered. Her words were clear, her eyes steady. She was sober. I was so surprised that I laughed and kissed her. "Merry Christmas, Mom!"

She grinned. "Merry Christmas, child."

I suggested that we go downstairs. "Do you need help?"

"Nope! I'll get there like I always do." She shuffled out of her room and slowly squatted next to the banister, then looked up at me reassuringly. "It's the safest way." She scooted on her butt until she reached the bottom step.

We moved toward the couch, where she told me how happy she was that I was there. I was disarmed but elated. I showed her the toys I'd brought for the church service and asked what she wanted for dinner. "Let's have something delicious. We deserve a good meal."

She frowned and shook her head. "I don't want you spending money. I'll finish the pizza I got yesterday."

"But it's Christmas!" I cried. "We should eat something special."

"Are you planning on cooking? I'm not."

I patted her hand. "Don't worry, I still don't cook, and I promise I didn't bring borscht. I'll run out right now and pick up something prepared."

"Nora went shopping a few days ago," she protested. "She stocked the freezer with Lean Cuisines and burritos."

I told her we weren't eating burritos. I went to the neighborhood's fanciest grocery store, where I bought close to a hundred dollars of premade London broil and roasted vegetables so she'd have plenty of leftovers.

She was still on the couch when I returned, staring out at the street, but her mind had wandered off. Her enthusiasm had been replaced by something heavy. I scrambled to reignite what little excitement had been there when I left. I gushed about the food I'd purchased, but she just nodded. Knowing how easily I could lose her, I grabbed the stack of unopened cards and set them in her lap. "Look at this huge pile! Why don't you open a few? We can find out what everyone's been up to this year."

She picked up a red envelope, then put it down and looked at the floor. The rug, which had been there for most of my life, was worn thin and dotted with dust bunnies.

I went over to the stereo. "I'd love to hear some carols. Maybe I can find that tape you loved, the New Agey one with all the bells? What was it called?"

"Oh, I don't remember," she said.

"Well there's gotta be something on the radio. I'd love to hear the *Nutcracker*. I'm so sick of the cheesy carols I've been hearing in stores, aren't you?" I immediately regretted what I'd said. The only stores she'd have been in were the liquor shop and drugstore down the block, and she probably hadn't even been to those since her aides ran her errands now.

I pressed the stereo's On button and fiddled with the tuner, but nothing happened.

"Don't bother," she told me. "That hasn't worked in years."

I asked if she wanted to sing and launched into "Rudolph, the Red-Nosed Reindeer." I stopped when she groaned, then bombarded her with stories about my life, teaching, and Marko, knowing there wasn't any point in asking for hers. My sentences landed on top of each other as my voice pitched higher and higher. I was doing exactly what she'd always done: pretending the situation was different than it was, fighting reality by offering a version of it that I preferred. But nothing I said pulled her into a conversation; she was refusing to play

"Happy Christmas" with me, just as I'd often refused to play along with her.

"Remember how we used to watch *I Love Lucy*? And *Cheers*? Which one did you like more?"

"What?" she blinked.

I glanced at my phone. "Mass starts in an hour. Do you need help getting ready?"

She clutched her arms and shivered. "It's so cold out."

"I know, but we're only going across the street, and you have lots of warm coats. Did Nora help you find something to wear? It looked like something was hanging off your closet door."

"I'm really tired," she said. "You're not tired from your drive?"

"Not at all. If you want, I can grab your clothes and makeup and help you get ready down here."

She repeated that she was tired, said she didn't have anything to wear and that it had rained the day before and the sidewalk was probably slippery. "That can be really dangerous for me. My balance has gotten so bad."

"I'll make sure you don't fall."

Her face was tense. She was quiet for a bit, then said that she didn't want to go.

"What happened?" I asked. "Don't you want to sing carols and give away these teddy bears? Maybe we'll see some neighbors." When she grimaced, I saw I'd said the wrong thing again. There were plenty of reasons that she might not want to see people.

I changed tack. "*I'd* really like to go," I said. "This service is really special to me."

"Then go." She patted my knee. "I'll just stay home."

"What if we took a cab to that Unitarian church you like? Their services are always lovely."

She was looking out the window again. There was no one on the street, nothing to see.

"Okay, let's skip church and get right to eating. I'll clear off the table and light some candles." I looked at the table and saw that clearing it would take a while. I thought again about how unprepared I was for what was supposed to be a special evening. Maybe I was the reason she was disappointed. She was actually sober, and I'd already emptied my bag of tricks.

"I told you," she said, and sighed, "the sidewalks are going to be slippery. I can't make it up the hill." She looked at her hands and rubbed her palm with her thumb.

"Well, let's think of something else. Maybe I could rent a movie, or—"

Suddenly, a conspiratorial smile spread across her face. A switch had been flipped. "You know what would be fun? A *drink*. We'll go somewhere fancy, like the Ritz!"

I glared at her. "You know I don't drink with you."

"But we never get to spend time together! I want to celebrate."

I pointed out that we were already spending time together. "We're having fun," I said, even though we weren't. "I know I can't stop you from drinking when I'm not here, but I don't want you to drink in front of me." I took her hand in mine. Her skin was cold and soft. "I'm so proud of you for being sober now. I'm sure it's not easy." I tried to sound encouraging. "You can handle not drinking for another night."

She crossed her arms.

"I'm trying to do something nice for you, Anya."

"Are you?"

We sat in silence until she announced that she wanted to watch TV. With a sigh, I helped her upstairs and flipped between the few channels she got until she decided on a crime drama. I stayed with her until she said she was hungry.

In the kitchen, I fumed as I dropped the food onto plates and stuck them in the microwave. It was only six, but the night was already a loud failure, and it was my fault. The only thing I'd done to give her a nice Christmas was hope that one materialized out of minimal effort. But if she wanted to spend the night watching TV in bed, we could do that.

When I presented the food, she poked at the carrots and parsnips. "What are these?"

"Root vegetables. They're very trendy."

We balanced our plates on our thighs and picked up the brussels sprouts that flew onto the sheets when we cut them too aggressively.

"Isn't this good? To think you wanted leftover pizza!" I said.

"Do you know what would make it even better?"

"What?"

"*Wine.*"

"Not happening," I mumbled, my mouth full.

She placed her plate on the dresser and wiped her hands on her shirt. "I need a drink, Anya." I looked at her and saw that another Anita had crept into her body. Her face was fixed in fierce resolve.

"I'm not buying you booze."

"Fine," she said breezily. "I'll get it myself."

I knew that she couldn't go to the liquor store alone; well, maybe she could, but it would be a pitiful and possibly dangerous journey. "Please," I said gently. "You're doing really well."

"Anya!" she yelled. "I *want* a drink!" Her thirst had been ignited. She'd made her decision, or her addiction had made it for her; it was a bully stronger than both of us. If she didn't get alcohol soon, she'd become increasingly difficult and angry, and we'd both be miserable.

She watched me as she tried to stand up. "I could fall, you know. It's so dark, the streetlamps barely do anything."

I thought about leaving in protest. If I did, I could go hang out with my sister and have a drink myself, which I really, really wanted to do. But she was my responsibility for the night. I'd been asking Alex for the opportunity to help for years, and I didn't want to fumble the one she'd finally given me.

"No," I finally said. "I'll go."

She immediately went sweet. "Thanks, darling. You know what I like, right?"

"I sure do," I said.

I walked to the liquor store through the frigid dark, under the church's tall, silent spire, hating her for putting me in the position she had and myself for caving to her.

I wished the smiling clerk a Merry Christmas when I walked in, and we chatted about the indignity of working on Christmas Eve, which I'd had to do many times when I was a cocktail waitress in Los Angeles.

When I dropped the wine, two double bottles of Chardonnay, on the counter, he raised his eyebrows. "Big plans tonight?"

I forced a smile. "It's for my mom."

He studied the bottles for a moment, then nodded with recognition. "Oh, I know your mother. Everyone here does, and the gals who work for her."

I stared at the ground, wishing I'd said the wine was for me so I could have remained anonymous. I didn't want to be the person with the notorious, drunk mother, the one buying that mother alcohol on Christmas Eve.

"You know little Nicky, the red-haired kid who works during the day?"

I said that I didn't.

He told me that my mom's aides usually bought her wine, but when she came in herself, Nicky always escorted her home. Not because she was drunk, though she often was, but because she could barely walk. I imagined my mother, with her sour breath and ratty hair, flirting with Nicky as he held her by her elbow and then waited to make sure she got inside.

"Thanks," I mumbled. "And thank Nicky for me."

The clerk pursed his lips. "My father's an alcoholic. It's hard. You don't want to watch, but you can't look away. When you do, you feel terrible."

"It's all terrible," I said. "Looking away, not looking away. What are we supposed to do?"

"Beats me." He laughed. "But if you find out, let me know." After handing me the heavy bag, he gave me his card and told me to call him if I ever needed help.

I put one bottle in the fridge, the other on the kitchen counter. For years, I'd refused to drink with my mother. It was a tiny act that made me feel that I was doing *something*, but it hadn't made a difference. "Screw it," I thought. "I deserve a drink."

My mom beamed like a kid who'd gotten the gift she'd wanted most when I appeared in her room with the wine and poured us each a glass.

She held up hers and cried, "Merry Christmas!"

I tried to make conversation during the commercials or when something interesting happened on the show, but her responses were mumbled and vague. Soon she stopped answering at all. She had what she needed: her bed, the television, wine, and cigarettes. She was finally having the Christmas she wanted. I was no longer needed. If anything, I was in the way.

After two hours, I called Alex to tell her I was on my way. She answered cheerfully, but when I told her about my evening, annoyance leaped into her voice.

"You bought her booze? You know this means she's going to miss Christmas, right?"

I hadn't considered that our mother drinking tonight meant that she wouldn't make it the following day. "I'm sorry," I stammered. "I couldn't keep fighting her. But just because she's drinking now doesn't mean she won't be able to come tomorrow."

When I went to say goodbye, my mother's smile was wide and wobbly. She was staring at the TV, but she couldn't tell me what she was watching.

I told her I was going to Alex's. "I want to be there when the boys open their presents in the morning."

"That's nice," she said. "That will be fun."

"Everyone's coming for a late lunch, so I'm going to pick you up at one. We've got a lot of great gifts for you. We all really want you there, especially the kids." I eyed the wine and guessed she'd had three glasses. There was hope. I reached for the bottle. "Let me put this in the fridge for you."

She batted my hand away.

"Mom, if you miss tomorrow, Alex, all of us, are going to be really disappointed."

"I'll be there," she slurred. "You're picking me up at one."

I started calling her at nine the next morning, but she never answered. Sometimes the machine would pick up, other times the phone just rang and rang. Marko arrived, and after my nephews jumped all over him, we discussed whether or not we should drive to my mom's and try to wake her, but we decided against it. If she was passed out, there was no way of getting her up. If she was awake, she'd be plastered, which meant she'd either put up a fight or be terrible to be around.

Her absence hung over the day. I trailed my sister through her house, apologizing over and over. She'd respond with a firm "It's fine," but I knew it wasn't.

When my nephews doled out presents before dinner, they stacked our mother's in an empty chair. When my uncle said grace, he acknowledged, as he always did, the family that couldn't be there because they were dead. He accidentally included our mother in the list.

My mom picked up when I called the next day. She was happy and drunk, but not so drunk that I couldn't understand her.

"You missed Christmas. What happened?" I demanded.

"Oh Anya, I was just so tired."

I reminded her that she'd promised she was going to come. She did what she always did when confronted: She didn't respond.

I told her that Marko and I were going to stop by on our way back to New York, to drop off presents and say goodbye.

My mother was drinking and watching TV when we got there. "You remember Marko, don't you?" I asked as I arranged the gifts in front of her.

"Polo!" she giggled, then composed herself. "Of course I remember him." She winked. "I always remember handsome men."

If it had just been me, she would have glanced at the gifts and returned to watching TV, but since Marko was there, she was animated and chatty. She still believed that a smile and a joke had the power to mask the stink of alcohol that surrounded her.

I was eager for her to open her presents, for her to see that we all cared about her. She unwrapped each mechanically and pushed the boxes off the bed. She didn't bother to act excited about any of them, not even the pair of fancy black pajamas from my sister and me. She criticized a calendar someone had gotten her and sneered at a chunky handmade necklace. I tried to see our gifts through her eyes and understood that they were unnecessary, junk. She needed and wanted very few things.

"We have to drive back to Brooklyn soon," I said, smoothing the comforter. "Do you need anything before we go? Are you hungry? I would have brought leftovers, but there weren't any."

"I'm having trouble sleeping." She rooted around her small night table and grabbed an empty pill bottle and waved it at me. "I'm out of my medication. Can you go to the drugstore and get me a refill?"

"Of course," I said, and was back in five minutes. She threw two pills down with a gulp of wine.

I told her about the books and games her grandchildren received from Santa, and said it would mean a lot to them, and to Alex, if she saw them soon. I reminded her that the eldest's birthday was in two weeks. "Have Nora help you get a present, okay?"

She pawed the bed looking for her cigarettes. When she only found empty packs, she asked us to get her some.

"Okay," I said. "Do you need anything else? Do you want the paper?"

"More wine."

"You don't need me to buy you more wine," I told her. "I'll get you the other bottle from the fridge."

She nodded at the wine on her nightstand. "That is the other bottle."

As Marko and I walked to the liquor store, I told myself that it was okay to buy more alcohol. There'd be much, much more. I was just buying one bottle.

She was already more relaxed when we returned. The drugs had kicked in. I opened the wine and made sure her cigarettes were within reach. I wanted to leave on a positive note, so I began telling her about the classes I'd be teaching during the upcoming semester.

She interrupted me. "I'm tired. You can go."

I looked at my mother and saw a stranger: someone I could hurt for but not love, or even like. I thought, *Fuck you, lady. I came over with presents, stories, and all the love I could muster, and you send me on errands and then on my way.* I wished her a Merry Christmas and left.

I spoke to her a few times over the next month because there'd been a sudden development with her health. Though her doctors insisted that "wet brain"—alcohol-induced neurological damage—was responsible for her mobility issues, they'd found excess fluid in her spine and thought draining it might improve her gait. She'd scheduled the procedure, which would require that she spend almost a week in the hospital, possibly in a fair amount of pain. She also had to be sober in the days leading up to it and while she recovered. I'd agreed to take off work so I could be with her before and after. I thought she'd be thrilled that surgery was an option, but when we chatted, she seemed hesitant about going through with it.

Five days before she was due at the hospital, we spoke on the phone as I was walking through SoHo.

"I'm canceling the procedure," she told me. "It's going to be painful, and I don't want to spend four days in bed."

I stopped walking in the middle of the street. A car honked at me, and I moved over to the sidewalk, where I collided with some tourists. I leaned against a building and glared at the sky. "You spend every day in bed and have for a long time."

She didn't respond.

"I know it's going to hurt, and I know that's scary. But it might help you walk better! Isn't that what you want? You should be excited! You used to be a dancer!"

She sucked hard on a cigarette. "I'm not doing it."

"This is a real chance to get better!"

"I'm not *doing* it," she said again.

"Okay, then I guess I don't have to come to Boston on Friday."

"You don't."

I hung up and stifled a scream. Why had I ever thought she might go through with it? I was as mad at myself as I was with her. For the past few years, she'd cited her inability to walk as a justification for her drinking, and I believed that it upset and depressed her, as it would anyone. By refusing surgery, she may have been admitting that although she'd love to be able to walk properly, she didn't want to change. If the surgery was successful, she'd lose an excuse and face the hope and expectation—her family's and doctor's—that she'd drink less, or even stop.

That Friday, I was home, unsure what I should be doing since I hadn't planned on being there. Marko was with his parents; his father had late-stage prostate cancer and they were meeting with a new doctor to discuss treatments.

My phone buzzed, and I saw it was Alex. I answered without thinking.

She said, "I have something to tell you," and I knew. I'd predicted this moment and had rehearsed it often. We said it together: "Mom's dead."

Nora had found her in her bed that morning. She called the social worker who coordinated our mom's care, and the social worker called my sister. They were both at the house. Our mom's body had just been taken away. I told Alex I'd leave for Boston as soon as I could.

I studied the winter sun slanting through the window. Everything was the same as it had been a few minutes ago, before my sister's call. Dolores was sleeping on the couch; I knew that if I tried to pet her, she'd bat my hand away. I turned in circles to see my apartment, then stood still.

My mom's death had been on the horizon for more than

a decade; sometimes it was close, sometimes far away, but it was never out of sight. I no longer had to wait for it. Finally, it had arrived.

I was calm as I called Marko, but the moment he answered, I surprised myself by crying. "My mother died." My words were caught up in my tears.

"What?" He was thinking about his father's imminent death, stuck for hours already in the hospital.

"My mother died," I said again, and my tears dried up. "My mother *died*."

"Okay," he said. "I love you. We're almost done here."

"I have to go to Boston," I said.

"I know," he said. "I'll be home soon."

When we arrived at my sister's five hours later, my brother-in-law, Raj, gave me a huge hug and told me how sorry he was.

"Thanks," I said. "Where's Alex?"

My sister came out of the living room. We looked at each other, hugged, and looked at each other again.

"So here we are," I said.

"Yup."

We all sat on the couch drinking red wine. Alex and I made lists of what we needed to do that night and over the next few days: call family, call more family, call my mom's friends, find a place to have her cremated, write and publish an obituary, find a church, organize a reception.

Our first stop the next day was the medical examiner's. They'd made an exception and seen us on the weekend. A kind and efficient older woman took us into a room with a round table. She slowly opened a manila folder and slid a large black-and-white picture of our mother's face across the table.

Her eyes were closed, her hair was spread out on a gurney, and her skin sagged toward her ears. I thought, "That woman in the picture is my mother, and that picture is a picture of a dead person."

The funeral home was next. We chose one not far from where Alex lived. It was a white clapboard house with black shutters, and Irish-owned. O'Someone's, McSomething's.

A large man with hammocked eyes greeted us and brought us upstairs to an office where he described what would happen: They'd receive the body from the medical examiner, cremate it, then release the ashes to us.

He gave us each a heavy binder of urns to browse and left the room. We saw that our mother's ashes could be housed in one that looked like a Roman vase, a football, or a horse's head.

When he returned, we said we didn't want an urn. Any urn.

"Perhaps," he stuttered, "you'd like go with something simple and elegant so you have a nice place to keep your mother while you decide what you want to do next."

"It's okay," we said in unison.

He straightened papers on his desk. "What we do in these instances is put your mother's remains in a tightly sealed bag and put that bag in a cardboard box."

Alex and I looked at each other and nodded. I smiled and said that was perfect.

We stood and shook hands. "We should be receiving the body from the medical examiner tomorrow, and we should be able to take care of your mother in the afternoon. We'll call you when she'd ready for pickup."

I made a move for the door, but my sister lingered. "In addition to calling us when you're finished, can you call us before you begin?"

"I'm sorry?" he said.

"I'd like you to call us before the cremation, so we can know when it's happening," my sister said.

"Of course," he said. "We'd be happy to."

We decided to hold the funeral at the Unitarian church that our mother liked. I had been to the church with her once for a winter solstice celebration on Christmas Eve, and she'd gone a few times on her own. The minister was a tall, calm woman who resembled Sarah Palin. She asked us about our mother so she could plan the service, and we told her everything. We wanted to be honest about her alcoholism, but we also wanted to celebrate her achievements and love of travel, and address the loss of Yuri and our father. She asked us what our religious beliefs were. Alex and I looked at each other blankly.

The minister explained that she wanted to use vocabulary that we were comfortable with. She could use the term "God," for example, but she didn't have to. She asked my sister what she'd told my nephews about their grandmother's death, explaining that she thought it was important to reinforce that story or belief in an official capacity.

"I told them that Noni has gone to live in the stars," Alex said, and she began to cry. The minister seemed relieved to see one of us get emotional, but by the time she handed my sister a box of tissues, Alex was done. She'd wiped her cheeks with her hands and blinked away whatever tears remained, but politely accepted the box and kept it in her lap.

I'd seen her cry only a few times. Alex thought feelings were an indulgence. She'd once gone to therapy, and when I'd asked about her session, she told me she didn't see the point. "I cried the whole hour," she told me. "It was such a waste." When I suggested that expressing her pain and frustration could be a good thing, especially since the burden of our mother fell so heavily on her, she'd rolled her eyes. I tried again. "If you cried, maybe you're more upset than you know. You're juggling so much between the kids, work, and Mom. Speaking to someone an hour a week sounds good for you."

"I'm too busy," she'd said. "And, anyway, I'm great at compartmentalizing."

Alex's phone rang as she drove us back to her house, and she handed it to me. "I think it's the funeral home."

When I answered, the man we'd met with said the cremation was done, and we could pick up our mother anytime. "Okay," I said. "Thanks so much." I hung up and relayed the news.

Alex's face turned red and her eyes filled. "He was supposed to call us before so we knew it was happening, not after! Why didn't you scream at him?"

"I don't know." My mind went blank, as it always did when someone was mad at me. "Do you want me to call him back?"

"No," she sighed.

"Why did you want to know when it was happening?"

"So we could have prayed, or meditated, or I don't know, done *something*."

I apologized and squirmed in my seat. Alex had cried twice in one day. We were experiencing our mother's death together, but her feelings weren't what I'd expected. I figured she'd feel unburdened, maybe even happy. I didn't know how to respond to her, didn't know if she wanted comfort or quiet.

Meditating or praying while our mother's body was turned to dust seemed too spiritual and reverent for my sister; that was the kind of thing *I* tended to want to do. But I hadn't thought of it in the first place and had forgotten about it altogether. I didn't know if Alex's desire came from wanting to acknowledge and respect that moment or from needing a specific time to say goodbye.

I asked again if I could call him back. "I'll yell at him," I said.

"Don't bother."

"Do you want to pull over and meditate?" I said anxiously. "We can do whatever you want."

Raj and Marko seemed uncertain how they should approach us when we returned. I took Marko up to the guest room and flopped on the bed.

"How's it going?" he asked as he stroked my arm. "Are you okay? Are you sad? You can be sad, you know."

I traced invisible shapes on the green-and-white bedspread. I was hyperaware of my body and movements, aware that I was empty. "If I'm sad," I said, "I'm sad for my mother."

That became my line. Whenever people asked how I was doing, I said that I wasn't sad for myself but was so, so sad for my mom and for what her life became. How could I be sad that my mother, the person she'd turned into, was gone? Wanting her to live longer, when she obviously didn't want to be alive, would have been cruel, even selfish. I was sixteen years older, but I felt the way I had when my father died— relieved.

The night before the funeral, Marko and I went into the drugstore where I'd worked throughout high school. The owner, his son, and everyone who worked there had been deeply kind to my family and me. They'd looked after me when I was little, and, when I was older, talked me through treatment options for my mother. They'd wait with me if I told them an ambulance was coming to take her to detox and let my mother's account go unpaid for months. I figured they knew about the funeral from the neighborhood, or from the obituary we'd published, but I wanted to invite them personally.

A young guy was working, and I asked to see Danny, the owner's son. Danny's smile evaporated when he saw me. He said he and his dad would be at the funeral; all of the staff who could be spared would be there. He asked if I needed anything, and I burst into tears. The young kid disappeared. I was so confused to be crying, and embarrassed by my gasps and wet face. When I tried to apologize, I couldn't get the words out. I waved my hands in the "I can't/I'm sorry" gesture, tried to make the "you get it" face, and backed out of the store.

"I can't believe that just happened," I hiccuped to Marko as we walked toward the restaurant. "That was crazy."

"It was." Marko laughed, then realized he wasn't supposed to be laughing. He put his arm around me and squeezed.

Marko and I were staying at my mom's house since my sister's place was full of guests. When we got in, he asked if I wanted a drink. "I'm good," I said. "I have to work on the eulogy. I haven't even started."

He laughed. "You know the funeral is tomorrow, right?" He gave me a long hug. I wriggled out of it, anxious to get to work, and sent him to bed.

I'd done what I typically did—put off a big task with the hope that the eventual pressure would produce genius I wouldn't otherwise be able to access. I took out a notebook and started writing, but the only things that came out were canned sentiments I'd heard elsewhere. I couldn't think of anything personal or remotely brilliant to say. After an hour, I gave up and went to look for inspiration.

The door to my mother's bedroom was closed. I peeked in and saw that it was almost exactly as I'd last seen it. Her dressers were littered with cigarettes packs and lighters, tissues and pill bottles, but her bed had been stripped, her stained mattress naked. The bottles, dirty plates, and glasses had been cleared.

I poked around her study, the room that would soon demand so much of my time, until I came across boxes of photographs, ones I'd seen many times as well as ones my parents had never shown me—photos from their wedding; of them in bathing suits and Santa hats atop camels; my mother in Boston, Beirut, alone, with us. I realized her life had inspired many of my dreams and goals; all of her travels, working internationally. I'd never been able to admit it because from childhood I'd positioned myself as separate from her. Later, I was only able to see her as a prisoner of her own weaknesses, a bedridden victim who had no dreams at all. I grabbed a bunch of letters and pictures, and returned to the living room and my notebook. What came out was a surprise.

I didn't cry at the funeral. Not when I walked in with my family, or when I saw how crowded it was and that so many of my friends had made the trip from New York. But I knew that I had to show some emotion. As I walked up to the podium to give the eulogy, I scanned the page and found a place where I could pause and perform at least a bit of grief.

On behalf of my family, I want to thank everyone for coming. It means so much to us to have you here to honor my mother's life.

As her daughter, and probably as anyone who knew her well, it's hard to know what person and life to honor. In a lot of ways, I think my mother led two distinct lives. The first part, which thankfully was the largest, was filled with passion, adventure, and achievement. She was a very sensitive person, and she put love into everything. She traveled the world, dedicated years of her life to environmental protection. She was a devoted teacher and, of course, a mother. One of the nicest, and most difficult, things for me to hear over the past few weeks is how much she adored my sister and me. How, though she had a million interests, we were really her life. She gave us a lot of love, and she also raised us to be strong and independent. On top of all this, she was also a lot of fun. She loved laughing and telling jokes, she could talk (and talk) to anyone, and she was a great hostess.

But my mother's life was also filled with tragedy. She lost her son, Yuri David, and then she lost her husband, my father, George. And I just think it was too much for her. These two people left her life, and they left enormous holes in her heart. I don't think she believed it was possible to fill them. She was so sad, and she turned to alcohol to deal with her feelings.

And we all know the rest. For so long we, her friends and family, rallied behind her, but she didn't believe in herself like we believed in her. I felt so helpless as I watched her sink further and further into her anger and grief. I also felt incredibly sad, angry, and confused. For so long I thought things might change, but eventually I accepted that they weren't going to. She continued to decline, and toward the end of her life, I know many of us felt that she just wasn't the person we knew and loved. I know it's going to take me a while to make sense of what happened to her, as much as you can make sense of anything.

People have told me that of the most difficult things to do after someone dies is to go through their belongings, but last night, I found some things that were actually very comforting, though I did feel a bit like a kid who was being really naughty by going through Mommy's stuff, and that she might show up at any time and scream at me. Now that she's gone, I can finally get to the good stuff, the stuff in the boxes on the top shelf that I need a chair to reach. This excavating is weird and it *is* sad, but I'm seeing and learning so many interesting things about who my mother was when she was not my mother, that I can't help but be a little bit happy and even charmed.

One of the best things about going through my mother's stuff is seeing all of the pictures, and I'm talking about thousands of pictures. My father was a wonderful photographer, and he documented everything, big and small, and I feel so lucky to have this window into their life. I've been poring over these pictures from the sixties and seventies, and I've come to a realization that's exciting to me now, but would have freaked me out when I was younger, when I definitely would have *never* verbalized it . . . but I think I'm ready.

My mother was *cool*. She was really, really cool. I feel lucky to have been her daughter (most of the time), but I would have loved to have been her friend. I wish I could have traveled with her. I wish I could have stayed up late with her, arguing about politics and philosophy. I *definitely* wish I could have borrowed her clothes, and I can't even tell you how badly I want to have gone to one of her parties. Of course that can't happen. And of course I can't pretend my mother didn't turn into a different person. But I *know* that person, and it was often not an easy relationship. Now that I have all of these pictures and letters and ticket stubs, I realize I can honor my mother by getting to know the woman I never knew.

We held the reception at a Persian restaurant that had been one of our mom's favorites. I was touched by the large turnout, and by all the stories people wanted to tell. Her friends told me things I expected and knew, but my friends, the ones I'd known for decades, told me things I didn't—how much they loved my mom, how stylish and glamorous they'd always found her. How she'd treated them with respect and interest, way more than their own parents, and made them feel welcome at our house. She never asked about school, only how they were, where they got their nose ring, or if they had music recommendations. And she listened to their answers.

Memories flickered before me. The time my friend Sindhu swung by with her gutter-punk friend Liam. My mother got to the door before I did, and after hugging Sindhu, she said, "Liam! What a wonderful name." She ran her fingers down the arm of his black leather jacket that he'd decorated with angry phrases and band names in silver paint. "Fabulous." Liam blushed and mumbled, "Thanks."

Another time during high school, when my mother was home for the weekend but, I thought, drunk enough that she was basically away, I was hanging out with people in our backyard, drinking her booze and smoking her cigarettes. When she surprised us by coming outside, I thought she was going to yell at me and kick us all out, but she greeted everyone enthusiastically. She went to over my friend Bart, a Vietnamese guy with long dreadlocks. After introducing herself, she said, "Your hair is wonderful." She asked if we needed anything, and when I said we didn't, she left us alone.

I nodded along to what I heard, accepting sympathy and saying "Thank you for coming" over and over, but I was in another time. A time when my mother was the person my friends remembered, the person I'd spoken about in her eulogy, when she was a person I hadn't known.

Part Two

I traveled often between Brooklyn and Boston in the months after my mother's death and was busy in both cities. In Boston, I was still cleaning out her house, moving things into storage, and helping my sister finalize our mother's estate. In Brooklyn, I was teaching and finishing my thesis. I didn't have enough time for even one of these tasks, or to be patient with Marko or my friends who hovered nearby and asked me, again and again, how I was *doing*.

Death liberates you for a short period of time. You get to do whatever you want. No one can be mad at you, and you never have to explain why you want to do something or not. Marko and I had a running joke—one of us would say "My mother died!" whenever we wanted to go out to dinner again, or take the train to Boston instead of the bus. I loved the excuse, but I never made it because I was sad. I wasn't. I'd preformed sadness at my mother's funeral but only because I thought I had to.

My friends, some of whom had been around for my dad's death as well, came over one by one to make dinner for me. They offered food with big eyes and sat, ready to listen to me cry or complain. But all I could do was scarf down their baked cod and crack jokes. They'd come expecting something that I couldn't give them. They thought they'd find me transformed, if only temporarily, by the loss of my mother, which would be particularly hard for me because I'd also lost my father.

I began to resent everyone's expectations. I became defiant, proud of my lack of sorrow. *Both* of my parents were dead, and I was fine. People who still had their parents seemed like wimps by default. And people who'd lost parents and were really sad about it? They were wimps, too.

It was easy, and enjoyable, to tell myself that my parents were *bad parents*. But I kept thinking that there had to be a primal connection that made all of that irrelevant. I retained my childhood fears about being defective, and they shook my bravado. I wondered if I wasn't sad because something was wrong with me.

I read grief memoirs, hoping they'd stir up sorrow, but they made me feel lacking as well. I wasn't devastated or depressed like those authors, and could not connect to the books' blue beauty. Sometimes, I'd get jealous. Not of the writers' pain, which was too powerful and destructive to envy, but of the relationships that had caused them to be so burdened. I thought it was incredible to be close enough to your parents, to love them so much that you were bedridden with anguish when they died, so comatose or unmoored that you ruined other relationships and found the world empty.

I justified my ambivalence by telling myself that I wasn't very close to my parents, and since my family wasn't a very happy place to be, there just wasn't much to miss. I felt lucky that my parents had died when I was youngish. I'd never have to put them into homes, witness their memories evaporate, or support them financially. But what I'd glimpsed in their early letters nagged at me. Instead of fading, my curiosity grew.

As I cleared out my mother's house, I filled boxes with my parents' most personal belongings and brought them with me to Brooklyn, where I arranged papers and photographs into piles on my bedroom floor. One was for the letters that my parents sent to each other. Another for those my mother exchanged with her lifelong friends Sylvia and Chip. There was one for the condolences we received after my father's death. Some were typed on official stationery from the European Bank for Reconstruction and Development and the Nigerian Banking Corporation; others were scrawled in store-bought cards, the sender's words written under a preprinted statement. There was a stack of my mother's speeches and reports for the Sierra Club; a stack of articles about my father from *The Economist* and *BusinessWeek*; one for photographs of him, one for her, one for them together. Some items lay alone and apart: my father's 1953 certificate of American citizenship, which stated that he was born in Poland, and which he'd corrected by hand to read "UKRAINE"; my parents' wedding invitation; the psychological and educational evaluations I'd started receiving when I was ten; and a soft doll, the size of my hand, that had belonged to Yuri.

I sat among these piles and questioned every item in them. I arranged letters chronologically, then by topic. I spread out photographs like decks of cards, picked them up, shuffled them, and spread them out again to see if something new was revealed. When they provided no answers, I stood and circled them, studying them from across the room as I paced and talked to myself. Depending on where I stood, the piles looked like a cityscape, an audience, an orchestra, or an insurrection.

I returned most often to the letters my father wrote to my mother because they were the most confounding. I read them silently and aloud until I could anticipate and recite long passages.

In July 1966, he wrote:

Life seems so much more mechanical without a loving sweetheart to look forward to—to talk to, to laugh with, to smile at and with. I love you dearly.

And in February 1971, he told her:

Whenever I leave you I feel a powerful and wonderfully terrible series of emotions . . . there is an emptiness inside me, a true aching of the heart. It is a longing and a dull sorrow for leaving behind that which I love.

His descriptions of his infatuation were unraveling lyrics of openness and devotion, and they made me furious. I'd always believed he wasn't able to be the person I'd needed him to be, and I had found that idea comforting. If he was deficient, then our bad relationship was inevitable. But his letters to my mother proved he was capable of tenderness and suggested that he'd chosen to behave very differently to me. I knew the love people had for a partner was different from the love they had for a child, but how could it be *so* different?

I spent months wrestling with this material and months ignoring it, pushing the piles to the edges of my room and pretending they weren't there as I graded papers, watched movies with Marko, or got undressed. I could have packed it back in the boxes I'd brought it in, but I knew I wasn't done. I returned to the piles, followed ideas, got lost, crawled back to reality, then went in again, hoping a new path would lead me to the answer of my biggest questions: How, and why, did they become the people they did?

One day, I decided to look further back. I picked up my father's high-school yearbook—he'd graduated from Hibbing High School in Minnesota in 1958—which I hadn't opened since I was a teenager, when it had been shelved in our living room next to *Nomads of the World*. I'd first reached for it to see what a dork my father had been, then went for it again a few years later when my aunt mentioned that my father had gone to school with Bob Dylan, then known as Robert Zimmerman, to see if Dylan had been a dork, too. Then again when I bragged to friends that my father had gone to school with Bob Dylan and needed proof.

When I opened the yearbook in my apartment, acceptance letters from Harvard and Johns Hopkins, which he chose to attend for premed, fell out, as well as a certificate from the National Honor Society. Accustomed to my previous interest, the pages fell open right to Dylan's junior-year photo. I had to wrestle with the ones that followed to find my dad.

In his portrait, my father chose to stare at the camera, while the other end-of-the-alphabet seniors looked into the distance. Next to his name was the phrase "Let's get down to business." His accomplishments and affiliations were listed to the right: student body president; president of the debate team; member of the German, science, and social studies clubs; the prom committee. Notes from his peers and teachers spoke to his work ethic and future success. "Keep on plugging the way you have been, and you will be on top, where you belong . . ."

Even as a teenager, my father was motivated by a desire to

be great and the expectation that he would be. When I was in high school, kids like him were a mystery. They had visions of their future, of themselves, big goals, and the diligence to work toward them. They seemed to understand that high school was an unglamorous part of the journey to real life. For most of high school, I operated on the belief that I would fail, that it was pointless to try because my future would be messy and forgettable. He put that belief in me. Who put his beliefs in him?

I let the yearbook dangle from my fingers and looked at my parents' things. I'd been working as if what I had would form a complete picture if I just arranged everything the right way. Instead of seeing piles of stuff, I saw the spaces between them. I could keep reorganizing and examining what I had—or accept that what I wanted to know could only be found elsewhere.

CHAPTER FIVE

Secret Garden

*T*here were only three people who could tell me about my father's earliest years: Aunt Lana and my father's friends Ruslan and Natasha, who were both Ukrainian immigrants. It was embarrassing to admit that I didn't know even simple details about the first years of his life: not the name of the village where he was born, the real circumstances of his family's departure from it, or what their life was like after they'd immigrated to America when he was eight.

When I told Lana that I wanted to learn more about my dad, she said she'd help me however she could. I offered to visit her and Uncle Gene in Connecticut, but she had a better idea. Her fiftieth high-school reunion in Hibbing was approaching, and she and Gene were taking a road trip through Minnesota beforehand so they could visit the towns her family had lived in. She invited me to join them, and suggested I go to the reunion as well. I could see where my father had partially grown up, and ask all my questions along the way.

I thanked my father's yearbook for calling up such a perfect situation. I flipped through it again and tried to make out the signatures below the well-wishes that filled its pages by matching them to the names under his classmates' photos. I wanted to speak with people who'd known him in high school, but when I couldn't figure out who his closest peers had been, I placed an ad in the *Hibbing Daily Tribune*.

The only person who responded was a woman named Donna. She remembered my father well, not just because they'd had classes together or because he was "different" and "serious" but because he'd given a rousing speech about his journey from Ukraine to America. In a letter, and then over the phone, she told me that his speech had been "Incredible. The story he told of his family's Ukrainian background was so compelling. He was an excellent speaker. I would venture to say that the seventh- through twelfth-grade students who heard his story in that huge auditorium have never forgotten it." I wondered what prompted the speech—it could have been part of his campaign for class president, or something he did as a member of the debate team. That he was so confident as a teenager wasn't surprising, but that he'd been so open was.

Before I left for Minnesota, I tried to banish my beliefs and assumptions about my father. If I was angry at him, or refused to believe he'd been anything other than the person I'd known, I wouldn't be able to learn anything new about him or understand who he'd been before he was my dad. I tried to replace my version of him with the boy Donna described.

Lana carefully plotted routes to and between the places they'd lived—Brainerd, Aitkin, Park Rapids, Grand Rapids, and finally Hibbing. She wanted to see their old houses and apartments, and had done as much research as she could beforehand. What she hadn't been able to find online, she looked for at local historical societies as we traveled. We drove separately to each destination, which allowed us to make our own detours. They visited a lot of lakes; I visited a lot of bars and went to a rodeo.

Brainerd, where their family had spent three years, was our first stop. We walked through the area they'd lived in, where streets were laid out on a lettered grid. It was full of modest, vinyl-sided houses fronted by yards made tall by weeds. They'd rented a small, two-family house on G Street, but we discovered the neighborhood now ended at H Street. There was a strip mall where G Street once ran; the site of their former home was now a Ca$h Wi$e Liquor.

Lana laughed. "That explains why I couldn't find G Street on any maps!" We had similar experiences in other towns. Most of their homes were no longer there.

As we walked along the highway that cut through the town, Aunt Lana spoke of places she remembered, some of which still existed and some of which had been razed, such as the factory where my grandmother had done piecework. Lana said that although the city was more prosperous when they lived there, their neighborhood had always been lower-middle class. I wondered what my father's vision of life in

America had been before he'd arrived, how hard it had been for him to assimilate first in New York, then again in the Midwest.

I asked question after question. When did my father lose his accent? Did they like American food? Did they feel as though they belonged? Lana's answer was always the same. She didn't remember. She'd been so young.

On our second night, I spoke with Lana in her hotel room. We sat at a round table while Gene lounged in an uncomfortable-looking desk chair a respectful distance away. I asked her to start at the beginning and tell me everything she could.

She placed her hands down and spread out her fingers. She'd heard the earliest stories of my father's life from her parents as well as from my father, and she'd expanded them with her own historical research. She didn't have her own memories; she hadn't been born when they fled Ukraine. She spoke slowly and paused often to think, correct herself, or ask Gene if what she'd said sounded right, if his memory of her memories differed from hers. It was never supposed to be her job to get such things right for me, but she wanted to.

My father was born in 1940, in a village called Rai. Rai means "paradise" in Ukrainian, but it wasn't paradise for the Ukrainians who lived there. At that time, Rai and the rest of western Ukraine was part of Poland, and Ukrainians were considered second-class citizens. They seemed to be subject to different laws and were frequently harassed by the police. Many had been agitating for independence for years. Paradise, to them, would have been more concept than place. It could have been Rai, the nearby city of Berezhany, or even Lviv. It would have been freedom, their own country, no reason to be afraid.

My grandfather Dymtro, whose own father had been a horse trader, was determined to go to college and worked to secure one of the few places allocated for Ukrainian students at the Lviv Polytechnic National University. He'd spent his childhood hiking and riding though the Carpathians, and chose to study forestry engineering in order to better know the land he loved. While at college, he met Irene, the daughter of one of the area's most well-to-do Ukrainian families. The baby of her family, the only girl out of five children, she'd grown up exploring the world alongside her brothers and was the first woman in her village to wear pants, have a bicycle, and try skiing. Strong-minded and -willed, she was a steady, straight-talking counterpart for my witty and soulful grandfather.

After getting married, they settled in Rai, where Dymtro managed forested land owned by a Ukrainian cardinal, and Irene taught grade school. My father was born at home, and my grandmother returned to work soon after his birth. Dymtro made enough money that the family was comfortable on his salary alone, but Irene enjoyed working and refused to give up her job. "She just wasn't the stay-at-home type," Lana said. In between classes, she ran back to their house to breastfeed.

Rai was quiet and woodsy, beautiful enough that a Polish count had one of his estates there. Surrounding his large villa was a park; one of the few photographs I found of my father as a small child shows him playing in front of the estate's sculpted pool as my grandmother watches, looking happy and relaxed. It's impossible to know if she was aware of the chaos that was coming.

As World War II closed in, an underground movement of Ukrainians tried to take advantage of the anxiety it was causing to weaken Poland's hold over them with violence, kidnapping, and murders. Factions of Polish nationalists who were determined to maintain control over the region retaliated with the same tactics. "There was a lot of Polish-Ukrainian stuff going on during that time," Lana said, "and it was very, very ugly." The Germans arrived, as well as the Russians; different wars on different scales. Everyone was trying to survive. Some went after people or groups they perceived as threats, others aligned themselves with those they thought would protect them, but who and what was safe kept changing.

One evening, my grandfather learned that his family had appeared on a "Polish list," a list of Ukrainians whom the Poles intended to murder. "You'd better get out," a coworker told him, "because if you don't, they're going to kill you." Lana didn't know if her family had been targeted simply because they were Ukrainian or because they were incorrectly perceived to be a part of the independence movement. While independence was my grandparents' great hope, along with peace, they weren't actively fighting for it.

My grandparents packed up what they could and threw it into their cart. They were supposed to leave that night with another family who'd found out they were on the same list. Just before they set out, my grandfather changed his mind. "He had a premonition or something," Lana said. "It spooked him enough that he risked staying until morning." A few hours after leaving the next day, they came across the bodies of the other family on a riverbank. They had been shot.

My father's family traveled through Poland, trying to avoid attention and sleeping wherever they could. At some point, my grandparents had to split up; my grandfather got on one train, and my grandmother and father got on another. My grandmother was horrified to discover they'd be sharing a car with Polish women who said things like, "If I come across a Ukrainian, I'll slit his throat!"

"Babtsia was terrified. Your father was very talkative, and she knew she couldn't control him. She told me she kept whispering, 'You cannot talk, you cannot talk,' because he spoke Ukrainian. It was one of the few times that my mother ever admitted to being afraid.

"There were a lot of stories of my parents trying to reconnect," Lana continued. "It was very haphazard. One time they were on a military train, maybe in Slovakia, and there was a bombing; your father and Babtsia had to hide under the table. They stayed in different places along their journey if my father could get some kind of work. One story I remember was that my father and a friend would buy sugar and then sell it at an inflated price. My mother always hoarded sugar." She laughed. "Maybe that's why."

They settled in Austria for a few years while they figured out where they could go next. That was where my father started school and Lana was born. My grandparents had wanted to go back to Ukraine, even if it was in ashes, but discovered they couldn't. There were rumors that when people returned, the Russians labeled them traitors and sent them off to the gulags.

They wanted to leave Europe and were willing to go almost anywhere. They could have followed other Ukrainians to Brazil or Argentina, but in 1948, they received the necessary sponsorship from friends of friends of friends who'd settled in New York. They sailed to America and moved to Manhattan's East Village, a fist of Ukrainian immigrants that offered their language and food, churches and schools, manners and memories.

I thought of what my father would have remembered of Ukraine and Europe, having left the first at four and the second at eight. Mostly images and emotions that didn't belong to clear events. Flashes of fear, his own and his parents'; panic and destruction. He'd have padded those fragments with the stories his parents told him and Lana, stories that were repeated until their children could claim ownership of them as well. This is what happened to *us*. What he didn't remember was remembered for him. They weren't the dead bodies—those of the family they didn't leave with—but they could have been.

After two years in New York, my grandfather's English had improved enough that he could get a job in his old field. He didn't want his family to suffocate in a tiny apartment, and he missed trees. He looked for jobs where there were forests, found one at a mining company in Minnesota, and moved his family to the closest town. That job led to others, and to other towns throughout the state, and soon he retrained himself to be a mining engineer. My grandmother hoped to become a nurse and worked as a nurse's assistant wherever they lived, but after a number of years she had to quit because she developed back problems. They didn't have a lot of money, but they had enough.

Although they were continually uprooted, the one steadying center in my father and aunt's lives was their Ukrainian identity. They were taught to read and write Ukrainian, the language spoken at home, regardless of where "home" was.

My grandmother told her children that everything they said or did was a reflection of Ukrainians in America. They always had to look nice and neat, behave like the cultured Europeans they were, and, of course, do well in school. But my grandmother's strong opinions and impulses were often conflicting. She insisted that her children be models of decorum, but said it was equally important that they think for themselves and be independent. She wanted her kids to be individuals, yet constantly reminded them that they were already a part of a very defined whole.

In Hibbing, there was only a smattering of Ukrainians, people who were too old for my grandparents to befriend and who didn't have kids their children's age. This meant my grandparents had to work extra hard to reinforce their heritage. They spoke often about Ukraine and the life and family they'd left behind, and subscribed to Ukrainian American newspapers. They talked politics and dissected events taking place in Russia or Hungary. My father began participating in these talks after he joined the debate team in middle school. Conversations about Communism and the state of Eastern Europe started before dinner and continued after coffee, and they were often heated. Aunt Lana explained that my father enjoyed pushing against his parents' ideas, even when he agreed with them. "He wouldn't get riled up, but *they* would get riled up, especially my mother. I think my parents respected how he acted, but also found it annoying." She sighed. "They weren't really arguing, but it all sounded like an argument to me. I hated it."

When I asked Lana what my father was like in middle school and high school, she said she didn't really know. "He was six years older than me, so I didn't pay too much attention to him. He was always busy with homework and activities. Of course he was always getting awards and honors." Though she was a strong student as well, I got the impression their parents considered my father the star.

"Did he have friends?"

"What?" She laughed. "Of course he had friends. When he wasn't doing schoolwork, he was practicing with the school band and the debate team. He was always hanging out with people."

I thought of him being pulled forward in school and backward at home. He was told to remember who he was while being pushed to become something more; to master being two things at once, belong twice. He hadn't just survived; he'd excelled. He spoke Ukrainian, started school in German, then went to school in English and was president of his class. Moving so often hadn't held him back. If anything, it taught him how to adapt and thrive anywhere. The qualities of his that I'd envied may not have been innate. Perhaps he'd had to fight to become the person he was.

I asked Lana if she knew about the speech my father gave in high school. When she shook her head, I told her about my conversation with Donna. She looked at me in amazement. "I didn't know about any of this."

I didn't confess that my father's willingness to share so much with people he didn't know, but not with his children, had begun to bother me. I couldn't deny that I'd never been interested in his life before, but it felt strange to have to go to Lana for my father's story, for my family's story. I felt that I was asking to be a part of something he'd wanted, or needed, to keep for himself.

His approach had been so different than that of his parents, and of Lana. Babtsia and Dymtro ensured that Ukraine stayed vivid for their children and reminded them who they were, and Lana had done the same for her kids. When I asked her about her choice, she said it was somewhat accidental. She'd never thought about raising her children to speak Ukrainian because she'd never really thought about having them. She'd married a Ukrainian, but only because she'd fallen in love with one, and together she and my uncle decided to keep their heritage alive by sharing it with their children. Their Ukrainianness was the result of circumstances my father hadn't chosen.

Maybe my father thought his story wasn't relevant to his daughters. It hadn't seemed relevant when he occasionally spoke of it. If I'd been asked, I would have said I was happy that my father didn't make me listen to his stories. But now I wished he'd told me so much more. I couldn't think of anything that might excuse the way he'd treated me, but I could imagine why he was so quick to grow frustrated with me. He'd had far more disadvantages and was able to do well in spite of them. He may have perceived my disabilities and behavior as weakness. Perhaps he thought he could make me tougher, and refused to accept that his methods didn't work. My character was too different, my enemy, somehow more terrifying.

ANYA YURCHYSHYN

My grandparents were the primary source of my father's connection to his background, which meant he was able to develop an American identity separate from theirs, but not a Ukrainian one. That changed when he moved to Baltimore to attend Johns Hopkins, where he became friends with Natasha, who was from the area. She told me that my father really honed his Ukrainian identity during college. A bunch of people their age—some who were from Baltimore, some who'd come there for school—formed a group that was part of the Federation of Ukrainian Students Organization of America, and my father was elected head. They held talks and dances, and attended conferences in Chicago and Toronto.

After not seeing him for decades, I reconnected with my father's friend Ruslan at his office in the East Village, a few blocks from my grandparents' first apartment. Ruslan was a frequent guest at our house when I was growing up. He and my father saw each other periodically during their childhood in Minnesota and reconnected when my father was at Johns Hopkins and Ruslan was visiting friends in Baltimore. A few years later, they were in Chicago at the same time, while my father was in graduate school, and Ruslan had helped him integrate into the local Ukrainian community. They were together again soon afterward in Boston, where they worked with a group of academics and Ukrainian professionals to establish the Harvard Ukrainian Research Institute. When he and my father weren't talking politics and working through the extensive beer list at their favorite German restaurant, they were talking politics at our house over my father's smothered pork chops. I loved having Ruslan over, though he smoked a stinky pipe, because he was gregarious and let me climb all over him and tug on the cuffs of his suit's brown pants.

After we embraced, I stepped back and saw that he hadn't changed much. His eyes were still wild behind his large glasses, his hands and arms still emphatic accompaniments to every sentence he spoke. Seeing him made me remember how much time I'd spent with him when I was young and how much I'd enjoyed it.

Ruslan did educational work with Ukrainian American youth. His office, which he shared with people who also worked within the local diaspora and immigrant community, was empty of people but full of their work. Chaotic stacks of books and files teetered on mismatched desks and chairs. He cleared off a chair for me and placed it across from his own.

He spoke for hours about my father, growing more excited as time passed, as if he were continually recharged by his own florid speech. While Lana had spoken carefully, Ruslan presided over our conversation like a raconteur. Memories and thoughts flew from his mouth with authority and force.

He started by saying that my father "marched to the beat of a different drummer" and did what he wanted without apology. He was driven by a need to succeed as well as a stubborn independence, which was why he changed his major from premed to business, disregarded his parents' objections to marrying my mother, and worked in "strange" countries. "Your father wanted to be a man who made a difference," Ruslan told me, "to change the world." Specifically, he said, my father wanted to change the world by contributing to the destruction of the Soviet Union.

I laughed, but when Ruslan frowned, I composed myself. I conceded that yes, my father seemed to hate Russia because of how it had treated Ukraine, but any hope of personally destroying the country was probably a fantasy. I told Ruslan I'd referred to myself as "Russian" once when I was little and had to explain the origin of my name, and had received a long lecture about it. My father had repeated, "You are *not* Russian, you are Ukrainian!" for what felt like two days. I'd said I was Russian because most people didn't know what Ukraine, or even "the Ukraine," as it was often referred to then, was—but I didn't tell that to my dad.

I also said that Natasha admitted that when she and my dad were in Baltimore, members of their Ukrainian student group would destroy anything Russian that they found—flags, signs, posters. Their hatred of Russia was a given. Once, she told me, she'd torn down a small Russian flag and stuck it in a bucket of paint. However, I wasn't aware of my father actually wanting, or doing, anything to destabilize Russia's power at any point in his life; he'd chosen instead to strengthen Ukraine. Ruslan argued with me and said that in the eighties, my father had been a part of a secret scheme that sought to undermine Communism by privatizing Bulgarian fruit farms. When I laughed again and pushed him to substantiate this outrageous story with details, he quickly dropped it and moved on.

My father didn't like to talk nonsense, Ruslan said. He only spoke when he had something to say, and then, he spoke firmly and directly. "Your father had a dignitas about him, and he wouldn't throw it away. He could not just talk to anyone at a party and go 'Hee-hee-hee, ha-ha-ha.' Some people have a rich internal life that they can't always project, and your father was one of them." Ruslan held up a finger to make sure he had my attention. "He had a secret garden inside. His soul was his garden. And this garden was where he was at home. He closed one door and opened another up."

I knew of such places. I'd searched for one in the junk room, and when I didn't find it there, I created one inside my head. My father was the reason I'd needed a secret place. Was the frenetic nature of his childhood the reason he'd needed his? If he'd built it when he was a child, why did he still go there as an adult?

Ruslan asked me if my sister and I spoke Ukrainian. I shook my head. "They sent my sister to a Ukrainian school for a little while, but she hated it so much that they gave up, which meant I never had to go. Sometimes he would try to teach me a few words from kid's books, but I didn't take it seriously enough for him." I paused. "Now, of course, I wish I spoke it."

"Well, kids don't learn language from books," he said. "He should have known that."

"He could have tried harder, but he wasn't really around a lot, and I wouldn't have wanted him to. But it meant that only he was Ukrainian, not us. When he started working in Ukraine, all we could do was watch. Not that we wanted to join him." I paused again, then said, "I've been wondering why he kept his pride and nationalism to himself, or for himself. I never knew it was as important to him as it was, and now that I do, I don't understand why he didn't share more of it with me."

We decided to grab a meal at a Ukrainian restaurant down the block once the light outside his office's dirty window dimmed. As I gathered my belongings, I asked Ruslan if he thought it was possible that the car crash that killed my father wasn't an accident. I'd waited until the end of our conversation to mention my father's death because it seemed much less significant than his life.

"Of course! He was murdered!" he bellowed. He waved his hand to indicate that the answer was a given, barely worth addressing.

It wasn't a given, not to me. Until I'd asked the question, I hadn't taken it very seriously. I'd expected him to say no.

After a moment, I said, "Why 'of course'?"

"When people wanted to follow up, everything disappeared! His car was gone. The van that hit them was gone. The driver was gone. There was nothing. No physical evidence, no crime scene."

It was the first time I'd heard anything about what happened immediately after my father died, details that broadened the picture surrounding what I'd viewed as an event isolated from motives and outcomes. I didn't know if Ruslan's statement was theory or fact, something he'd imagined or something he knew on good authority. I'd never looked into the crash myself. Doing so hadn't ever occurred to me. A wave of shame about my ignorance, about my deep lack of knowledge, washed over me. I didn't know what to think, so I smothered my reaction. "Later," I told myself. "Later."

After dinner, I walked to the subway. Third Avenue was crowded with college kids ready to get drunk. I wove between them and sped through crosswalks, holding my hand up when taxis honked.

I thought about Ruslan's stories and tried to find connections to what I'd learned in Minnesota. What froze in the blur of so much movement? What could my father clutch, what was there when he opened his hand? Himself. No one had to tell my father that if he needed another self, and a place where he could be that self, it needed to be kept inside, where it was safe. For years, his parents had demonstrated how to survive; he'd escaped with them, stayed tense with them, quiet. He knew how easily home could be destroyed.

My father had adapted but never to the point of losing his true self. When you don't want to give in or give up, when you refuse to relinquish what you love or even hate, when whatever you are doesn't fit or hurts too much, you bury it somewhere secret. You always protect it. An intruder, anything dangerous, is cause for retreat or attack.

Perhaps my father thought he wouldn't need such a place when he met my mother. From their letters, I could tell that she didn't just give him a feeling of love; she made him feel safe. She might not have known that he had somewhere inside of himself where he could disconnect and disappear. In the beginning of their relationship, he'd had no reason to withdraw and protect himself. But when problems arose a few years later, this place was still available. She wouldn't know where he'd gone, or how to reach him.

CHAPTER SIX

Kiss of Fire

*W*hen my mother was twelve, she went to visit her father. My grandfather Roman had left my grandmother Helen a second time, for good, after my mother was born. My mother and her family stayed in Chicago while Roman moved to the suburbs with his new wife, Josephine.

My mother didn't tell anyone she was going. There was nowhere she was expected to be after school; no one would worry or wonder where she was unless she missed dinner. She was fluent enough in public transportation that she could get herself into the suburbs by bus and find his home, though she'd never been to it.

Like every other house on the block, her father's had a narrow patch of lawn. She rang the bell and waited.

Roman opened the front door.

"Hi, Dad!" she said. She spoke with an announcer's boom and cheer to play up the surprise.

His tight face went slack when he saw her. Before he could say anything, Josephine came up behind him in a dress from a nice store.

My mother said, "Hello, Josephine."

Josephine nodded, whispered in her husband's ear, and disappeared. Roman brought his face to the screen. "You can't be here."

My mother held his gaze.

"We have company, and they don't know about you. You have to go." He didn't wait for her to respond. He shut the door, trusting she would leave.

She did.

My mother needed to tell this story at least once a year. "My own father!" she'd rage to me, my sister, whoever her audience was that time. "His own daughter!"

I met Roman and Josephine only once, when I was about ten. My mother and I and were visiting Aunt Arlene, who then lived in the Chicago suburbs, during the summer. Arlene had managed to create some sort of relationship with Roman and he knew my older cousins, though not well. My mom didn't ask me if I wanted to meet him, she just told me I was going to one morning as I ate breakfast. I slumped in my chair. "I don't want to."

"You have to," she said coolly. "They're picking you up this afternoon."

"Are you coming?"

She took a small sip of coffee, then shook her head.

"Why do I have to meet him?" I wanted to hang out with my teenage cousin Susie, play in the backyard, read, do anything else. I pushed my cereal bowl away.

"Because it's important," she said, and nudged the bowl back. Perhaps she'd surprised him by insisting that we meet. As she had when she was young, she was forcing him to acknowledge her, and her daughter as well.

My mother and I waited for Roman and Josephine in front of Arlene's house. Tension locked her body when they arrived, and it rushed into mine as her hand gripped my shoulder. She greeted them from her position on the stoop, then shoved me toward their car.

Roman was small and grumbly, Josephine pretty and polite. As he drove, Roman asked me short questions about school. I gave him short answers. I was good at talking to adults and knew I was supposed to ask them questions as well, but even basic conversation seemed dangerous. What was I supposed to know or not know? How could I trust any of his answers? I knew it was important to my mother that I be there, though I wasn't sure why, but also sensed that I wasn't supposed to like him. Instead of asking about the wrong thing, or saying something bad, I tried to look fascinated by whatever was on the other side of the window.

They took me to Santa Land, a small Christmas-themed amusement park that blared carols even in summer. Every time we approached a ride, Roman asked if I wanted to go on it, and I said yes, even the ones for little kids. "If I go on them all," I thought, "we'll have to leave." I rode alone as he and Josephine watched with stilted grins. He tried to buy me a snowflake T-shirt, a stuffed elf, and ice cream, but I wouldn't let him.

When we pulled up in front of my aunt's house at the end of the day, I said "Thank you" and leaped out of the car. My mother opened the door for me and waved quickly in their direction.

"How was it?" she asked as I kicked off my sneakers.

"Boring," I shouted, then went to the kitchen to look for snacks.

My mother learned of Roman's death in 1998 through her cousin Chrissy, who saw his obituary in a local Chicago paper. She mailed it to my mother, and I was home from college when she received it. She read it on the couch as I sat next to her, then crumpled it in a ball and tossed it on the carpet. "It says he's survived by his wife Josephine and his stepdaughter, Teresa. No one bothered to mention me or Arlene, his *real* daughters."

"Well," I ventured, "that's not really a shock, is it?"

Anger fixed her face, then a ripple of heartache disturbed it. She swiped a cigarette from a crumpled pack, lit up, and took a drag. After a long exhale, she sniffed. "What an asshole."

I put my hand on her knee. She kept her gaze on the far wall, then she stood with a jerk and said she needed a nap.

I looked up Roman's obituary, thinking it might reveal something about the man who had betrayed my mother and her family, while preparing to visit Chicago. It was cursory and brief—a list, not a life. The only helpful information it offered was the full name of Josephine's daughter, Teresa. A quick search revealed that she was still alive and living in Chicago. I wanted to know more about Roman, his illness, and his life with his second family, so I wrote her a letter explaining who I was and what I was hoping to learn, and sent a copy to the two different addresses I found online. With enough warning and explanation, I thought she might be willing to meet me while I was there.

As I had with Aunt Lana, I'd called Aunt Arlene and Chrissy and told them I wanted to know more about my mother. Arlene told me she'd be visiting Chrissy in a few weeks; they both suggested I join them in Chicago. I was relieved they were open to having me monopolize the time they'd planned to spend with each other.

Chrissy lived in a large suburban house that reminded me a bit of my parents' because it was filled with Asian art and fancy rugs. When I pulled up in front of it, Chrissy and Arlene bounced out to greet me with squeals, and we hugged eagerly.

I hadn't seen either of them since my mother's funeral four years before.

I'd always known them to be cheerful and fun. They were constantly teasing each other and cackling so hard that they ended up gasping for air.

The three of us spent days in Chrissy's small kitchen, draining bottles of white wine, looking at pictures, swapping stories and theories about my mother, talking over one another, making long digressions, and jumping between topics as I grilled them for details about my mother's life.

My mother's family lived on Chicago's west side in a predominantly Polish neighborhood populated by factory workers and plumbers. Their small two-bedroom apartment was above a drugstore and across from a bakery where Arlene and my mother bought strawberry-filled paczki on Saturdays.

Arlene was three and a half years older than my mother, and Chrissy was a year younger. Chrissy and her older brother lived in a nicer part of town, but Chrissy always begged to stay with her cousins because she wanted to be with the girls. The three of them often spent summer days at Riverview Park and North Avenue Beach, or playing in alleys.

When I was a child, my mother frequently reminded me that she grew up *very poor*. Arlene and Chrissy confirmed that. "My family didn't have much," Chrissy said, "but your mother and aunt? They had *nothing*." They would never have been rich, but they had "nothing" because my grandmother was a single mom and worked a menial job at a candy factory.

Helen and Roman were introduced by my great-uncle Eugene, who knew Roman from high school. Eugene was seeing my grandmother's younger sister, Genevieve, and he set up Helen with his friend in the hopes of increasing the chances of his own dates being sanctioned. Helen and Roman married after a year of dating.

Roman had gone to welding school, but he hated welding and working in general. Arlene believed he may have left his job while my grandmother was pregnant with her and was still looking for work when she was born in 1941.

After Arlene was born, Roman went into a manic state and bought a lot of things the family didn't need and couldn't afford. "I don't know how you could buy things on credit in those days," Arlene said, "but he supposedly bought six suits, an organ, and a boat—"

Chrissy interrupted. "I heard he went out to buy a new

refrigerator, because he and Helen were living in this small place and had a little tiny refrigerator. He wanted a bigger one for his growing family."

"Fine, he bought a boat and a refrigerator."

"No." Chrissy giggled. "He left to buy a refrigerator but he came *back* with a boat."

When Roman's behavior didn't normalize, Helen had him involuntarily committed. He was institutionalized for somewhere between nine months to a year and a half. He never shared his diagnosis, but Arlene's guess was that he was bipolar, though that term didn't exist at the time.

I asked Arlene if he'd displayed similar behavior before she was born. She said she didn't think so, but her mom told her that she knew my grandfather was unhappy when she first met him, and she hoped she could change that by marrying him.

"Oh God!" Chrissy sighed. "Don't women always think that?"

Roman's mother went behind Helen's back and had him released, and he stayed with his parents for a while. "My mom didn't know where he was for a long time, but one day, he showed up," Arlene explained. "And she took him back! Then she got pregnant with your mom. I don't know if he got a job then or what. Maybe there was something with Western Union. Then your mom was born, and he left the next day."

Chrissy leaned toward me. "I don't know if you know this. Your mom was a breech baby. The doctor had to break her clavicle in order to extract her from the birth canal. She was in intensive care forever. Even after Helen brought her home, your mother was so fragile that she couldn't be held for several months."

"I didn't know that," I said, then I paused. "Did I? I don't think so." That seemed like the exact kind of story my mother would have loved to tell. She'd been a victim from the start, a broken baby immediately abandoned by her father. What life could she build on such a faulty foundation? The only reason I could come up with for why she hadn't told me about her birth was that its difficulty reminded her of Yuri.

I thought of her arriving into the world in a state of animal pain, needing so much comfort and only receiving the lightest strokes from my grandmother's fingers. It could have had lasting effects on her personality. Babies who aren't touched often struggle to form attachments, empathize with others, and regulate their emotions.

When Roman left, my great-grandmother, whom Arlene and my mother called Buscha, moved in so she could supplement their income with her Social Security. She was a worn-down woman who took pleasure in wearing down others. She spoke enough English to complain to butchers and give orders, but she preferred going after people in gruff Polish. She and Helen worked at the same candy factory; Buscha worked the day shift while Helen worked at night. When Buscha arrived, she claimed one bedroom for herself, so my mom and Arlene moved into Helen's room. Arlene slept on a thin cot with squeaking springs, and my mother shared Helen's bed until she was fifteen.

"*Fifteen?*"

"Oh yeah. She didn't get her own bed until I went to college, and even then, they still shared a bedroom."

When I thought of having to share my bed with my mother, my skin got sticky. I would have considered it an intrusion, even as a small child. But my mom may have found the warmth of her mother's body comforting. My mother and grandmother always had been very close; perhaps sharing a bed for so long was one of the reasons why. When Helen died in 2005, my mother pulled her darkness even closer. Her mother died because she was old; at the time, I didn't get why it was so devastating, but learning this made me see my mother's reaction differently.

Helen had dropped out of high school after tenth grade so she could help support her parents, but she was determined that her daughters would be well educated. She monitored their performance in school and expected them to go to college. She saved money in order to pay for ballet and Polish dance classes, and for horseback riding lessons in Lincoln Park. Though she worked five night shifts in a row, she took her daughters on long bus rides on weekends so they could visit art museums downtown.

"We never just sat home," Arlene said. "And Anita and I wanted to! Do you know how long it took for us to get to the Museum of Science and Industry without a car? We had to stand in the heat or the cold waiting for the El . . . Once we got wherever we were going, we had a great time, but we always put up a fight."

My mother might not have wanted to go to museums, but, Arlene told me, "she always wanted to be out and doing things. Your mom was always goofing off, telling stories, making jokes. We walked up and down streets, played kick the can, roly-poly, and hide-and-seek in the alley with whatever other kids were around. We'd be out all day. There was no adult supervision."

"Your mother was such a cutie," Chrissy added. "I remember her running around in these silky magenta shorts that my mom made for her—not for me, mind you—with her curly blond hair, and thinking, 'Wow, I wish I had her shorts, I wish I had her curly blond hair.'"

Sunday was the only day both Helen and Buscha had off, and it was the one night that the four of them ate together. "Every Sunday," Arlene said, "we ate together, and every Sunday we had a family argument." Buscha would cook pot roast with gravy or sausage and potatoes, and she'd have a glass or two of wine while she cooked, and a few more during dinner. "Meals started off okay, but after some wine, Buscha's mind just went *pshh*. She'd say all kinds of critical things about our mom to her face, and my mother would get weepy. I'd get upset and defend her. 'Don't talk to my mom like that, that's not nice!' But it didn't make a difference." Buscha was relentless, and she used Arlene's protests as fuel, telling Helen, "Look at how your kids behave. No wonder your husband left you," which caused Helen to cry even harder.

Sometimes Buscha hosted a little party on Sunday instead of a miserable dinner. She invited friends of her husband's and her cousins, Helen and Arlene's uncles. They played bridge and rummy, complained about their bosses, and wondered if the Italians were moving in.

Company meant my mother and aunt could wear the frilly dresses their mother had made for them by hand. My mother was a ham, dancing until she got applause, practicing card tricks, and reciting the ads for toothpaste that played on their radio when it wasn't broken.

One of their great-uncles, the husband of Buscha's dead

sister, always asked my mother to sit on his lap. She did, and as he'd stayed in whatever conversation or card game was happening, he slowly worked a hand between her thighs and into her underwear.

Arlene didn't know what was occurring; my mother didn't tell her about the molestation until decades later. She said the abuse never went any further, and that she didn't even understand that it was abuse for years. Arlene confronted my grandmother about it, and my grandmother said she'd never had any inkling that was happening. My mother never told her, neither as a child nor as an adult.

My mouth went bitter as I considered that my mother, fizzing with excitement and eager for attention because it felt like love, had been molested repeatedly in front of people who should have protected her. There really was no supervision, even when adults were around. Arlene kept talking, telling me that my mother had never seemed scared of this man—they'd both adored him. When he put on his coat at the end of the night, my mother would beg him to stay.

It was hard to hear this. My mother could have hated what was happening but felt she couldn't stop it. Or perhaps this man's caresses made her feel special. Maybe any male attention felt like love and could briefly fill the space left by her father.

As a child, I would have been scared and repulsed if I'd heard this story. Like when I'd learned about Yuri, I would have been overwhelmed to know how much pain my mother had endured and afraid of how her turmoil threatened my safety. Hearing about these incidents decades after they'd happened, and after witnessing what my mother did to herself, I went cold. I had to force myself out of fantasies where I appeared in my mother's childhood kitchen in my clothes from the future and violently swept her off of that man's lap, and him out of her life and family. I felt sick and complicit for not having stopped him. As I sat there, I understood that my mother had kept some stories to herself, ones that she should have shared with someone. Being abused, and not speaking about that abuse, could have taught her that her pain and body didn't matter, and been yet another factor that would later lead her to alcoholism.

My mother told me so little about Roman that I'd always assumed he was completely absent from her life, but Arlene said that he took her and my mother out on occasional Fridays. I was surprised that he felt even that much duty to the daughters he'd discarded.

"We would meet him on the corner, he didn't come to the door. We'd have to go half a block, stand on the corner. We could have been kidnapped! Your mother didn't like it as much as I did. I had fun; I was happy to see him. He took us to little amusement parks or to the circus. If I wanted cotton candy, I would get cotton candy. If I wanted a turtle, he'd buy it for me. Anita stopped going after a while, I don't know why, but I kept going." Arlene said that he didn't seem mentally ill or "off," but he was quiet.

My mother's decision to stop joining them struck me as a pointed refusal to recognize Roman's paltry effort. Occasional afternoons or evenings didn't make up for his disappearance, and she didn't want him to believe that they did.

He gave Helen money when he could, but it wasn't enough. When Arlene was eleven and my mother was eight, Helen consulted a lawyer about receiving child support. The lawyer returned with good news and a big question. Yes, Roman was working and could pay child support. But was she aware that he'd married someone else?

She wasn't. She barely spoke to him. Even though she was angry and embarrassed that Roman had left her, she hadn't divorced him because she didn't want to be excommunicated from the Catholic Church. That was also why she'd never remarried, though she'd had boyfriends who'd expressed interest. But when she learned Roman was married, she had to divorce him. Arlene wasn't sure when he'd remarried, but thought he may have met Josephine during one of his hospitalizations. She remembered hearing that Josephine may have also dealt with mental illness, perhaps in the aftermath of her first husband's death.

"When your mom found out about Josephine, was that when Josephine found out about her and you guys? And that he'd never bothered getting divorced?"

Arlene took a sip of wine and said she had no idea.

He told Josephine at some point, and the way my mother told the story of her surprise visit made it sound like she'd met Josephine before. But he was still hiding his first family from most of the world, and my mother would have become even angrier with him than she had been; he'd been haplessly playing father while living a secret life.

Arlene didn't know why my mother stopped joining the excursions with their father, but she thought that my mother was brave because when she decided she *did* want to see him, she sought him out.

I told her I knew the story of my mother showing up at Roman's. "She *was* brave," I said. "It took a lot of guts to go there alone. It was a kind of 'Fuck you.' "

Why had she gone to see him that day? To remind him of her existence, of his mistakes and choices? Did she hope that he'd invite her in, and they'd spend a nice afternoon together? She may have wanted his love, but according to Arlene, my mother wasn't interested in forgiving him. If she'd wanted to needle him, she would have at least succeeded in making him uncomfortable. But that was undercut by his rejection, his literal denial.

Teresa never contacted me, so I reached out to her again after I'd been in Chicago for a few days. I didn't want to call her; I wanted her to call *me*, to want to talk. I wrote two short notes and delivered them to the addresses I had. Both were in humble neighborhoods on the outskirts of the city. At the first, the current resident informed me that Teresa hadn't lived there for years, but that he'd received my original letter and given it to her cousin. At the second, I slipped the note into the mailbox mounted next to the door.

On my way back to Chrissy's, I stopped by a supermarket to pick up flowers and wine. When I got back into my car, I turned it on and found I didn't have the strength to drive the few remaining miles to her house. I turned the car off, pushed the seat back, and stared at the roof.

There'd been so much noise all week. Every day I had absorbed more and more information. Sadness whirred beneath every discussion, and my mother was the center of each, even the ones that weren't about her. When I wasn't talking with Chrissy and Arlene, I was replaying our conversations as I drank in the kitchen while everyone else slept, or in my dreams when they came. My mind was always finding or making connections between stories, coloring them in and extending them. What had stopped me was the car's intense silence, so loud that it stung my ears and made me notice they were raw, and that the rest of me was, too. I was wrung out but still wet, yet I couldn't go completely limp. I had more interviews, more people to see and conversations to carry with humor and graciousness. I groaned as I sat up and started the car again, thinking about what Arlene had told me the other day.

My mother was a natural performer and loved embarrassing Arlene in public. Sometimes when they were riding the bus, my mother would cause a scene as a joke. She called her sister "Hortence Anastasia Waskavinska," and when the bus was crowded, she'd loudly exclaim, "Oh Hortence, will you behave yourself?" or "Hortence Anastasia Waskavinska, what's *wrong* with you?" while Arlene held her bag in front of her red face.

My mother's mischievousness and spirit had one particularly infamous display. At her school's end-of-year picnic, when she was in the fourth grade and Arlene was a seventh grader, my mother ran onto the makeshift stage at the end of the talent show and broke into a rendition of Georgia Gibbs's 1952 recording of "Kiss of Fire." She rocked her hips and tossed her hair, giving her best impression of a femme fatale, and crooned about being a "slave" to "devil lips" in front of a scandalized audience of nuns and children.

"I was *so* embarrassed," Arlene told me. "But even then, I was impressed by her stage presence. It was really incredible."

"Did the nuns call your mom?"

"Not that time, but other times. They threatened to kick Anita out of school."

"Kicked out!" I cried. "Why?"

"She was caught passing notes to a boy. I don't know if he wrote it or she did, but it said, 'If you want to kiss, I will.'"

I laughed. "I did stuff like that at the same age. I think that's pretty normal."

"Not in Catholic school!"

"Your mom always had a way with men," Chrissy said. "Whenever we went to a dance, she got the good-looking guy immediately. She never had any trouble attracting them. She was a big flirt, but she wasn't obvious about it. She just had a way about her, smart and vulnerable at the same time. I think a lot of guys found that very appealing." She spoke of witnessing my mother flirting with men and having them "wrapped around her finger" in minutes. I'd seen similar things as a child, my mother receiving extra attention, men lingering in her presence, and sensed there was something different and charged in those interactions.

"I'm a big flirt, too," I admitted.

Arlene and Chrissy feigned shock. "No, you?"

"I can't help it!" I laughed. "I flirt with *everyone*. I always thought it was my personality, but maybe I do it because I watched it work for my mother." I'd never considered this before, but it made sense. Flirting with people made basic interactions more fun. The attention was validating, probably more than it should have been, and whomever I flirted with generally seemed happy to participate. My behavior only caused problems if someone took it to mean that I was more interested in him than I was, or when I was dating a guy who was insecure.

While I was in Chicago, I also visited my mother's best friend, Sylvia. We chatted on her balcony, smoked her thin cigarettes, and drank instant iced tea. Sylvia had been a constant presence during my childhood. Every time we went to Chicago to visit my grandmother, we'd see Sylvia as well—she'd stayed in the city and had a family—and she would also visit us in Boston. She and my mother talked often on the phone and quickly regressed at the sound of each other's voice, giggling and gossiping and making squeaky kissing noises into the receiver. Though they were grown-ups, theirs was the kind of friendship I'd always wanted to emulate when I was a child: intimate, necessary, and exalted. Despite my problems in middle and high school, I'd been able to cultivate and maintain friendships that were far stronger than the ones I had with my relatives. I often put more into my friendships than my romantic relationships because I found those alliances more rewarding and permanent. I'd loved few partners as deeply as I loved my friends.

At my mother's funeral, Sylvia handed me a stack of letters and postcards that my mother sent her over their five-decade friendship and said, "These are yours now." In these letters, my mother confessed her deepest secrets and fears, details of her life both exciting and mundane, and gushed about her love for her friend. In 1973, almost twenty years after they'd met, my mother wrote Sylvia from London and explained, for possibly the thousandth time, how special she thought she was. "How do I love thee, let me count the ways . . . I've made several friends since I have been here but none will ever be as precious as you. Really, truly, you are a comfort, an excitement, a lasting you. I feel happy whenever I think of you."

I asked her to tell me again the story of how she and my mother became friends. They were in the same first-grade class at the local Catholic school. There were around sixty kids in one room, and at first they didn't know each other. "Your mother was a *talker*." Sylvia laughed. "Me, I was quiet. I didn't dare step out of line. Finally, the nun had had it with your mother and said, 'Change your seat and sit next to Sylvia. Maybe she'll teach you to be quiet.' So we sat next to each other. Your mother *still* wasn't quiet. That's how it all started."

My mother's father was absent; Sylvia's had died. "We had that as a bond from the very beginning," Sylvia explained. Her mother remarried and had more children with her stepfather. Once she and my mother became friends, they spent their afternoons together because Sylvia didn't like being at home. After school, they'd walk to my mom's apartment so she could drop off her bag and they could play. After a few hours, my mother walked Sylvia halfway home as they held hands and then parted with a hug.

Sylvia told me that when they became friends, she began praying every night for the opportunity to sleep over at my mother's house before she died. She demonstrated, placing her hands together and looking up. " 'Please God, don't let me die until I get to sleep over at Anita's.' And I did pretty soon after that. We slept with your grandmother in that one full-size bed. I slept over lots of times after that. I became a part of the family. Helen was so sweet. She was so good to me."

We both smiled at her memory. "My mother was always really sweet to my friends as well," I said. "She really encouraged my friendships when I was young, made sure I had sleepovers and got to spend time with the kids I was close to."

Sylvia and my mother had more in common than missing fathers. Both were Polish, short, and had curly blond hair. "We were twins," Sylvia said. "We did everything together. We had to do everything the same."

Wanting to have everything that the other had became a problem when it was time for their first communion. Sylvia's family had more money, and her mother bought her a beautiful dress. When my mother saw it, she realized the one Helen had bought her wasn't nearly as nice. So she begged and pleaded and ranted and raved until Helen gave in and bought her the same dress.

Hundreds of children were receiving their first communion on that day because the bishop was in town. My mother and Sylvia made sure they sat together so when they went up to the communion rail, they could be next to each other. A cloth was laid over the rail so the children wouldn't be tempted to touch the Eucharist. As Sylvia and my mom stuck their tongues out for the bishop, they put their hands together under the cloth and linked pinkies.

"That's adorable," I said.

"It was, but we were hardly angels. We were very unsupervised growing up, so we found lots of time to get into trouble. Your mother was an instigator; she had a lot of courage. The trouble that I got in, I got into because of her." Her smiled puckered around her cigarette. "We started smoking in third or fourth grade; that was all your mom."

"She always said that *you* were the one who got her smoking!"

"Me? I would never have had the nerve!"

One of Sylvia's favorite stories was about their prom. They'd double-dated, worn puffy dresses and tiaras. After the dance, the couples went out to dinner, per tradition. "Your mom and I had the brilliant idea of switching outfits. So we went into the bathroom, switched dresses, and came out. We thought it was the funniest thing in the world, we got such a kick out of it. Our dates were not amused."

They'd always intended to go to college. "We both had wanderlust," Sylvia said. "We wanted adventure. That was one of the good things about both of us coming from humble backgrounds. We were always striving for more, and we wanted to travel more than anything else. Your mom traveled a lot more than I did, though. I was a little jealous, I think, but I was happy for her."

"Did she talk to you about my father's decision to work in Ukraine? Was she angry that he made that choice and went somewhere for so long without her?"

"She did. She resented Ukraine because he felt closer to Ukrainians than he did to his own family. And I think a lot of that was just loneliness, and being with a kid who was out of control." She gave me a tight smile and I hung my head.

I thought of how I treated my mother when I was in high school. I hit her and I held a knife on her, and she'd just taken it. I spoke quietly. "Did she complain about me?"

"I wouldn't say complained, but she was frustrated. She just didn't know what to do with you."

"When I think of how I behaved as a teenager, I feel terrible. I gave her hell." I sighed. "I feel so guilty for everything

I put my mom through when she was already going through so much."

"Good!" She laughed. "Kids should feel guilty about stuff like that." When I winced, she quickly added, "But you know, you can't be too harsh on yourself—that's part of growing up. Adolescence is an awful time; you say and do terrible things. So you can't . . . you can't punish yourself."

"Well, I do," I told her. "I feel a thousand times worse about what I did now than I did then."

When I was leaving, she took my hand. "There was a lot to your mom. She had so many positive things going for her, but she had her demons. She did the best that she could, so there's no blaming her, there's no thinking less of her. She was human."

"I spent a long time blaming her for the problems I had with my father," I said, "struggles I had as a young adult, for her drinking. But I don't want to. Not anymore."

We hugged. She was smaller than my mother, and skinnier than my mom had been at the end. When we held each other, I felt that we were holding my mother between us.

"I hope I don't cry when you leave." Sylvia's eyes were already full of tears. "I lost her so many years before I really lost her. It's such a big, big sadness."

The next morning, as I was getting ready to drive out to the second address I had for Teresa, I decided to call her first. If a machine picked up, I wouldn't leave a message. If she picked up, I'd hang up and jump in my car.

After a few rings, a woman answered. I froze, then started speaking without meaning to.

"Is this Teresa?"

"It is." Her voice was thin and testy.

"This is Anya Yurchyshyn," I said. "I'm the woman—"

She cut me off in a voice far stronger than she'd answered with. "I got your letters. I didn't respond on purpose. It was embarrassing to have that letter forwarded by that other family because that was from forty-five years ago."

"I didn't mean to upset you. I just want to ask—"

"I don't want to be a part of this! It's in the past. I have enough grief."

I knew that conversation was probably the only one I'd have with her; my sympathy was overridden by my desire to know what had happened. I rushed to appeal to her. "There has been a lot of grief in my life as well, as there was in my mother's life, and I'm just trying to understand what happened—what Roman was like as a father, and if you knew that he had children from another marriage."

She said, "I'm not ready for this," but continued anyway, speaking in fragments that were difficult to connect. "Roman was very secretive. He was hiding a lot of things. Roman never spoke to me about having other children. That was one of the things that bothered me."

"So he didn't tell you about his other children? Who did? Your mother?"

"We always had his family over for dinner on Sundays and no one said anything."

"That must have been so upsetting."

"My mother went into a terrible depression."

"After she found out?"

"I didn't find out until my mother went into her post-menopausal depression."

"So your mother hid this information from you, or do you think she didn't know, either, and finding out—"

"I had a lot on my plate having them sick for a long time."

"You took care of them? That must have been very difficult."

"It was! Of course it was. I wish someone would ask if I needed something instead of always asking if they could have something from me."

"Is there anything I can do for you, Teresa?" I stuttered. "I would love to help in some way."

"Just leave me *alone*."

I couldn't make much sense of what she'd told me, all I knew for sure was Roman eventually caused his second family as much pain as his first.

I spent a few more days speaking with some of my parents' roommates, walking around my mother's old neighborhood and the University of Chicago campus with her friend Chip, then ended the trip with my friends Chris and Meredith. Meredith, a midwife, was working an overnight shift when I arrived.

Chris was one of my most important friends. I spoke to plenty of people more than I spoke to him, but I spoke to few people as eagerly. Sometimes we avoided calling each other because we knew we'd talk for hours. When he still lived in New York, he'd often bring a list of things we needed to discuss to whatever bar or restaurant we met at. We never got through it. Once, we both admitted that we didn't know how we'd felt about something until we discussed it with each other. We enjoyed sharing the new developments of our lives as much as discussing events from the past, revisiting favorite stories about awkward parties and weirdos we'd dated until events from each other's history became part of our own. As we launched into this familiar pattern, I realized we were mimicking my mother's behavior that I'd so often complained about. Telling and retelling stories we knew by heart. I did it because it felt so good. It reaffirmed my bonds with people, explained what we had and where we'd been. But my mother's were most often sad. She'd been touching a wound to remind herself who she was.

I told him everything I'd learned—my mother's traumatic birth, her molestation—as he doted on me, serving me braised pork and custom cocktails. I explained that I was starting to understand the neediness I'd observed in her when I was a child. My grandmother's devotion wasn't enough. Roman's flight left a cavity that couldn't be filled by other people's love or traveling the globe. I was still dealing with issues from my own childhood; hers must have haunted her as well. But I hadn't ever understood that; being my mom meant she was supposed to be perfect.

I was more affected by hearing her stories from other people than I'd ever been by her own telling, and by the ones she'd never shared with me. Without her insistence that I view her as a victim, I could see her as a person who'd experienced an enormous amount of loss and be furious at myself for not being sympathetic when she needed me to be.

Chris told me that he and Meredith were going away for the weekend, and I asked if I could stay at their house while they were gone. I was driving to Minnesota in a few days, and when Chris said yes, I lied to Chrissy and Arlene and told them I was leaving early. By this point, I couldn't handle more stories or sorrow. I wanted to be alone, enclosed by silence.

I'd been filled up with so much information but felt empty, pressed flat and thin by a weight bearing down on my body. I padded through Chris and Meredith's house, foraged for food in the fridge, popped Klonopin, watched hours of Netflix, and poured myself drink after drink.

My last night, I saw I was dirty and disheveled; I looked like my mother. Her pain hurt me so much that I'd needed to turn the world, and my brain, off. For so long, I'd considered her weak, but simply hearing of her burdens and horrors had caused me to take to bed for days and drunkenly hope that tomorrow wouldn't come.

CHAPTER SEVEN

Mountains

$\mathcal{M}$y parents met in 1964 on a bus from Chicago to Washington, D.C., which had been chartered by the University of Chicago, when my mom was a freshman and my dad was in his second year of graduate school.

He was already sitting on the bus when she arrived, escorted by Helen; my mother was still living at home because the dorms were too expensive. As she boarded, her mom loudly reminded her to call once she got to D.C. and to *be safe*. My mother took the seat behind my father and returned her mother's wave with a sigh.

They were only a block into the trip when he turned to

her and started flirting. "Be safe," he teased. "Don't talk to strangers."

She rolled her eyes and told him that she was going to D.C. because she figured the city would soon be her home. She was majoring in political science and hoped she'd get a job in Washington after she graduated, one that might lead to something at the United Nations or in the foreign service. Blushing, she confessed that she was on her first big trip. She'd never even been out of the Midwest and was just as excited to see the mountains they'd be passing on the drive as the city's famous sites. She'd never seen mountains before.

My father was charmed by her eagerness, but he explained that she wouldn't be seeing any mountains on that trip. The bus would be far beyond them by sunrise.

She was disappointed, but said she'd see them another time.

"You're very brave," he said. "Traveling to a new place on your own."

She asked if there was something she should be afraid of.

He said there wasn't, then asked, "Is someone whisking you away when you arrive?"

She laughed. His interest gave her confidence. There wasn't. What about him? Would a motorcade be waiting for him outside of the bus station?

He said no, he wasn't even staying in D.C. but was continuing on to Baltimore. He told my mom he was visiting friends from college, but that wasn't the truth. He was going to see an old flame, one he was still pining after.

She listed the places she planned to see over the weekend, then the ones she hoped to see during her life: the Parthenon, Germany, and the Great Wall of China. She felt suffocated and stuck in Chicago, and was determined to have a life full of movement and freedom.

My father told her he'd been born in Ukraine and moved to America when he was eight. He'd seen lots of Europe, though he didn't remember much of it. There were many places he wanted to see as well; that's why he'd switched his major from premed to business while he was at Johns Hopkins, and was now working toward a joint JD/MBA. That was the best path for a career in international business.

They smiled at each other, recognizing shared interests and motivations. They wanted similar things and were determined to get them.

My mother gave in to her tiredness first. She made a bed for herself using her sweater as a pillow and her coat as a blanket. My father stayed awake as the other students followed her into sleep. The hum of conversation was replaced by the heavy breathing of the passengers and the growl of the engine.

People were moaning for coffee when my mother woke up. She was looking out the window at the gray of the approaching city when my dad placed a piece of paper on her lap. The side facing her was blank. When she flipped it over, she saw he'd drawn a picture of mountains, a range that filled the entire page and seemed to continue beyond it.

My parents didn't tell me how they met. I constructed the above from what they'd told their friends and family. It was an auspicious beginning to their relationship. My mother wanted to see the world, and my father had done what he could to show it to her.

What did they see when they first looked at each other? My father's hair was black, his skin olive. His hooded eyes were magnified by thick glasses. My mother's long platinum hair shone from constant brushing. She tried to deflect attention from her sharp chin and crummy teeth by penciling in her eyebrows, which were fair and sparse. She made the blue of her eyes pop by packing matching shadow onto her lids.

My mother had gotten into the University of Chicago on a scholarship and was still finding her footing. I imagined her feeling overwhelmed when she walked its storied campus. Her Catholic-school education was less rigorous than that of many of her peers. Their parents were lawyers and professors, not factory workers who didn't finish high school. But Helen's expectations were as high as anyone else's, and my mom planned to surpass them.

My father was in graduate school and on a path that seemed long and clear. Sylvia told me that my mother liked that he was in law school and that he was older. His age and intellect probably made him more attractive than the guys my mother sat next to in class.

At school, she was surrounded by young women like herself, whose ambitions were much bigger than the opportunities available to them. Like her friends, she didn't intend to work hard and prove she was as capable as any man, only to graduate and stand behind one as a wife or a secretary. If she met someone she wanted to marry in college, he would be someone who expected great things from her as well as from himself, and wouldn't place his career before hers.

My mother moved into the dorm her second year, and her roommates became lifelong friends. Knowing how gregarious my mother was, I asked her college roommate Linda how much they goofed around, talked about boys or movies or music. She said, "We had really heavy-duty discussions, we didn't gossip. We talked about ideas. We had so much work, and we always had to read stacks of books and write treatises and essays. It was amazing we survived."

When I asked my father's friends and roommates to tell me what he was like at that time, I always heard the word "serious" first. They said that sure, everyone at the University of Chicago was serious, but my father was even more so. He socialized occasionally, but was mostly a loner. He'd hung a sign above his desk that said, "Once in a while I want to be with a smart person, myself."

My parents started hanging out once they returned to campus, meeting often in the library since they both had so much work. "They were doing their little mating dance between the stacks," Sylvia explained. After they'd been dating for a few months, my mother returned late to her dorm and told Linda that when she'd met my father that night, "There was a glow on his face. He looked so happy to see me. I knew he loved me."

She spent more time with his friends than he did with hers. My father loosened up around her, talked and joked more. Even if he was quiet, he appeared to enjoy watching her socialize, and admired how she'd jump into conversations and hold her own on political theory, current events, and art. No one seemed to think anything of their age difference; it was common for graduate students to date undergrads. "However much younger she was," one of his roommates told me, "she was clearly his intellectual equal. He wouldn't have been attracted to her if she hadn't been mature and capable of matching his intelligence."

They were a striking couple. The girlfriend of one of my father's friends told me, "Your mother and father were such an interesting contrast in appearance. Your mother was very beautiful, so blond and fair. Your father was dark." He was serious and focused, while she was "lively and witty, and spoke beautifully. Your mother just sparkled."

My father proposed in 1965, almost two years after they met. He was in his last year of graduate school and was moving to Boston to begin a three-year training program at the Bank of Boston. They decided my mother would finish her degree in three years instead of four, so she could join him. Knowing that my mother had been hoping to work in D.C. or for the UN, I wondered if moving to Boston for my father's career was a difficult decision. But none of her friends said that she'd expressed such concerns, only that she was worried about the extra work that graduating early would entail.

A new job, a new city, rushing to finish college early— these were exciting inconveniences. They believed they could weather them together and worried about a far bigger obstacle to their future: my father's parents.

His parents would have been disappointed with any partner who wasn't Ukrainian, but they were furious that my mother was Polish. That was far worse to them than the fact that she was from a poor, single-parent family. They raged at my dad and demanded he call off the engagement. It didn't matter that my mom's family hadn't lived in Poland for two generations; her people had been terrible to theirs. Neither of them were surprised by this reaction—they hadn't approved of my mother when she was his girlfriend—but they were hurt. The rabid opposition of his parents didn't make any sense to my mom. Her background should have been as irrelevant to them as it was to her.

My dad begged her to be patient and asked that she try to understand his parents' perspective. One evening, her friend Chip found my mother dozing off over a large book in the library. When he asked what she was reading, she showed him the cover—an encyclopedia of Ukrainian history.

My parents spoke of their dreams, where they wanted to live, work, and travel, but I learned from my father's friends that he interrupted these fantasies with two stipulations. The first was that they'd raise their children as Ukrainians. He was willing to defy his parents by marrying her, but his Ukrainian identity was as important to him as it was to them. The second was that she'd let him "go back and contribute" to Ukraine if he was given the chance. It may have been easy, even romantic, for my mother to agree to these conditions. Raising their future kids as Ukrainian sounded exotic, and she assumed that he'd never have a chance to act on his duty toward his homeland. No one expected Ukraine to ever gain independence.

After they got engaged, my mom went to Europe for the summer to study German. My dad decided he'd meet her when her courses finished so they could take their first big trip together. While they were apart, they sent each other letters full of longing multiple times a week.

I have just finished a most hectic evening working on one of my papers, but I just have to stop and think a bit about my dearest scrump. Just the thought makes everything much more pleasant. Thinking about you sweetie,

> I fly away to Austria and sit beside you and together
> with you drink in all of the wondrous things that make
> life and the world around us so exhilarating.

In Europe, my mother was in places she'd always fantasized about. Simply walking down the street made her euphoric. The "kindness, warmth, and hospitality" of her host family, and the "mountains consumed in clouds and the greenness of the countryside" were so overwhelming that one day, as she returned from mass, she started crying. "I just could not contain it all and was just weeping as I was walking—everything and everyone is just too beautiful for words."

She missed my dad as much as he missed her. "You're so wonderful, darling. I love you and appreciate you so. I really believe all my experiences, all the people I meet, every one now culminates in you."

These were the letters that shook me when I was cleaning out my mother's house. I'd been so convinced that they'd never been in love, but the passion I found in their letters was undeniable, enviable. My parents were intoxicated and confident; each new declaration was more emphatic than the last.

Their fevers were interrupted with conversations about my dad's parents' continued anger. After visiting them over the Fourth of July, he wrote,

> My mother is quite committed to seeing that I'm happy,
> even though she may be not too happy with my decision.
> My father, however, is unapproachable. I'm becoming
> more and more convinced we ought to go off and elope."

My mother's response was composed over multiple days, and included attempts at German, stories of dancing and drinking and problems with her camera. When she reached the topic of his parents, she was firm but diplomatic.

It's still difficult for me to understand your family. How can your father be 'unapproachable'? Doesn't he appreciate you as another man, and can't you speak to each other as such? How, love, can you maintain such a patient attitude?

He countered,

You suggest that I am too patient. I have not been very patient and my earlier discussions of this subject at home have produced bitter arguments. I would certainly be much happier if my parents approved but if you are suggesting that I can force my parents to change their opinions simply on the basis of the fact that I think I am right, then I think you are being somewhat unrealistic.

After defending himself, he softened his tone.

My only concern is whether you are willing to accept the fact that they are and probably will be for some time opposed to our marriage, even after the fact. I would hope that if our love is strong then their oppositions will have no effect on your happiness with me. Therefore, I ask you to please accept their opposition as something which is a product of many things neither of us can perhaps fully understand. I ask you to love me, to make your happiness with me—in the end everything else will turn out right.

His letters usually included instructions for how she should handle potential suitors. He insisted that she tell "any fresh Austrian or other Salzburg Institute inhabitant to go out and yodel in the traffic, or under a snow avalanche." A few weeks later, he said, "I know you must be knocking them dead . . . make sure the old (and young) lechers stay their distance, remind them that nothing is more violent than the wrath of a Cossack." These comments were more playful than possessive, but the distance probably made him insecure. He knew the men she was meeting might be as taken with her as he was.

I was awed by the strength of my father's feelings, their colors and fire. My mother's wild emotions, her love of the world and him, seemed to give him the opportunity to share parts of himself that he'd kept hidden. Quiet for so long, he now composed letters full of poetry. I read them again and again, spellbound by their beauty. My mother must have done the same.

> Your leaving didn't fully hit me at first . . . I walked among the columns on the lower level of the campus and then out into Halsted. I walked up that street—past the interchange at Congress, whirring with traffic even on a quiet Sunday afternoon,—the pigeons were more interesting than the cars,—I walked up Halsted, looked into Greek shop-windows, into the bars, at the blank, reddened faces of the men that frequent the vacant lots, alleys and curbs of the areas. I turned onto Madison and just walked. I didn't show much emotion, I don't know if I really cared, I just walked, they just stood, slept, stared blankly, no one really saw anyone, I just

walked. I really didn't lose my composure until I had
reached closer to lopping Madison, those blocks just
before you reach Canal. I guess there is only so much
that you can passively accept—out of the corner of your
eye, on those side streets, those buildings just behind
that vacant lot along the street,—you see them—it re-
minds you of a prison, a concentration camp, are they
animals or human, but they are there—those buildings where they sleep for fifty cents, they have fire
escapes running down their whole length on one side,
and all the windows and doors open up on them—and
they stand there, sit, hang, without shirts, the heat is
tremendous—the bars come up to their waists, there are
dozens of them on each floor, floor above floor and on
each floor—long iron gangplanks they stare, they stare,
stare, stare,—there is little sound—almost a picture, a
frozen stare, blank, completely blank, but you know
they are living, you can almost smell the sweat, but you
just keep on walking, you barely hesitate, you just keep
walking. And I kept on walking, I passed a theater and
then another, I went in, the movie was stupid, stupid
because it tried to recreate the depth of reality in the
childish imagination of moralized history.

Enough of this moroseness, but perhaps it conveys
better than anything else, how much I miss you and the
emptiness of being without you.

I struggled to reconcile the enormity of these people's
young love and optimism with the behavior of the couple
who'd raised me. Believing that they'd never been in love, as

I had for so long, was much easier than knowing that they had been. Accepting this gave me something entirely new, and unexpected, to mourn. Falling out of love, or waking up in the middle of a life that you didn't want, was one of the most painful things I could imagine.

My mother thought she had found someone as full of feeling as she was, and who offered her a love she'd wanted her entire life. That love and my dad's defiance of his parents were more powerful than any oath.

When they returned from Europe, my father moved to Boston and my mother went back to Chicago. They wrote to each other constantly. My dad didn't talk of his new job or coworkers, just of his longing.

> It's a cold and rainy night in dear old Boston . . . I miss my precious darling. We could be sitting here together— huddling warmly so that the chilling draft from that slightly open window would not be noticed—and, perhaps, even without a word, we would gaze out together into the darkness and hear and see the sounds.

My mother's responses were just as affectionate, but also anxious. She talked about wedding expenses—$70 for flowers, $300 for liquor: "You have to figure four [hundred] drinks for one hundred people"—and the stress of applying to four different graduate programs while also battling a heavy academic load. "The exam question is unbelievable. I've spent all night on Aristotle and haven't gained any headway." She returned often to the expense of the wedding, but even more often to her feelings for her fiancé.

210

How I would love to lose myself into you now. Instead, I must to Plato and Aristotle. There is NO JUSTICE IN THIS SORRY WORLD . . . A honeymoon doesn't matter as long as you will be there to squeeze my hand and we're together . . . like we should rightly be now . . .

My father's parents continued to oppose the wedding as it approached. When my father didn't bend to their wishes, they told him they wouldn't come. When this didn't change his mind, his mother finally gave in and said she'd attend. Dymtro was livid and declared that she couldn't go, and she told him that he couldn't tell her what to do. Her decision was a necessary sacrifice; her duty to her son was as strong as the one to her husband.

She tried and tried to convince him to go as well, and when he wouldn't agree, she sought help. She called Ruslan and begged him to convince Dymtro to attend. Ruslan agreed because he knew how badly my dad wanted his parents there. Irene made Dymtro drive to Chicago the night before the wedding, and they met Ruslan outside of the dorm where my father's bachelor party was being thrown.

Ruslan was impressed with Irene's determination. "All this stuff your grandmother did," he told me, "standing up to her husband, driving all that way, it must have been very unpleasant."

He got into their car and spent an hour talking to, and sometimes arguing with, Dymtro while Irene listened. Dymtro said his son was insensitive. Acting out both sides of the conversation to me, Ruslan said, "What do you mean insensitive? He loves her. What's sensitivity got to do with it?"

Ruslan knew he wouldn't succeed if he made flowery statements about America being a melting pot or love's power to transcend differences. He told me that he understood Dymtro's resistance. "It was the remnants of this nastiness that happened to him in his early years; he transferred it to her," he told me. "Every day, the Poles caused you grief. They stopped you, asked for your identity card. They wouldn't let you go to the university because only twenty-five Ukrainians were allowed to attend, and they already had their twenty-five." Dymtro wasn't upset because my mom "did some wrong to him, or she did some wrong to his son. It was the accumulation of old injustices."

"I told him, 'This is uncomfortable, the Ukrainian/Polish thing. I agree with you." But he said it didn't matter if they agreed or what they thought, because "this is what George wants to do, and he is going to do it, no matter what."

The wedding was in less than twenty-four hours. My father had made his choice; now Dymtro had to do the same. Before returning to the party, Ruslan looked at him and said, "If you don't come, you're going to lose your son."

His appeal worked. My dad's parents made it to at least part of the wedding. Some people, including my mother, remembered them only attending the reception; others remember seeing them at both the ceremony and the reception. Lana told me that she had no idea; all she remembered was being worried about looking fat in her bridesmaid dress.

The ceremony was at the University of Chicago's Bond Chapel. Guests sat on the bride's or the groom's side, per tradition, which meant the crowd was split between Poles and Ukrainians. Strangers did not introduce themselves or ask who they were related to. Even the people who already knew each other didn't chat. "The tension between the Polish side and the Ukrainian side was intense," Chrissy explained. "You expected them to go after each other with swords."

The wedding was conducted by the chapel's priest and an Orthodox cantor who spoke Ukrainian. The reception was held at a modest faculty club. Guests were serenaded by a strolling violinist as they ate traditional Polish food and later danced to a raucous polka band.

When my parents danced, guests thought they fit together perfectly and moved as if they were a single unit. When my mom grew tired, my dad picked her up, kissed her, and "carried her around like a prize."

CHAPTER EIGHT

Shamefully Happy

$\mathcal{A}$fter the wedding, my parents moved into the small apartment my father had rented for them in the Back Bay. He liked the gas lamps that lit the streets at night, the neighborhood's grand brownstones, and that it was close enough to the financial district that he could walk to work.

He'd established a simple life while he waited for my mother. He put on one of his two suits in the morning, spent the day learning about loans and credit reports, then returned and made himself a modest meal and drank a beer or two.

Though she had been excited to get married, my mother wasn't prepared to be a wife. She sent her former college roommates a letter detailing a "day in the life of a young newly" that demonstrated just how different she was from the "budding balaboosta" she thought she was supposed to be:

> Boy, married life is ultra cool . . . sleeping till noon . . . reading the paper in bed till 1 p.m. And ah, the lovely afternoons . . . lying around drinking beer and reading my darling husband's old *Playboy* magazines . . . Sometimes, however, ugh, I have to get dressed and go to the grocery to buy more beer, frozen pizzas, and TV dinners . . . gourmet foods.

She included a sample of the nightly conversations that she had with her husband.

> "What the hell did you do today . . . this goddamn apartment looks just like the day we moved in."
> "But darling, you know I haven't been able to find a maid yet, and besides, I get all worn out, looking thru the yellow pages . . . have another beer and shut up."
> Since we haven't bought a television yet, our delightful conversation, moistened with Schlitz, continues till the wee hours and then we rollllll into bed and . . . AH, begins another delightful day, around noon or so.

She acknowledged that she probably wouldn't be able to maintain this languorous state forever. "Things may change ten years from now, when we have beautiful, talented, and intelligent little ones . . . I may have to get up a bit earlier or even have to cope with a nanny."

My mother's visions of marriage were gauzy and romantic, a formalized version of the life she and my father had had in Chicago and Europe. They'd spend their days discussing books, reading aloud to each other from the newspaper, and wandering through museums; their nights, watching foreign movies or debating politics as they drank in bed.

As time went on, though, my father had less time and attention for her. His training program kept him away until seven. He brought work home because he wanted to get ahead of his peers and because he enjoyed it. He expected my mother to have something for them to eat when he returned, and that their home would keep becoming more of one as she unpacked and decorated. He didn't want her to be a housewife, but since she wasn't yet working, he thought she could do something. She did very little. Dodging domestic responsibilities could have been a feminist protest or laziness. Or, it could have been a way to deal with the frustration she felt upon realizing she now had to compete for my father's attention.

Boston was conservative, not nearly as vibrant and diverse as Chicago. A friend of my mother's told me that although both of my parents were outsiders in that somewhat provincial city, my father blended in. "That gray suit," she said, "fit him like armor." He was an expert at adjusting to new environments. He understood how he was expected to behave at the bank and knew how far he was allowed to deviate. He chose to keep his beard, but otherwise looked the part.

My mother, however, "did not fit the image of the Boston woman." She had the education but not the pedigree. She didn't want to play the part of a banker's wife or be a

ANYA YURCHYSHYN

homemaker who volunteered at museums. She enrolled at Northeastern for her master's in political science, and found work as an editor for environmental and antiwar publications.

At parties with my dad's coworkers and their wives, she was one of the few women working or in school, let alone doing both. She rounded out his somewhat two-dimensional work persona by charming his superiors with wit and compliments and ingratiating herself with hostesses.

Some of my father's Ukrainian buddies from Chicago and Baltimore, including Ruslan and Natasha, ended up in Boston as well, and soon he was part of a tight group of young Ukrainian academics and professionals. "It was a totally different community from the kinds that usually formed around churches," Natasha explained. "It was more intellectual."

Their group worked to bolster Ukraine's international profile and broaden the conversation about its history and current problems. They hosted talks with scholars, read the latest books about the country and the region, and discussed ongoing problems with human rights and corruption. They wanted to inspire other Ukrainians to be proud of who they were and become involved in establishing its place in the world. Their efforts contributed to the establishment of the Harvard Ukrainian Research Institute in 1973, which they supported through a smaller organization that conducted fund-raising, published articles, and promoted its efforts. "We all revolved around the institute," Natasha said.

My mother wasn't interested in being a part of this group, probably because my father's friends referred to her as "the Polish girl." "The whole community knew your dad married a Polish woman," Natasha said one afternoon as we chatted in her wide, leafy backyard. "It was as if he married an American. It was negative."

"He *had* married an American," I said. "I know why his parents were upset, why did his friends care? They were young intellectuals, and it was the late sixties!"

"You were supposed to marry your own kind. You were almost excluded from the community if you married out." She sighed. "*I* married out. It didn't matter that Joe was at Harvard with the rest of them." Her husband was Italian American, and like my mother, he wasn't very welcome.

My mother and Natasha became friends, and my parents often went on double dates with Natasha and Joe to the beach or dinner. Their friendship worked, Natasha said, because Joe was also an outsider. Neither my mother nor Joe had to worry about the conversation falling into Ukrainian, which often happened when the group was larger. Despite their friendship, Natasha said my mother "didn't have time" for the group as a whole, and believed that was because "she hated Ukrainians."

After being rejected by my father's parents, my mother was probably frustrated to find that the same nationalism ran through his peer group. She wasn't Ukrainian, but otherwise she had a lot in common with them. I don't know if my father ever encouraged her to study Ukrainian so she could assimilate, or if she considered studying the language after finding herself in the middle of yet another discussion that had switched from her language to his. She may not have been very interested in ingratiating herself with people who seemed determined to reject her. Her decision not to learn Ukrainian or find another way into this group, and my father's failure to involve her, meant she was excluded from a big part of his life that would soon become even more meaningful.

In 1971, my father was offered the position of the vice president and director of corporate finance for the bank's London branch. My parents were excited to live abroad; my mother was also probably excited to get away from the Ukrainians. Even more thrilling was the six-month leave that my father had negotiated. When he asked his supervisors for the time off, they told him no one had ever done such a thing, but my father was happy to be their guinea pig. He'd work for a few months in London, make sure things were in order, and create protocols for how things would run while he was gone. He and my mother had discussed traveling through the Middle East and Asia when they were in Chicago, and they wanted to do it before they had children or my father's work made such a trip impossible.

They began their trip in Denmark, where they purchased a used, cream-colored Land Rover that took them the more than twelve thousand miles across India, Iraq, Iran, Afghanistan, and finally Nepal. I'd heard about this trip as a child, though not many of its details. I learned more about it from the letters my mother sent Sylvia once she was back in London.

> My mind is still full of a million impressions of proud Turks, Afghanis glorious in full beards and turbans, Arabs in flowing robes, people bathing in the holy Ganges, graceful sari'd women sliding through the countryside. The mastery of architecture and ceramics of Iran, the stirring biblical cities of Iraq, the marvels of Kashmir, the incomparable glory of the Himalayas.

She was particularly moved by Benares, describing the Indian city as

> a prayer where one is surrounded visually by temples, shrines, and one hears the sound of sacred bells and holy chanting. Oh the serenity of Buddhists at Sarnath, where Buddha preached his first sermon and where he received enlightenment.

My mother also shared their inevitable lows. Their car broke down in rural Turkey on "what had to be the worst road in the world—we had two flat tires in one night and due to all the bumps, our Land Rover lost all its screws." My mother stayed with the car while my father walked to "a teeny village in the middle of nowhere" and found a man to look at the car. He said the problem was the carburetor, and he offered to fix it with wire so they could get to a real town with a mechanic. When the car jack my parents had bought in Denmark failed, the man gathered a group of locals who "formed a human jack" and held the car up while he patched the faulty part. He insisted they take the rest of the wire in case the carburetor gave them more trouble. He "refused to accept any kind of payment. He pointed at Allah above, and then to his heart."

They had a different sort of car trouble in India, where my mother said the roads were a "nightmare" because they were jammed with "people, bulls, cows, oxen carts, bicycles." She claimed she lost twenty pounds during this portion of the trip—which meant she would have weighed eighty—"not to food but to tension." She found driving in India so stressful that she often wasn't able to eat at the end of the day.

They met a young Dutch couple, Theo and Annemarie, making a similar journey when they got stuck at the Iran–Afghanistan border, which had closed early for Ramadan. They parked their vehicles on the side of the road and shared bread, cheese, and cookies as they swapped stories and boiled water for tea over a low kerosene flame. In the morning, they hugged and planned to meet again and spend Christmas together in Kathmandu.

Kathmandu was my parents' final stop. They set up an informal bazaar in front of their small hotel to sell their camping equipment, clothes they no longer needed, and their battered truck.

Theo and Annemarie arrived, and they celebrated Christmas together as planned. My father bought a small pine tree and put it in the corner of their hotel room and topped it with a star he'd fashioned from gold paper. They ate ham from tins for dinner and drank too much Nepalese beer. A few days later, they gave away what they couldn't sell and flew to Europe. They remained close with the Dutch couple, whom I met many times when they traveled to America with their daughters. When I spoke with them about the trip, they said my parents were both incredibly brave, but that my mother seemed a bit "traumatized." They had the impression that she'd started the trip enthusiastically, but that my father pushed her limits of comfort and safety and she was eager to return to Europe.

Once they were back in London, my father began traveling through Europe, Asia, and the Middle East for the bank, visiting companies involved in aircraft chartering and container leasing, as well as those interested in shipping natural gas to global markets. His job was to assess requests for credit and to identify companies that might be in need of a loan.

My mother began working for the Sierra Club's London office, where her primary responsibility was influencing the UN's negotiations of the Law of the Sea Treaty. It was an unpaid position, but she took her job as seriously as my father took his, and buried herself in books and reports on oceanic environment and underwater mining. These were topics she'd never even thought about, but soon she was an expert on them. She was overjoyed to be part of the international political community, where she was one of only a few women. She became the club's London representative and was their delegate at the UN Conference on the Human Environment in Stockholm in 1972, which resulted in the creation of the United Nations Environment Programme.

My parents rented a duplex in Mayfair and decorated it with rugs and sculptures they'd acquired during their trip. They hung their favorite photographs from their adventures next to bright, abstract posters. Soon those pictures shared space with nudes of my mother and her growing belly. One of their friends told me, "George had photographs of your mom everywhere, naked, this beautiful big bump. He really celebrated her." My father documented the curves of her changing body in portraits taken in bathroom steam or in the squares of light thrown by their tall living-room windows.

My mother found pregnancy "wonderful." She told Sylvia that toward the end she "felt sort of sad, knowing that I would miss the feeling of life thrusting about. It's such fun to actually sit there and watch your tummy gyrate, wave, and jump."

Still very pregnant two weeks after her due date, labor had

to be induced. My father booked a private room and read to my mom from Kurt Vonnegut's *Welcome to the Monkey House* as her contractions increased, then held her hand and coached her as the delivery began. My mother told Sylvia the birth "was not bad at all." She didn't remember the pain, just the "incredible moments of watching your baby being born, slipping out from you into the world."

They named their daughter Alexandra. My mother thought she looked like a "sphinx, brooding and ageless." My father pulled out his camera and began taking photos of their baby. When a nurse placed Alexandra in a cot in the room, he "kept running back and forth to the little crib to see his daughter, who was lustily crying."

My mother "felt a tremendous surge of love for her daughter from the very beginning." When Alexandra cried, she cried too. When she thought ahead to "all the tears which shall inevitably be a part of her growing up and how I might not be able to prevent them," she was devastated. Motherhood would, in many ways, be "painful," she concluded at the hospital, realizing that "mothers are very vulnerable people." But all the same, she marveled at the "great bond" she felt "to all women," especially her own mother. "How many of my tears caused hers?" she wondered in a letter to Sylvia.

Alexandra, with her dark hair and complexion, took after her father. "I think George enjoys everyone saying how much she looks like him," my mother reported. He was always "playing with her, watching her, coaxing smiles from her, changing her messy, messy diapers. It's true, she really is daddy's little girl."

When Alexandra was six weeks old, my father had to go to Asia for three weeks, and my mother teased he'd be gone for half their daughter's life. "I hope this won't happen too often," she wrote Sylvia, "as babies need both parents."

In addition to worrying about the frequency of my father's work trips, there was tension around Alexandra's baptism. My father wanted her to be baptized in a Ukrainian church, while my mother didn't want her to be baptized at all. "How can I teach her things I really don't believe in?" she asked. "How can I encourage her to go to church when I don't?" She thought my father saw baptism as "a ritual, a national symbol, a kind of 'Ukrainianization' of his daughter," but said he was a hypocrite because he wasn't religious either. "The ceremony itself rather repulses me," she continued. "It's a lot of exorcism. How can a child be possessed by the devil?" Alexandra did get baptized, but not for years. We were baptized at the same time, when I was three and she was seven. In the one picture I have of the ceremony, we are sprawled out in our godfathers' arms as they struggle to hold us.

When Alexandra was two months old, my mother told Sylvia, "I feel as if she is a wonderful present, which someone may yet take away. She is a pure delight. I truly adore her, am incredulous that 'she came from me.' . . . What was life like before? . . . I am shamefully happy."

I'd always thought my mother didn't really want to be a mother. I knew she loved us, but she seemed to find the work of being a mother a drag—the cooking, the cleaning, refereeing fights over what TV show to watch or what cereal to buy. I wasn't able to sense the love running under her annoyance with the drudgery. Reading her descriptions of her initial joy forced me to reconsider my previous ideas. Having children brought a deep richness to her life—at least at first.

While she was pregnant, my mother took a Lamaze class and became good friends with another young mother-to-be, an Englishwoman named Sue, whom I would come to know well. My mother often told me about how much she relied on Sue as a young mom. In addition to having the emotional support of someone who was also bouncing between the extremes of new motherhood, its joys, loneliness, and uncertainty, she had a Sherpa. Sue would accompany her to the chemist and remind her that diapers were "nappies," pacifiers were "dummies," and to ask clerks not if they "had" an item but if they "did" them. Every time she spoke to Sue, saw Sue and her family, or someone mentioned England, my mother launched into an impression of herself fumbling at a shop after Alexandra was born.

As herself, she'd say, "Do you do dummies?" Switching into an outrageously bad English accent, she then gave the reply. "Hmmm, we *did* do dummies, but I don't know if we *still* do dummies. Let me ask Nigel. Nigel, do we do dummies?"

After my mother died, I went to London to visit Sue, who I hadn't seen in over a decade. As we reclined in her backyard or wandered through her community garden, whose paths were lined with bright peonies and clusters of lavender, she told me about the beginning of their friendship. She told me that they talked on the phone constantly while they were pregnant and got together often after they'd given birth to their daughters. "When a child is little, they're easily transportable, so we'd

meet in the park or go to a museum or spend the evening together. If we had sitters, we'd see a film. When we saw each
other, we'd of course talk about how the girls were getting on,
but not for very long. Most of the time, we'd talk about the
political things I was involved in or the work she'd been doing
before and wanted to do again."

She and my mother were frustrated to discover that, since
having children, people only wanted to talk to them about
their babies and seemed to believe that their children were the
only things they thought about. "If you're a woman who has
always worked, and I had always worked, it's a shock. Your
opinions don't seem to matter to anybody; you're just somebody who looks after children. But your mom and I shared a
tremendous amount ideologically, and we needed to be able to
talk about those things."

What Sue said helped me understand something I hadn't
been able to as a child, and echoed things I'd heard from my
friends who'd become parents: You can adore your children
and your time with them but still resist the expectation that
you've been changed so dramatically by motherhood that you
no longer care about the things you once did, or that your previous life should be over. My mother didn't want her identity
to be "mom." She didn't get satisfaction from doting on her
kids or cooking or even playing much with them. She was far
more interested in the world outside of her home than inside
of it. Alexandra is the same. Her children are a big part of her
life, but they are not all of it. She's a mom and, determinedly,
many other things as well. Like my mother, she has refused to
be reduced.

I asked Sue if she'd met other wives of my father's coworkers. Sue had, and she didn't like them. "Your mum could not have been more different from them," she said. "She looked more student-y; we wouldn't spend much money on clothing." The other American women were extremely wealthy and well dressed. "Their husbands worked for banks, and they were all massive. Your mum looked like a creature from a different planet, and so did your dad. These people were *so* vulgar. They would be saying this awful right-wing crap, and your mum would contest it all the time. They thought we were both flaky as a consequence." These women treated my mother and Sue as if they were ditzy teenagers even though, Sue explained, "She'd already done a huge amount of things. Your mom was much, much more traveled than they were."

My mother and Sue took to each other instantly, but Sue worried that she might not like my father because he was "a part of this international banker world," and thought he might not like her, or her husband, Martin, who was a painter. But they all got on "very well. I think he was quite surprised that he liked being with us. He and I had a good relationship as well, as Martin and George had a good relationship. They shared a lot of similar interests. We had a tremendous time together; your father had a terrific sense of humor. Your mother was a good foil for him."

One of the many things Sue appreciated about my father was his tactful generosity. He was aware of the fact that she and Martin didn't have as much money as he and my mother did, and he often offered to pay for dinner or movie tickets, and when they didn't let him, which was most of the time, he made sure they went to restaurants they could all comfortably afford, or my parents would just have them over. "He was extremely generous and understanding; it was a relief not to have to worry about spending too much when we were all hanging out, because we had other friends who weren't as conscious of the issue."

I asked her how my parents got along. "Did my father respect my mother?"

"Oh yes," she said. "He respected her intelligence, he valued her opinion, and he knew that the work that she was doing was significant." Like his friends in grad school, she thought their relationship was equal and balanced. The dynamic I saw later hadn't been established yet.

My mother returned to the Sierra Club part-time to draft two treatises—one on air pollution, and one on noxious substances other than those causing air pollution—and to represent it at the IMCO's monthlong International Conference on Marine Pollution. She was happy to be working on something "constructive," but found it hard to be away from Alexandra. She told Sylvia: "On a few occasions she has been weeping and clinging to my legs as I attempt to go out the door. It can be heart-wrenching."

My mother went to Geneva for more environmental conferences with a female coworker, who told me the meetings were interesting and fun, and they'd had a great time together. They encountered plenty of sexism, mostly from diplomats or other government representatives. The field of environmentalism was less sexist than many others, she explained, and she and my mother came with the inarguable credibility of the Sierra Club. During that trip, and the others that followed, she and my mother hung out together in the lobby of the Hilton Intercontinental when they weren't in meetings to network and promote their agendas. They called it "lobbying in the lobby." It was effective, in part, because they were "young, attractive, and smart," so people wanted to talk with them.

My mother discovered she was pregnant again in 1973. She told Sylvia, "I'm not exactly pleased, as I can't imagine someone else to distract me from precious Alexandra, whom I enjoy so much. But," she conceded, "with this attitude I may have delayed indefinitely, never feeling the time was right."

I was terrified to reach this part of my parents' story because I knew how tragically it ended. Everything I learned about their early marrige and parenthood, even its happy moments, sounded like terrible foreshadowing. Each turn of the story was expected, and each made me cringe.

My mother's ambivalence about having a second child continued after Yuri's birth. She told Sylvia that she

> missed Alexandra so much while I was in the hospital and felt I was thinking more about her than Yuri. I was away from her for six full days, coming home the morning of the seventh and so excited to hold her again.

A few months later, she wrote

> You asked about my feelings and if they were the same this time, and again I will say honestly but with guilt (I have decided parents are always guilt ridden about something) no, frankly. This is not to be measured in love but rather excitement and the awe that I remember describing to you after Alexandra's birth. I suppose one can never relive the super high of a first thrilling experience

although childbirth and the delivery was certainly again enthralling.

Yuri was

more complicated than Alexandra was as an infant, cries a lot more and is just more intense. They tell you second babies are easier—don't believe it. He is rather funny looking frankly and I add with some feelings of guilt, not as pretty a baby as Alexandra, who was chubby, round, and not bald!

Yuri and Alexandra didn't look related. Yuri had my mother's fair complexion, which made Alexandra's seem even darker. Her mess of deep brown hair made his bald head look blue. Alexandra was also much more robust, with a huge belly and arms ringed with deep creases, while Yuri was slight, almost skinny.

When he was ten months old, he developed a cough that turned into pneumonia. Yuri was admitted to the hospital, but he didn't respond to medication, and it soon became clear that something bigger was wrong.

When I was cleaning out my mom's house, I found a slim, brown notebook that she kept during this chaotic time. She'd recorded each horrid development in spare language and short sentences, and used only six of its pages. Her entries brought me as close as I'd ever been to such an enormous loss; it told me what my parents didn't and couldn't. I was haunted by the enormity of their pain, and it consumed me. The notebook was the most revealing item I had found; I never read it without crying and wishing it hadn't needed to be written.

Feb 17—Rapid shallow breathing; doctor
Yuri taken into hospital

18, am—oxygen tent set up
pm—tube feeding

19th general anesthetics—"desperate for diagnosis"
blood tests continue

20th—no change; outside consultation

21st—Dr. comes; I am told to live from day to day. Heart
enlarged—low antibodies

As doctors performed test after test and tried different med-
ications, Yuri's body slowly shut down. Finally, they discovered he'd been born with an immune deficiency. He'd looked
"funny" because he'd never really been healthy. Pneumonia
wasn't the problem; the problem was that his body couldn't
fight serious infections.

My parents were at the hospital together as frequently as
they could be. Alexandra visited Yuri a few times at the beginning of his stay, but was mostly at home with a nanny.
One of my parents returned home every evening to give her
updates and explain again that Yuri was sick and that they
needed to be with him.

22nd—@ 11:00 am. Yuri stops breathing; resuscitation,
yields his spirit and dies.

24th—second death; make arrangements

Yuri is dead by the end of the notebook's first page. I don't know what happened between the above two entries, but it seems he came close to dying on February 22. Perhaps doctors kept him on life support for those last two days.

My mother did not record her reaction, or my father's. When she'd told me about Yuri's death when I was ten, she'd said my father had cradled their son's body and whispered "My son, my son, my son" as he cried, but that wasn't in her notes.

When I spoke with people who knew about Yuri's death, they told me the story my mother told them; their versions were violent and vivid, so bright they were blown out. One person said my father lurched through the hospital wailing and throwing himself against walls. He'd screamed "My son," not whispered it. Another person said he'd screamed those words in Ukrainian: "*Miy syn, miy syn, miy syn.*"

25th—post mortem—lungs infected

27th—cremation

March 2, Sunday—ashes scattered in Cader Idris

My mother told me that when they returned from the hospital, they had their nanny take Alexandra for a few days. I imagine them wandering the apartment raw with sorrow, falling into furniture and onto the floor, pushing each other away when their rage surpassed their sadness.

My mother wrote

When will the tears stop burning? The immediate tension of the first three days has passed. The horror and absolute shock has gone somewhat and by Wednesday, March 5th, my arms ache to hold a son who was once mine. I would sell my soul to the devil to hold and cuddle him again. I don't know if I have accepted his death yet as each nite I dream we are at the hospital again and if he is dying, I can caress him back to life. But most of the time he is still alive."

When Alexandra returned home, she was confused. She made statements about Yuri and asked questions, experimenting with words and truths so she could figure out the change that had occurred. These were small punishments for my mother, who had to help Alexandra understand what happened to her little brother, to understand death.

March 9—At bedtime, Alexa crying about angels and Yuri. I find out Robbie has told her he is an angel. Then she says he is sleeping. I worry about how many explanations she has heard.

March 10—Alexa says Yuri in hospital and I say no otherwise she would visit him and I would be with him. She seems to understand this and says, "He has died" but I think I can tell her eyes are looking for what it means.

March 13—Putting on her socks, Alexa says they are too small and are the baby's. "Yuri is in hospital." No, I explain. If he were, we would be there with him. "He has died, but he's happy," she says. Yes, I say. "Can we bring him home again?" Oh god, if only we could.

March 13 (cont.)—Last night I lay in bed trying to fall asleep and I wondered with great pain what little Yuri must have thought those last horrible days and those moments he was dying. It breaks my heart to consider he saw only strange faces leaning on his chest, trying to resituate him. How I pleaded for them to let me come in—perhaps if he could have seen his mother, however cloudily—heard my voice. But in reality he was alone in his last moments. What must have been going on in his mind?

Yuri's death tormented my mother. It tormented my father as well, but I have no record of his pain.

Later in the month, she went to Geneva for work, hoping that being out of London and having something to do might distract her.

March 21–23 I give my speech—rather well. Meet old colleagues at weekend conference. Shaking as I walk in. Forcing myself to "act normal."

24–28 Geneva. Role playing and I long to scream and cry.

Early April—Alexa must have dreamed about Yuri or remembered the last time she saw him in hospital. She said, "Yuri . . . I kissed him and said be better."

I still think of all old and new emergencies. How often I sang to him the words, "And if you take my hand, all will be well when the day is done." I really believed I could protect him always.

Am answering all the letters and cards which were sent. It's more than painful.

Sue said that she called my mother often during this time because she sensed something was wrong. She became more worried as each call continued to be ignored. "One afternoon your mother finally answered," she told me. "I asked, 'How have you been, how's Yuri?' And she blurted out, 'He's dead.'" Sue's voice began to wobble. "We spent the next three hours on the phone. She just talked and talked about Yuri. Her description of your father holding his body was just awful."

At one point during their conversation, my mother abruptly began talking about a film in a cheerful voice. Sue was confused. A moment later, my mother apologized and explained, "George came into the room. He doesn't like to see me like this." Sue thought that my father felt my mom shouldn't be dwelling on Yuri's death or "maybe he just didn't want to hear it again. I went out almost immediately to see her, and she talked through what had happened, the absolute nightmare of it." The one person who understood her grief didn't want to hear about it, and wouldn't share his. Both of my parents must have been dissecting the events surrounding Yuri's death, finding ways to blame themselves and obsessing over what they could or should have done differently. My mother needed to share her pain, but my father made her bear it alone.

His parents came to visit a few months later. Instead of providing help or comfort, Irene attacked my mother. My mother shared one particularly terrible exchange with Sylvia.

The second night she cornered me and said, point-blank, without any thought that it might hurt, 'How could you let the doctors murder your son?' She is an amateur health nut and really believes that the penicillin treatment caused his suffering and death. God, the pain and incomprehension that welled up inside me.

My mother was haunted by her mother-in-law's accusation. "The last time I was at the doctor's, I found myself breaking down and asking whether my sweet Yuri should have been given penicillin. Please dear one," she begged Sylvia, "mum's the word about this unreal episode as I could never bear to tell anyone else—my mother, even George, how troubled I have been."

My parents were isolated from each other, barely communicating about the tragedy that was possessing them. My mom was "troubled" by the idea that one of her decisions contributed to her son's death, but she didn't want my dad to know that she was thinking such things or that his own mother's insensitivity contributed to her pain. What awful feelings to be alone with. Did she try to tell him or make him listen, or did she worry that my father hadn't wondered about the penicillin, and that if she suggested it, he would suddenly conclude that she was guilty? Swallowing her grief, and having to act happy not just for her daughter but for her partner, who was supposed to support her, had to have been another kind of death.

As I learned more about this time, I wondered if this was when my mother began relying on her childhood ability to perform as an adult, to act like a person who was happy instead of one overwhelmed by misery. Her reaction to my father's death years later might have been fueled by everything she hadn't been able to say or do when her son died. After containing her feelings for so long, she had an opportunity to finally let them out. If she'd been able to speak about Yuri, maybe my father's death wouldn't have been as destructive as it was. She'd have only been dealing with one death, not two.

I considered how I dealt with grief and realized I didn't have much experience actually feeling it. I'd never been as sad as my mother and didn't know how torturous it was to hide such despair. But there had been times after my mother died, such as when I visited the drugstore where I'd once worked, when I'd erupted in tears. I hadn't been aware of my pain, but I also hadn't been able to muffle it when it arose. Like my sister, I thought I was good at compartmentalizing. But as I spent more time with my parents and my memories of them, my feelings would seep out and reveal I wasn't as skilled as I believed. I constantly had nightmares where I screamed at my father or followed my mother through the house begging to be seen. I'd wake sweaty and tangled in the covers, pulsing with rage and gasping for breath. And once, after I'd gotten my nails done, I started crying because my manicurist insisted on zipping up my jacket for me so I wouldn't mar the polish. That simple act, and the smile and pat that accompanied it, made me feel taken care of, looked after, and my reaction showed me how desperate I still was for maternal attention.

In 1975, my father received a six-month assignment in

Kuwait, and he and my mother were separated for part of it. While they were apart, they continued to write to each other. After a visit to Kuwait, my mother wrote:

Dearest Love,

Here we are "at home" but as home is where the heart is, it's very empty without you. Already—no not already, but the moment I left your side, I've missed you . . .

. . . My future awaits your nearness. Do love me soon. I kiss all of you.

He replied:

It's been ten days since you left. The first few days seemed to drag out forever. I became very restless and depressed. Yet I really couldn't get myself to get up to do anything. From morning to night seemed like such a long time. Somehow this state is beginning to change a little—although I don't know whether to ascribe it to just getting used to the realities of life here or whether I am beginning to think about the fact that I'm not going to be here much longer . . .

. . . I wish I could hold you and crush you against my chest—I miss you very much.

These letters prove that their love was still there, even after the tragedy that had ravaged them. They seemed to be trying to close the distance Yuri's death had placed between them.

The following year, my father was made the senior vice president and area head for the Middle East and Africa division, and the bank moved them back to Boston. My mother didn't want to leave and told Sylvia that she felt Yuri was in London. But she didn't have a choice; she had to follow her husband.

My parents bought a town house on the flat of Beacon Hill. It was a new home, but Yuri lived in my mother's dreams and more often in her nightmares. She put framed pictures of him on dressers and chests but my father moved those pictures to drawers. I'd see those photographs a few years later but could not see what my parents did—the child they hadn't been able to save.

CHAPTER NINE

Unternehmungslustig

*T*hough my mother missed London, she was relieved to return to Boston. She was closer to her mother and Sylvia. She could keep working for the Sierra Club and be with old friends. Boston was normal and known, a place where things went well, where her son might not have died.

For my father, Boston meant new professional opportunities and being back with his Ukrainian friends. He enrolled Alexandra in Sunday Ukrainian classes at the local Orthodox church. He hadn't been able to teach her Ukrainian because he wasn't around enough to speak it to her, and my mother couldn't reinforce the lessons in his absence.

But Alexandra hated Ukrainian school and tried to stay home every Sunday. Our dad made her go anyway and forced her to review what she'd learned while she squirmed and told him that she was bored. When he was traveling, which was often, Alexandra fought harder to stay home because she knew our mom would cave and let her.

My father was furious when he discovered my mother's delinquency. She'd agreed to raise their children as Ukrainians before they'd gotten married; her refusal, whether the result of laziness, compassion, or defiance, was a betrayal. But his anger did not lead to change. Alexandra stopped going, and I was never sent; my father's heritage, which he'd so badly wanted to share with his children, never became ours. When he moved to Ukraine a decade later, he went to a place that was important only to him, where no one in his immediate family could even ask for directions.

Sue and Martin, and their children Sophie and Joseph, visited my parents soon after they'd returned to America. Sue said they had "the most fantastic time," eating lots of seafood, exploring the city, and watching their daughters play together, but my mother was still devastated about Yuri. Every night, she made Sue stay up with her while she guzzled brandy and "went over what happened, talking about it all again and again, and speaking of how critical your father's parents had been of her." Sue had the impression that my father still didn't want to hear my mom speak about their son or her persistent miseries. The one person who understood and listened to her terrible pain, my mother told Sue, was her own mother, Helen.

My parents' Hungarian friend Lili was the only person who remembered my father ever sharing his own pain. My dad agreed to join her for dinner shortly after Yuri's death, and Lili "had no idea that he was coming with such devastating news. It was awkward," she told me, "because at that particular moment, my sister was there with her husband. If I had known, I would have said 'Don't come tonight.'" My father "just poured out his heart" to her and her guests. "He told us the whole story. He wasn't crying, but he was destroyed."

Perhaps my father silenced my mother because her anguish was a reminder of his own. Instead of engaging, he retreated into himself. If my mother had been allowed to talk about Yuri ten nights in a row and then again on the eleventh, she might never have started speaking so often of her tragedies. Being silenced may have convinced her that no one ever listened to her or could understood all she'd lost.

During Sue's visit, my mother confessed that she and my father wanted to have another child but were struggling to conceive. Her periods were irregular, and she believed that was a physical manifestation of her grief. One evening, as Sue went to check on Joseph, she heard my parents' voices in his room. From the top of the stairs, she saw they were kneeling at his crib and watching him sleep. His eyes still on Joseph, my father whispered, "We'll make another one, won't we?"

They did. I arrived in 1977. I didn't know that my parents' joy was mixed with sorrow, that I shared my crib with a ghost, or that when my parents looked at me, they saw the threat of unbearable pain.

As a child, the only cause I could find for my father's viciousness was myself. The "why" of his actions expanded when I learned more about a story my mother had told me when I was young. She'd admitted it was a lie when I was an adult, and when other people shared their own very different versions of it after she'd died, and after I better understood the effects of Yuri's death, I finally gained a bit of insight into his rage.

I have bright scars all over my scalp. I can't see them, but hairdressers always ask me about them. I tell them what my mother told me. When I was one and a half, I collided with a metal lounge chair as I crawled through the living room and "cracked my head open." My mother wept in the cab that took us to the hospital as blood soaked through the towels she'd wrapped around me.

Sometime in college, when I was briefly in Boston for a holiday, I came home late and slightly high on Ecstasy. Feeling friendly, I decided to chat with my mom instead of rushing past her door like I usually did. I chirped mindlessly about my classes and roommates, then stumbled into a story about my most recent visit to a hair salon. The colorist had asked about my scars, and I'd told her about cracking my head open.

I wasn't sure that my mother was listening until she turned to me and said, "Did we never tell you the truth?"

"The truth about what?"

She whispered, "We didn't want you to be afraid of cats."

I said, "What?"

She took a long sip of wine and told me what really happened. When I was an infant, I'd been attacked by Krupskaya, the Siamese cat my parents had had for years. I'd backed her into a corner thinking we were playing, and when she'd gotten scared, she'd lashed out, latching onto my head with her hind feet, shredding my skull and severing part of an eyelid. My mother was in San Francisco for work at the time. When she returned to Boston, I was back from the hospital and bandaged up.

People spoke low on the television. Its yellows and reds flashed across the walls of her room. I touched my head reflexively. "What happened to Krupskaya?"

"She was gone by the time I arrived. When I asked your father where she was, he said, 'You don't want to know.'" Her eyes widened as she waited for my response.

"You don't know what happened to her?"

"He wouldn't tell me."

I stared at her. "You have no idea?"

She shook her head so vigorously that her glasses almost slid off.

This story felt different from the ones she usually told. It didn't have a tidy ending. The look on her face, expectant, nervous, made me suspicious.

I called Alexandra the next day. "Do you remember what happened to Krupskaya? Were you there?" She would have been six at the time.

"I might have been at school. I remember being told to stay away from the cat while you were at the hospital. She was alive, and some adult was with me, maybe a babysitter. Dad probably had her put down. Krupskaya," she clarified, "not the babysitter."

"But if he'd put her to sleep, he would have said that. He wouldn't have been all ominous . . . 'You don't want to know.'"

"What else would he have done?"

"I don't know," I said. "He could have done lots of things."

Krupskaya came up while I was in Chicago with Chrissy and Arlene. We found a picture of her in a photo album. As Arlene cooed over the picture, Chrissy said that "Krupy" had been the most darling cat.

"She was not darling!" I screeched. "She ate my face!"

Chrissy told me to quit being so dramatic. "She didn't eat your face. It's right in front of me. It's still there."

I told them what my mother had told me and asked if they knew what happened to Krupskaya.

"I heard they put her to sleep," Arlene said.

"I thought your mother was there," Chrissy said. "Your mother told me your father bashed the cat to death against the wall."

"He bashed her against a wall? In front of my mother?" I'd imagined many ends for Krupskaya, but never one so violent. "She told me she was away on a business trip, but she didn't say if my dad was watching me or a babysitter."

Arlene tapped her finger on the table. "The babysitter wouldn't throw the cat against the wall."

Krupskaya also came up when I spoke with Sylvia. At first it seemed like a non sequitur. I'd asked if my mother ever spoke about my father's temper, and she responded by asking if I remembered Krupskaya.

"I don't, but I know that she attacked me. My mom told me she was away when it happened." I said that my father wouldn't tell my mom what he'd done, and I shared the different stories I was juggling: that my father had killed the cat in a fit of rage or had her put to sleep.

"I think the violent one is accurate. Anita was covering for your dad. She took you to the hospital. Krupskaya was gone when she came home. She told me what happened, and she was very upset about what had happened to you as well as what happened to the cat. She was shocked by what he did, how he did it."

I leaned forward. "How he did *what*?"

Sylvia smiled weakly and looked away.

My mother had probably been aware of my father's fear and rage; she'd tugged at his feelings for years and could have been frightened to see that when they unfurled, they were as big as hers, or bigger. Something had stopped her from telling me the truth. She told me that they didn't want me to be afraid of cats, and we did get another one, a Siamese we named Mischa, who was swiftly declawed. But maybe it was my father she hoped I wouldn't fear.

If my father killed Krupy, and it seemed that he did, it was because he was scared of losing me. My basic fragility must have reminded him of Yuri, so he tried to keep me safe by policing my behavior. He exploded when I fell down the stairs and burned me when I couldn't stop playing with the stove because such events called up a pain he couldn't bear to experience again. Watching me move through the world meant constantly watching the beginning of a story that ended terribly. It ignited the fear and anger he'd been suppressing over Yuri death's and maybe even frustration that he'd been given a clumsy daughter instead of another son. I understood his desperation to protect me after losing Yuri, but I still did not understand why he'd attacked me as I did homework and refused to back down when it was obvious his approach wasn't working.

To learn who my father was when he wasn't being my father, I sought out the coworkers he'd spent so much time with. Although it had been two decades since his division was disbanded at the Bank of Boston, most of my father's peers from the twenty years he worked there were still in touch with one another. It only took locating one person for me to be connected to many more who were eager to talk to me about him.

Over breakfasts in hotel lobbies, drinks at university clubs, lunches, coffee, and Skype, I was regaled with stories about my father. One man told me, "There was kind of a mad-scientist quality to him. He was an eclectic man who happened to be a banker. He was not a banker who somehow became eclectic. He loved going to funky places, the funkier the better." Because he was always in a rush, his staff nicknamed him "the Blur." When they suggested that he slow down, he charged past and told them, "It's harder to hit a moving target."

According to one of my father's coworkers, the bank was "extremely conservative, but the Middle East and Africa division was like a financial artists' colony. Some people might say it was full of misfits. It was a weird and wonderful hodgepodge of people and characters, and they were *characters*. People from all kinds of backgrounds with different abilities, different educations, different languages—different everything." One man, who was in his seventies, told me with boyish glee that whenever people from the European division walked by, he and his cohort shot rubber bands at them.

Multiple people told me that my father gave them their big professional "break." He didn't care where they'd gone to school or been employed before. One guy was working at a motorcycle shop when he was hired. Another was a security guard. Both went on to have prominent roles in the division. The ex–security guard said my dad "recognized the value we could create, and respected that we were different." He hired people he could trust to be imaginative and take well-calculated risks. They told me that my father "was interested in the quality of our thinking. He wasn't looking for people who were going to maintain. He wanted people who were going to get on their feet and get out there."

No one explicitly referred to him as a father figure or called him paternal, but that's how his behavior sounded to me. I was frustrated that this group of misfits got the dad I'd wanted. He'd purposefully hired people who were "different" and let them work in their own ways. He knew people had particular minds and abilities, and found eccentricities valuable. The qualities he'd celebrated in his staff made him furious when he saw them in me.

But as I thought more about it, I realized that he and my mother actually had allowed me to be different in certain ways. I started dying my hair at twelve, wearing makeup and dressing like the personal assistant of the Mistress of the Dark, and they never interfered. Most kids I knew didn't even shop for themselves; their parents controlled their appearance. I'd once told Alexandra how upset I'd been that neither of our parents had been sympathetic to me in middle school, when my appearance and behavior provoked so much malice. She'd shaken her head. "Maybe they wanted you to know that being an individual came with consequences that you had to be able to deal with. *They* had to deal with them! Everyone in our neighborhood talked about whatever you were wearing, the color of your hair . . . I know Mom found it annoying, but she and Dad probably admired your guts." I hadn't felt gutsy; I'd struggled with the consequences. But my sister was right. They'd let me suffer, but they also let me experiment with boundaries and self-expression.

I met with a Nigerian American woman who'd worked with my dad in the '80s and she explained that whenever he traveled for work, he tacked on a few days at the end for his own adventures. "We all used to tease George about his boondoggle trips," she said, and laughed. "Let's say there was business to be done in Damascus. He'd take a few extra days to go to Aleppo, Palmyra, to shop every bazaar for the rattiest rug he could find. If it didn't have enough holes, he wasn't buying it."

A Lebanese coworker told me he'd been roped into one such trip while he was in Syria with my father. After their meetings, my father insisted that they go to Hama, a city north of Damascus, which was supposed to have one of the oldest mosques in the world. "Your father all of a sudden told me, 'We need to go see that mosque.' I didn't even know it existed, but I said, 'Okay, let's arrange a cab.'"

The driver had to be convinced to take such a long journey. "The way the driver was looking at us, I knew something wasn't right. He dropped us off a mile from the mosque. In Arabic I said, 'What's going on?' The driver said, 'It's a military zone, be careful.' Of course we immediately got lost. We asked someone where the mosque was, and the person said, 'I can't tell you.' As we went along, I realized we were being watched. Eventually, your father took out his map, which is the worst thing to do."

I was surprised that my father would make such a rookie mistake. "You never take out a map! Even I know better than that."

He nodded. "Now *everyone's* watching us. We went a little farther until finally we saw a wide, empty area. The whole downtown was rubble. It was like a bulldozer came and opened a soccer field. That's the first time I heard your father swear. He said, 'They blew up the fucking mosque. How could they do something like that?' We were in the open area, and people were looking at us with binoculars. A few people started coming over to see who we were and listen to us talk. I told your father, 'Well, we're probably going to be asked pretty soon what we're doing here,' And he said, 'Yeah, let's go. Nothing here to see.'

"We went back to the cab and the driver said, 'Did you find what you were looking for?' I said, 'Well, we found the spot. But I don't think you want to know what we found.' He said, 'I'm not asking any questions.' "

A man who worked with the bank in Cameroon told me that my father once asked if he could see where he grew up. Flattered, he arranged for a weekend visit to his village, which was "deep in the African forest" and required a long drive over terrible roads. "We went to a beautiful beach on the Atlantic Ocean," he said. "He saw fishermen's traditional houses and smoked fish ready to sell to traders. After dinner, your father insisted we see some local entertainment and dancing. He was very happy. Your father was an open-minded intellectual; he loved Cameroonian culture, the cooking and palm wine."

In Nigeria, my father made the same request of a man he'd become close to over multiple visits to Lagos. "Your father wanted to see places, which, ordinarily, he would not have been able to see," the man shouted over Skype. "We went to my hometown, Benin City." He described how impressed his parents were when he brought my father home. His mother said, " 'So this is your friend from Boston?' I said, 'He's not my friend, he's my boss.' That was a plus. My father was a very serious person. He said, 'Son, I'm sure you are doing a good job, otherwise your boss would not come to the house with you.' They were very proud."

My father's coworkers also told me stories about my parents traveling together. One of my favorites took place in Nigeria as well. My parents went to the northern city of Kano to visit one of the bank's outposts with one of my father's coworkers and his wife, and someone in their group decided that they should meet the emir. However, the emir did not meet with women. My mother and the other woman said their husbands were only going if they could go, too. My father contacted the emir's staff and convinced them to make an exception.

The emir sent two gold Mercedeses to their hotel, one for the men and one for the women. When they arrived at his mansion, they were greeted by his staff and lines of drummers and trumpet players. The emir received them while seated on a pedestal and addressed the women directly, warmly inquiring about their impressions of his country and asking many questions about Disney World.

I'd wondered how my mother negotiated the role of "banker's wife abroad." I was told she was polite when she needed to be, opinionated when it was appropriate, and kind to people regardless of their "status." She knew that she "needed to be the right person at the right time." Only in small groups or with certain people did she confess boredom or annoyance. One man said that my mother once came up to him at a dinner party and whispered, "I don't know how you put up with these people."

I loved hearing about my parents' travels because I knew the world had delivered the thrill and gravity they sought. They were determined to see everything they wanted to, even the things they weren't supposed to see. I was an equally brazen traveler and often sought out experiences that were dangerous, or had the potential to be. In Turkey, children snuck me into a decrepit mosque after seeing that I was trying to observe a prayer service. In Zambia, I paid a man to bring me into the off-limits area surrounding Victoria Falls so I could swim at its edge; he made his way through the still waters of the Zambezi's fringe using a stick not to steady himself but to scare away crocodiles. He watched as I swam to the rim and clung to slimy rocks while being battered by the rapids. When I returned, he congratulated me for avoiding being swept away. In Johannesburg, I met an older Xhosa woman who was training to be a *sangoma*, or traditional healer, and went with her to her village to observe her days-long induction. Outside of Durban, I learned that Nelson Mandela would be speaking at a school opening a few hours away, and hitched a ride to hear him. That day, like so many others, I was in awe of the abundance of the world and intoxicated by its different people and possibilities. When I was younger, I wanted to believe that I traveled the way I did because that's who I was, and that I had developed my interest independent of my parents' influence. As an adult, hearing about their travels forced me to acknowledge what I'd tried to deny. Many people discover traveling on their own, but I owed my interest in it to my parents. They'd given me a gift. Despite everything, they'd given me many.

Each time I spoke with someone who'd worked for the bank in Africa, I thought of my mother's story of the woman who'd said that Africans were "used to losing their children." I didn't think it would be the kind of thing that someone else would remember. If they did, they might not want to admit that it happened.

I heard the story anyway, or a version of it, as I ate lunch with a man who'd spent a long time working for the bank's Zimbabwe branch. He said, "I remember on one occasion, your mother joined your father in Zimbabwe. They had dinner at our house in Harare, and your mother had a meltdown."

"Oh?" I said casually.

"We were sitting around after dinner, and I started talking about pre-independence days, when there was white rule in Zimbabwe and the medical facilities weren't open to Africans. Your mother completely broke down, and your dad had to take her back to the hotel. Later your father apologized, saying it was the lingering effect of the death of your brother. Anything involving medical treatment that wasn't right or wasn't proper struck a chord with your mom."

There was no mention of his wife's maid losing a child, but it had to be the same story. I wondered if he was covering something up so he didn't look bad. My mother hadn't said she'd broken down. Was my father embarrassed? Did he chastise my mother in front of their hosts, or offer her the comfort she'd needed?

"Do you remember what year this was?"

"It would have been in the early eighties."

"My brother would have been dead for more than five years at that point," I said, as much to myself as to him.

Though my mother traveled with my father often, he took the majority of his trips without her. I would have been aggressively angry at such an unequal dynamic, jealous of his adventures and opportunities. He was working, sure, but my mom knew he'd always find a way to include a few thrills. While she was taking care of their kids, he was roaming souks and drinking palm wine. I had to remind myself that she and I were different. She could have enjoyed having a break. When he was home, she had to listen to him yelling at me, see me buckle under his words. His demands for silence and the loud quiet that settled around him whenever he isolated himself in his own thoughts caused resentment, anger, and confusion. It could have made her want even more space, space where she could be the person he didn't want to see.

Did my mother wonder, as I now did, where the man who'd wooed her so passionately had gone? What had he done with the love that once flowed freely? By that point in their marriage, she might not have missed my father while he traveled. But she must have missed the person he'd once been.

She filled this hole with new men. There was Bob, whose visits I was happy to keep secret because I enjoyed them so much. I found a Polaroid of Bob with me and Alexandra among my mother's things. The two of us are holding live lobsters that would soon be our dinner. My sister was in Wonder Woman Underoos. I was in pajamas. Bob, tan and bearded, is crouching down to be in the frame with us and beaming at the woman holding the camera.

I mentioned Bob to Chrissy and asked if she knew of my mother having affairs. She said that she'd once asked my mother if she had any "male companions, what with George being away so long. She said she did. I got the impression he was in Boston. She didn't make it sound like she was madly in love with this guy. It was, you know, recreational."

I used this as leverage when I asked Sylvia the same question. "My mother told Chrissy that she'd had an affair, or affairs. Did she ever talk about other men with you?"

Sylvia crossed her arms and gave me a stern look. "When your best friend tells you something in confidence, it's not just for the next ten years, you know."

"So that's a yes." I grinned.

"I can think of a couple of occasions, when your dad was traveling, or when she was traveling, going to Sierra Club or other environmental things, that she came into contact with men who had similar interests. I know there were times she brought men home when you girls were there. And, you know, your dad was just *gone*."

"When you say 'similar interests,' do you mean cleaning up and protecting beaches, or having sex on them?"

"Oh, I don't know." She laughed. "Stop being salacious."

It's easy for me to assume that my mother had relationships with other men because my father wasn't as loving as she needed him to be. She may have been seeking attention and affection more than sex. Though I rarely saw my father be tender with her, he could have been very loving when they were alone. Maybe she couldn't be sated because he didn't want to acknowledge every part of her, particularly her ongoing grief over Yuri, or because her needs were too great for any one person to meet.

Yet my parents' relationship wasn't passionless. Chrissy told me that there were times she stayed with us when my father was away, and when my father returned from his travels, "They were at it in the bedroom within two hours." Many of my parents' friends said that though he wasn't extremely affectionate, it was obvious from how he looked at my mother that he adored her. I wasn't able to see that adoration at the time, but it was revealed in the thousands of photographs that he took of her.

When I asked my father's coworkers from the bank if they had any knowledge of him having affairs, they looked horrified. "I just don't think your father was interested. He was always so busy," someone told me.

There were rumors that he'd had an affair while he was in Ukraine, but when I spoke with his alleged mistress, Irene, a German woman who'd since moved to Canada, she assured me that they'd only been friends, and cemented her case by telling me she was a lesbian and that my father knew her girl-friend.

Irene and I met for dinner in Brooklyn's Sunset Park after corresponding for months. We embraced firmly after spotting each other in the Mexican restaurant I'd suggested. After we sat down, she told me that one of the reasons that she wanted to meet me was to see how much I was like my father.

Surprised, I said, "I'm not like him. Not at all."

She raised her eyebrow and took a sip of her beer.

"How did you meet?" I asked.

She said they'd met at an art gallery. "I was alone, and your father was there alone, and the gallery was empty, so we had to talk to each other. Your dad wanted to create a social life for himself and other people because really, there was nothing to do in Ukraine at that time. But there was art, and your father and I shared that interest."

"So what *did* you do?" I asked.

"Anything. Everything. If someone managed to find a bottle of Moldovan champagne, we'd drink it. If your father heard of an interesting village somewhere, we'd hop in the car." She laughed. "One really hot day we were hanging out on the banks of the Dnieper, and I decided to swim across it. Your father told me I shouldn't—the current was too strong, and the ships were moving faster than they looked—but I didn't care. I jumped in and started swimming. It was nearly impossible and utterly terrifying. Your father saw me being dragged downriver, so he rushed over a bridge to the other side. I could see him running up and down the bank in the distance, trying to figure out where I'd emerge." When she finally made it to shore, my father helped her out of the water and said, "I told you it was dangerous, but you're not the kind of person who listens."

I said, "Neither am I."

She smiled. "Neither was he."

When I asked for her take on the car accident she said, "For me, the accident was just that. I never saw or heard anything related to his business dealings at the bank or the venture fund that suggested he had enemies or was afraid of something. Traveling at night was risky because the roads were poorly lit and not properly maintained. Add to that Soviet vehicles with bald tires and worn-out mechanics, and the likelihood of an accident is high."

After dinner, Irene and I went for drinks at a bar that we quickly discovered was also a brothel. We took the only available table, ordered two Coronas, and watched women in ill-fitting clothing and sloppy eye makeup circle the room with trays they bopped off their hips. They bent over and talked to the men, sat on their laps, and laughed at their jokes. Sometimes one would lead a customer through a door in the corner.

"I've lived in New York a long time," I said, "but this is my first brothel."

Irene knocked her bottle against mine. "You are like your father," she said, trying to speak over the music. "You and he share the same quality. We have a word for it in German." Irene grabbed my notebook and pen and wrote "*unternehmungslustig*." "It means 'very enterprising,'" she said, "in the sense of travel and adventure."

I looked at the word. "I guess I am pretty *unternehmungslustig*."

"Your father was good at creating something out of nothing, and in Ukraine, there was nothing. He always tried to have a good time, and to make sure other people were having a good time."

I told her how difficult it was to imagine my father as that person. "It's hard for children to know their parents, and hard for parents to be themselves around their kids. You're describing someone I never had the chance to meet." Irene nodded as I continued. "I guess I'm a lot like my dad. I always thought he was a boring, uptight banker. I had no idea how much risk and flexibility his work required or that when he wasn't working, he was determined to find or create adventures. And I thought he was the determined one, not me, because I was so unfocused for so much of my life, but now I am crazy determined and bristle when someone or something tries to restrict my freedom. I've created a life that allows me to do whatever I want to do so I don't have to disappoint people the way he did, or resent them. I always thought I took after my mother because I'm really sensitive, and I never wanted to be like my father because I didn't like him, but now . . ."

"Now," she said, "you know that your father was *unternehmungslustig*, and that you are, too."

Part Three

*A*s I spent months, then years, going through what my parents had left behind and speaking with those who'd known them, new people emerged, not the parents I'd known but passionate, successful, and curious individuals who tried really hard to get things "right."

What was the correct or "true" version of my parents? Was it the one I'd experienced, or the one I was learning about as I read their letters and spoke with their friends and coworkers? Could both exist at once? Was it possible, or wise, to let the things I didn't know about them, or images I'd never had, overshadow the ones I did? That seemed like a form of magical thinking, one that was seductive but also a little dangerous. Was accepting this new story a denial of my own? Or was my refusal to acknowledge their other personas the ultimate, immature act of disrespect?

How much could I really understand about even the most basic aspects of their worlds? I valued being able to go wherever I wanted, when I wanted. I didn't want children. In many ways, my life was more expansive than my parents' because I had so much freedom. I hadn't considered that in other ways, perhaps I was stunted. No kids or marriage meant I'd experienced none of the sacrifices, joys, and deep vulnerabilities that accompany each. I'd done many hard things, but I'd never tried to do what they'd done.

I stopped thinking of my parents as my parents, and began

seeing them simply as people. I wondered and worried about their relationship as I read their early letters even though I knew how their young love ended. Often I found myself commiserating with them. How does anyone get this shit right? If my friends and I were constantly talking about our relationships and entanglements, our hang-ups and fears, they must have been talking about the same things with their friends. Did they freak out or falter? Did they see things happening and wish they could stop them, then watch them happen anyway? Of course they did. People don't "get over" things. They keep living as best they can.

The questions that sparked my interest in them, in who they were and what happened to them, had been answered. My father had experienced great turmoil as a child, was smart and intense. He took risks and didn't want to be held back from pursuing what was most important to him. And he loved, really, really loved, my mother. My mother had an equally hard childhood marked by the absence of her father and of the love that she craved. Wildly intelligent, she fell in love with a man whose ambition helped give her a life that was full of adventure, at times better than she'd dreamed it could be.

It was also full of loss on a scale I hadn't known and prayed I'd avoid: absent father, dead child, dead husband. Though I wished my mother had tried harder to stop drinking, I no longer thought she was weak for drinking herself to death. When I considered the pain my mother woke up to every day, I thought, "I wouldn't want to get out of bed, either." I felt guilty at how dismissive I'd been of her grief. If my sister and I had acknowledged her suffering as she'd wanted us to when she spoke repeatedly of her losses, would she have felt heard and then fought to get sober? What if we'd seen her the way she'd needed to be seen?

My parents experienced one of life's worst tragedies: They lost a son. My mother was hobbled by grief that she couldn't share because it was too hard for my father to listen. My father's career took him farther and farther from my mother. She detested his absence and the responsibilities it forced onto her. They never had the chance to be reunited, to see if they could work through and past their many problems.

After years of feeling like my parents owed me something because of how they'd treated me, I now felt like I owed them something. I'd unearthed so much suffering and had nowhere to put it. I couldn't erase it from their lives or my own. It wasn't enough to know them better. I couldn't change how their stories ended, but perhaps I could change our relationship, which was still alive and always would be.

CHAPTER TEN

The Painter's Honeymoon

$\mathcal{I}$t was difficult to determine when my mother began drinking seriously, when my father became aware of her problem, and what he'd done—or hadn't done—to help her.

I remembered my mother making martinis while I was young. They turned her face pink and loosened her smile. But I didn't remember ever seeing her drunk. When I asked Alexandra if she remembered our mother drinking, really drinking, while we were young, she could only summon one memory. We were having dinner at a Thai restaurant. Our mom was drinking, and our parents got into an argument. She didn't come home that night. Alex didn't know if she went to a hotel, or if she slept at a friend's. "I remember thinking that she still wasn't there the next morning, but she was back when I got home from school. She was in bed, and her whole face was swollen. Dad was sitting with her; he hadn't gone to work. I asked her what was wrong, and she told me she'd had an allergic reaction to a mosquito bite. That probably wasn't the truth, but I didn't know any better."

"Did that kind of thing happen a lot?" I asked.

"Not that I remember. But she *must* have had a drinking problem during our childhood."

I reread the psychological assessment I received when I was ten and found something I'd previously missed. Under "family situation," the therapist had written

> there is some concern on father's part that mother might drink too much. It is reported that she drinks one to three hard drinks per night, but it is stated that this does not interfere with her overall functioning.

When I discovered these sentences, an alarm sounded. Though he'd downplayed it, my father, who I'd considered to be a very private person, was bothered enough by my mother's drinking to mention it to a therapist. He claimed that it didn't interfere with her life, but my sister and I were convinced that it did. Like me, Alex remembered our mother snoring through our mornings and our father getting us ready for school when he wasn't traveling. As adults, the only explanation we could find for such behavior was drinking. "I would never let my husband get away with that, and he wouldn't let me just sleep all morning," Alex said. How do you handle the kids and then go to work and make the money?

I didn't remember the day my father officially left for Ukraine a few years later, which seems strange, because it would have been a happy one for me. But my friend Hillary did because she came over after he departed, and she recalls my mother being wasted. I may have noticed that my mother was drunk at the time, but the memory of that day disappeared. My father's absence allowed my mother to drink more heavily, and was probably one of the reasons that she did. She started once I was in my room for the evening and slept it off while I was at school. After my father died, she tried to keep herself together for my sake while taking opportunities to drink excessively when she could. Looking back, I realized that she probably went to our cabin in New Hampshire so frequently when I was in high school because she could get as bombed as she wanted to while she was there. I was so thrilled to have the house to myself on the weekends that I didn't think about why she was going so often or why she never checked in on me, and because I wasn't sad about my father's death, I didn't find her behavior strange. Now I know that instead of leaving their child alone after such a momentous event, most other parents would have tried to be available for them. But I wanted to be away from her, so instead of wondering or worrying about what she was doing, I worried only about what I could get away with.

As we sorted and swapped memories, Alex told me she'd once had to leave a college formal because one of our mother's friends called the school to say she needed to be taken to detox. She didn't have a car, so her date had to drive her two hours to Boston, and he helped her get my mother to the hospital. This sounded so similar to my own experience, when Eli helped me take her to the emergency room.

"If you were in college, I was in high school. Where was I?" I asked. "How did I not know what was happening?"

She said she had no idea.

"We were living in the same house. Even if I was sleeping at a friend's, how could she have been messed up enough that her friends knew she needed to go to the hospital? Why would they call you and not me?"

She shrugged.

"Why didn't you tell me?"

She thought for a moment. "I guess I figured you knew, and I felt that it was my responsibility to do something about it because I was older." She was right to assume that I knew. I thought back to when I was in high school and my mother's friends told me that she was in the hospital for exhaustion. I'd accepted that explanation and moved on, never considering that she might be in detox instead. I'd asked my sister how I could have missed what was happening, but I knew the answer, and it made me ache with shame. My mother was hiding her drinking, but she didn't have to try very hard because I was so committed to not seeing her. It didn't seem possible that I could have been as oblivious as I was, that I could have ignored her so successfully, but it had been easy. When problems arose, they fell to Alexandra first, and she took care of them for all of us.

"Were you trying to protect me back then?"

"Maybe," she said. This incident, of which I wasn't even aware, was one of many that my sister shouldered for me. She constantly tried to shield me from our mother's drinking and its effects. The summer after my freshman year of college, I'd decided to go to Saint John Island, thinking I'd spend a few months working in a restaurant. I'd never been and had no experience in food service, but it sounded fun, and I didn't want to return to Boston and live with my mom for even a few months. I thought my sister would think it was a terrible idea, but when I told her about it, she said that I should absolutely go.

She bought my ticket even though I'd saved up for one, accompanied me down there, and spent a few days camping on the beach with me and helped me find a job. I figured she wanted a weekend in the islands and for me to have fun, but later she told me that what she'd cared about was making sure I didn't have to be at home with our mom.

I heard stories about my mother's drinking from many of the people I was speaking to, and though I couldn't pin them to specific years, many took place earlier than I'd expected. My mom told Sylvia that my father once threatened to take my sister and me away when we were younger because she was drinking too much. Sylvia added, "I think it was a threat to shake her up. I don't think he would have done it. But he did have a temper, and he had the evidence about the drinking to hold against her, so it was possible that he could have gotten the two of you removed. I think she was always a drinker," she continued. "She never got over Yuri's death, and she was alone so much after it happened. Knowing her, and knowing how fragile she could be, how much she *loved* babies, and having to deal with it by herself . . ." Her voice trailed off.

A couple who was close to my parents told me that before he started working in Ukraine, my father told them that he was worried about my mom's alcohol consumption. "We didn't know how to respond," they said. "Your dad was worried and aware that there might be a problem, but didn't know what the answer was. And," they added, "your mother always denied anything about her drinking."

So my dad knew enough, and was worried enough that he'd said he'd take my sister and me away, spoke about it to a therapist, and with my mom's friends. I couldn't understand why he hadn't done anything.

My mother may have wondered what happened to the person she'd fallen in love with; my father may have done the same. I'd only ever considered that she might have resented him, but he had plenty of reasons to resent her as well. My mother drank heavily, caused scenes, and missed her children's mornings. Though she'd worked hard for the Sierra Club, her career hadn't turned into what she'd once hoped it might—she'd delivered no fiery speeches at the UN or forceful testimonies before Congress. That may have been because my father prioritized his career over hers; she might never have had the chance to pursue the jobs she'd really wanted because she followed him to Boston, then London, and soon, had to be home with the kids. Or, after graduating from college, she may have realized that she didn't want to work as hard as she'd thought she did, or felt she wasn't actually very ambitious when she compared herself to her husband. And how did my father's temper and treatment of me affect their marriage? He hadn't wanted to marry a drunk, but she hadn't wanted to marry someone who would bully their child.

While talking with my parents' friend Lili, the woman my father had spoken to about Yuri's death, I asked if she remembered taking my mother, sister, and me in after my father had been particularly hard on me. I didn't remember it, I said, but my mom had told me that Lili had provided us refuge. Could she recollect that evening or my mother complaining about my father's anger?

She told me that if she had, she didn't remember it, either, but said she'd once let my mother stay with her after she and my father had a huge fight.

"I don't remember them having big arguments," I said. "They bickered, but they didn't yell, at least when I was around."

I thought she was going to say more about that episode, but then saw her mind was on something else. After a long silence, she said, "You know about the abortion, right?"

The shock on my face told her that I didn't. She grimaced and glanced away.

"No. Was this after I was born?"

She nodded. "Things were bad between them at that point; they didn't feel it was the right time to bring another kid into the family. George went with her to a clinic. They wouldn't perform it because she'd had problems with pregnancies in the past. They told her she'd have to have it done in a hospital the next day. I remember when they came back, they were both upset. Your mother wanted a drink so she made one for herself and for me. Your father was annoyed. It was two or three in the afternoon, too soon to start drinking. He disapproved and he let it be known." The following morning, they had the procedure at a hospital.

We stared at our mugs as I tried to form words. "I've had an abortion," I finally said. "I don't want kids. The decision was easy. But my mom . . ." I played with my napkin as my voice faded.

"Once in a while your mom talked about what it would've been like had this child been born," Lili said, "but I don't think she had any real regret because the situation was really bad at that point." She didn't remember when "this point" was—I could have been three, five, or ten—or what specifically made their relationship so bad that they didn't want another child.

I considered what their problems could have been. Their lack of communication, my mother's affairs—though I didn't know if my father knew about them—my father's treatment of me, the imbalance of their careers, and my mother's drinking. You don't need to have big problems to not want another child, but both of my parents were so devastated about Yuri, I imagine that the decision was difficult. I trusted that they made the right choice since, as Lili said, they weren't getting along, but if they had been, I imagined they'd have welcomed another child. I was surprised to find myself feeling sad to hear my parents' friend say that their marriage was, at least at one point, "really bad." I thought it had been weak when I was little, but I hadn't cared about them then the way I'd begun to. I no longer wanted my earliest observation confirmed; I wanted it to be contradicted so I could hear they'd been happy because now, that's what I wanted for them.

But that wasn't the case. I understood that by the time my father took the job in Ukraine, my parents' relationship was so broken that the position offered not just a life-changing opportunity but a break from my mother. Deciding to work there would have been more difficult if he was worried about her behavior. But if he'd been fighting with her about her drinking for years, and she'd shown him that she wasn't willing to stop, he had even more reason to go. He refused to sacrifice his biggest dream to be with a person who'd disappointed him repeatedly.

Even if their marriage wasn't riddled with problems, my father had gotten my mother's permission to work in Ukraine decades earlier—before they were married. He'd told her that he'd go if he ever had the chance and she'd promised she wouldn't stop him. Bound by something she'd said so long ago, she asked Natasha to "convince George to not go to Ukraine" for her. But Natasha couldn't. She told my mother, "You're talking to the wrong person. I'm doing the same thing.'" Like Natasha and so many members of the diaspora, my father wanted to be a part of the historic changes taking place.

When my father moved to Ukraine in 1990, it was an exciting and tumultuous time; many people referred to it as "the Wild East" because it seemed to lack laws, or people interested in enforcing the few laws that there were. I was told there was "industrial-level Mafia and industrial-level prostitution." Every kind of vice was available, but you couldn't find paper, paper clips, or pencils—things necessary for an office. The chaos was part of its charm, another reason to be there. There were huge food shortages because supply chains weren't established. Markets rarely had milk or sugar, and people waited in bread lines for hours. There wasn't anything to buy, even if you had dollars. "There was the occasional gourmet international store that no one else could afford," Alexandra told me.

"You could sometimes find something you wanted, maybe a jar of Nutella that had expired two years before. You'd think, 'Eh, good enough.'"

In addition to establishing a central bank, my father and his colleagues had to create a new currency; Ukraine had always used rubles, which were not convertible on international markets. I was told that prior to independence, the only thing banks did in Ukraine was take "paper bags of money from Moscow and dispense it to various ministries." My father was engaged in a nation-building exercise that required skills honed in Western countries and economies, where there are checks and balances, and transparency. A Canadian who was there at the same time as my father explained that in the beginning, Westerners were enthusiastically welcomed by the Ukrainian parliament and members of the business community, though their feelings soon cooled. "We were telling Ukrainians in government to do things that were directly opposed to their personal interests. Their interest was to become the new capitalists in the world they knew was coming. We were telling them to open up opportunities to everyone, but they wanted to be the only ones with opportunity." My father and his peers stopped being invited to meetings with the minister of finance, their closest government counterpart, because he no longer wanted to hear what they thought. My father became a vice chairman of the bank, but left shortly after he was promoted. "The chairman," I was told, "was totally incompetent, and your father was caught in political issues. There was a lot of graft and corruption."

Instead of returning to Boston as he said he would, my father chose to stay longer. My mother felt increasingly abandoned. She wanted her husband to come home, to want to come home. I was angry on her behalf, but I sympathized with my father's position. How could he have said no to such an opportunity? It was something he'd fantasized about. Should having a partner or children stop him from living his lifelong dream? I don't know if my mother ever begged, or demanded, that he return; she knew that working in Ukraine gave him a sense of purpose and brought him happiness, and decades earlier she'd promised that she wouldn't stop him from going. She must have been happy that he had such an extraordinary opportunity but disappointed that she didn't have the same chance. I don't know what my mother's equivalent of getting to work in Ukraine would have been, but my hope is that she would have taken it. I would have been furious with her, because it would mean I was left alone with my father, but as an adult I would have celebrated her dedication to her career. She would have only been able to do that, however, if my father was willing to stay in one place and be responsible for me. I doubt if he'd have been willing to do what she had.

My father's next project was establishing Ukraine's first venture capital company with a firm that was owned by our neighbor. To learn more about what they did, I spoke with his old boss—the man who my mother felt screwed her over after my father died—and his wife. They'd reached a settlement eventually, but my mother remained convinced that she hadn't gotten everything that she should have. I was worried about seeing them after everything my mother had gone through with them or had put them through, but I avoided that particular topic and so did they.

David told me that he and my father invested up to $50,000 in "bread-and-butter businesses that could be picked up and moved to another location in town: sewing operations, travel business, nails and hardware, companies with no assets." Their small staff was a combination of local Ukrainians and members of the first group of Peace Corps volunteers in Ukraine. The corps worked with companies to convert their Soviet financial operations to international accounting standards. The Soviet accounting system didn't have contracts for profit, so people didn't record their expenses; if they did, they often kept two sets of books. The fund developed a two-day accounting course for anyone who wanted to take it, though their clients were required to. As people began approaching them with ideas for new businesses, my father saw that none of them knew how to prepare a business plan, so his staff also taught potential clients how to write those as well.

David's wife, Betsy, told me that when they visited Ukraine, my father showed them "all kinds of galleries and brought us to studios to meet different artists. He wanted to know what the intellectuals and artists were thinking, where they were headed. He didn't just care about business."

I asked David what he thought about the car crash that killed my father. Was he certain that it was an accident?

"I've thought about this a lot," David said. "It was an accident. I went to the site. I was there a week later and the tire tracks were still there. It was an absolutely straight country road. It wasn't three lanes, but it was definitely a good, solid two lanes with kind of ditches and trees and fields on each side. Allegedly, it was a head-on collision with a van. The people in the van were supposedly drunk or had been drink-

ing. There's no way that somebody would have used that as
the way to kill somebody. There were no cell phones then, so
some guy would have been standing beside the road and said,
'Now he's coming, go get him.' Who's going to do a head-on
collision? It just doesn't make sense.

"We had no enemies," he continued. "We were a source
of money for people. Your father was respected by everybody.
If he had lived, he could have really played a major role in
the country. He had all of the key elements. He understood
it. People loved him, and he gathered younger people around
him. He was a Pied Piper."

I said that my mother understood why his work was important, but that she couldn't, or didn't, share the connection
that he felt so strongly. Betsy told me that my mother had
ranted to her about how terrible Ukraine was after she'd visited. "I totally sympathized with her," she said. "That was no
place to be the wife of somebody in your father's capacity."

One of my father's close friends in Ukraine, Elizabeth,
whom he'd known vaguely from the Bank of Boston and who
came to Ukraine with the Peace Corps to launch its first business volunteer program in the former Soviet Union, joined
him for the Kiev Ballet's performance of *Spartacus* in 1992
on the first celebration of Ukrainian Independence Day. The
program was chosen for its symbolism, the slaves throwing off
their shackles and rising up against the Romans. The national
anthem was played beforehand, and she witnessed an electri-
fying swell of emotion. "Everybody just magically stood up,"
Elizabeth told me. "People were singing, cheering, crying in
the aisles. Your father said, 'This was a forbidden song in the
old days. You could be sent to Siberia for singing it.'"

My father was witnessing changes he thought he'd never see and creating a new life, while my mother was stuck in Boston with me. "She was responsible for everything," one of her friends explained. "It was overwhelming. I do remember it being so important and such a huge honor that your dad had been asked to go and do this. It was such a big thing." My mother comforted herself with that belief, which was reinforced by her mother-in-law, the occasional press that my father got, and alcohol.

My father knew she was angry, and that she was drinking. While Alexandra was interning in Ukraine the summer he died, he told her that our mom had gotten so drunk after the two of us went to sleep the previous Christmas Eve, he'd had to carry her to bed so we wouldn't find her passed out in the living room the next morning. He had the impression that she'd drunk that much to show him what his absence was doing to her. He didn't know what to do or how to help her, or wasn't willing to. He saw his wife getting worse, angrier and lonelier, but obeyed his obligations to his country, not to her.

In 1994, on my parents' twenty-seventh anniversary, my father gave my mother a card with a picture of Lord Frederic Leighton's *The Painter's Honeymoon* on its cover, in which a young woman in a billowing green dress snuggles against an artist.

Dearest Anita,

But who would have guessed it would last twenty-seven years and still be going strong?

I still feel just like the young artist in this painting—

inspired, completed, and warmed by your presence in
my heart and in my soul.

Our love shall last forever.

Did my mother read this and think, "Yeah, right"? When
my father took his job with the venture capital fund, he told
her that he hoped he'd be able to run it from Boston after a
few years. Did she believe him? Was he committed to that
plan? She'd never find out. A few months later, he was dead.

My mother had shared a nightmare she'd had after my father's death, where he told her he'd been murdered but couldn't
name his killer, though she never told me that she wondered
if it was something that had been purposefully planned and
executed. But she shared her fears with her friends.

"She talked about hiring an investigator," one of them
told me. "No one in Ukraine had investigated the accident
properly. Your mother said there was a lot of corruption,
and that the accident was suspicious. But she didn't know
how to go about it. She didn't speak Ukrainian, and she
lived halfway around the world." She'd spoken about her
concerns with David, and he'd told her what he told me:
My father had no enemies, there was no reason to kill him.
He said the same thing to a journalist from the *Boston Globe*.
One of the two articles they ran on my father's death states,
"The government is currently conducting a routine investigation of the collision . . . Everyone at the company feels
'that this truly was an accident.'" However, among these
and other articles, I found one from the *Ukrainian Weekly*
that stated, "The U.S. Embassy in Kiev . . . has reported that
an investigation by Ukrainian authorities is proceeding" and

that "Some of Mr. Yurchyshyn's close friends and colleagues in Ukraine suspect he was a victim of foul play." The piece does not go into the reasons that foul play was suspected, and I don't know if my mother knew their sources or contacted them. But this sentence alone would have been enough to stoke her fears.

My father's friends weren't the only people who doubted that the crash was an accident. One night, as I was drinking wine with Natasha and discussing my parents, she told me that the FBI contacted her about my father's death a few years after it occurred. "I got a phone call," she told me. "The guy said, 'I'm from the FBI. I would like to talk to you. Can I take you out for coffee or something?' I'm not going to say no to the FBI. We went out for Italian. He said, 'I have a question for you. You're a friend of Yurchyshyn's, right? Was he killed? Was he murdered? What is your opinion?' I'll never forget that."

It took me a moment to recover. "The FBI? What did you say?"

"I said that I didn't know. I said, 'If I hadn't driven on that road, I could give you a definite opinion. But I can't, because I have, and it's dangerous.'" Because she'd witnessed how treacherous the road was, she couldn't say with certainty that it wasn't an accident, but if she hadn't traveled it herself, she would have said it was murder.

"Why was the FBI contacting you so many years after the accident?"

"Don't know," she said. "You can't get much information out of them. I think your father was killed," she continued.

She'd asked my dad why he'd left his first position with the bank in Ukraine, and he'd told her, "Corruption. I cannot ever work with people like the ones who were in charge."

"But he died two years after leaving the bank."

She picked up her wine. After a long sip, she said, "We don't know what other connections he had."

I'd always known my father's accident might have been something more, but I'd never had a reason, or the desire, to investigate. The FBI's interest in his death, and his colleagues' doubts, raised my own for the first time. Natasha didn't tell my mother that the FBI contacted her because so much time had passed after the accident, and she didn't want to upset her. But my mother would likely have been eager to talk to that man, to learn more and take the opportunity to act on her concerns.

Although my mother was alive for sixteen more years, there wasn't much for me to learn about her life after my father died. Most of her friends' stories were the same as mine. They tried to help, it didn't work, they tried again, and again, then gave up.

One of her oldest friends told me that my mother called her one morning and begged her to get her wine. When her friend explained that she would always offer to help my mother if she wanted to give up alcohol, but that she wouldn't be her drinking buddy, my mother lashed out. When she knew she needed help, she'd call someone and ask them to get her to a short detox program. One person who tried to help her told me she'd once contacted different clinics to see who had space and learned that most would no longer take my mother. They'd found her uncooperative and uncommitted to recovery.

The couple with whom my father had shared his concerns about my mother's drinking told me that after his death, they worked hard to get her into a prestigious recovery center in western Massachusetts. "We had such hope," they said. "We worked so fucking hard to get her out of her house and to get her there. Your sister was there with us. It was impossible to even get intake appointments and interviews there, but we got one for her, which meant, if she was accepted, she was set. Alexandra was as hopeful as my husband and I were. We got there, and they spoke to your mom and Alexandra together, then spoke with them separately. Your mother didn't pass the interview because she wouldn't say that she needed or wanted help. We were all so disappointed and angry. Your sister was just crushed. During the ride back to Boston, Anita was just talking away like we'd just gone to Dunkin' Donuts or something. It was the crummiest day." These friends, and others, retreated as they grew increasingly frustrated with my mother, and as they found themselves responsible for their own parents, sick spouses, and grandchildren.

The only person who knew my mother better than I did during the last chapter of her life was my mother's favorite aide, Nora, who spent close to three years taking care of her. I met Nora for the first time at my mother's funeral, then later in her cozy Cambridge house.

"When I started with your mom, it was tough," she told me in her musical brogue. "I didn't think I could last. Then, as I got to know her, we got really close. I felt like she was family. I think about her almost every day."

"I know that she really adored you."

"I adored her, too. She was such a loving, sweet lady. We had days where I would get upset with her. I'd tell her, 'The reason I get upset with you is because I care for you.' She didn't want to hear it. She had a tough life. Your mom went through a lot of squalls." She sipped her tea. "She talked about the grandchildren all the time. And you and your sister as well. She loved you all so much." Her chin quivered as she spoke.

"That's nice to hear," I said. "She didn't make much of an effort to see anyone, though I know she probably couldn't. She missed most holidays."

She nodded. "The holidays were tough. She would get all excited about a month before, and then boom! She'd slip up."

Nora talked about dealing with the rats and mice that had taken over the house, combing my mother's hair, and how she tried to get her to drink wine instead of gin because when she drank gin my mother was more likely to hurt or soil herself.

Talking with Nora meant I couldn't avoid confronting how isolated and miserable my mom had been during her last years. Despair cleaved my chest. I shivered, then considered how much smaller that momentary pain must have been than what my mother experienced daily.

"Thank you for being so good to her. You did something that my sister and I weren't able to do." I didn't want to take care of her myself, but I felt guilty for spending such little time with her. I know that seeing her more wouldn't have helped, but it might have given her a little happiness. Then again, I thought as I remembered our last Christmas together, my presence didn't seem to bring her much joy. If it had, I would have seen her more often. Four years after her death, I still bounced between believing that I could and should have done more and thinking that I couldn't have done anything that would have made a difference.

Nora last saw my mother two days before she died. It was an unusual interaction, because my mother asked for a hug. She and Nora never hugged, but as Nora was leaving that evening, my mom requested one. "I hugged her. I walked out, came back in, and gave her another one. It was so strange," she murmured. "I wonder if people know when they're passing?

"When I went in that Friday, I didn't go to her bedroom right away. I heard the TV going upstairs. I said, 'She's watching her television.' I went in the kitchen because she loved to eat. I made Thai food for her. I was probably there ten minutes. I go up to her bedroom, and I was like, 'Oh God, no.' She was blue in the face. She looked very peaceful, though. It looked like she was sitting on the bed then decided to lay down. I think your mom, she's at peace now," Nora said, crying quietly. "It was lonely for her in that big house."

"Yes," I said, wiping a tear from my face. "It was."

CHAPTER ELEVEN

The Giant's Seat

*F*our years after her death in 2010, my mother's ashes were still in a cardboard box in my sister's attic. Alexandra and I had debated getting a plot for her ashes in a Boston cemetery or entombing them underwater in a coral reef built to evoke the lost city of Atlantis, but nothing felt right, so nothing was done. I was grateful for our indecision when I learned from my mother's diary that our parents had spread Yuri's ashes on Cader Idris in Wales. From the moment he'd died, my mother longed to be with him again. I could reunite them. When I asked my sister if I could spread our mother's ashes in the same location, she agreed. "I can leave you some," I told her. "If you want to spread some somewhere else, or do it together, I understand."

"Take them all," she told me. "What else are we going to do with them?"

The night before I flew to Wales, I gathered the documents I needed from file cabinets in my sister's attic: my mother's death certificate and a card from the funeral parlor I hoped would act as a "proof of cremation." I brought them and the small, heavy box that held my mother into my sister's guest room. Worrying that Alex might change her mind and want to spread some on her own or use them in a memorial at some point in the future, I decided to take only half. Sitting on the floor with a ziplock bag, I opened the box and saw the ashes for the first time. They looked like dirty flour.

I shook some of them into the bag. These were the ashes I'd leave behind. My mother tumbled out in streams and spurts, a spectrum of grays and whites that were occasionally lighter than bone. It wasn't just dust; chunks that looked like knuckles fell by themselves. I kept telling myself that this was my mother, but it seemed too strange to be true.

After ten hours of travel with my mother, who looked like a lovingly packed bag of blow, I landed in Cardiff, picked up a rental car, and drove across Wales. Cader Idris was at the southern end of Snowdonia National Park, a huge swatch of land that touched the very top of the country and, for a long section, ran rough along the Irish Sea. On two-lane roads narrower than most bike paths, I drove past glittering lakes and a patchwork of green forest and farms. The landscape looked as though a special-effects artist created it; it was more perfect than nature, more real than real life.

I'd booked a room at the inn closest to the base of the mountain. When I checked in, the owner, a tall, affable man, informed me that the building was older than America. It was quaint and cramped; brown wooden beams lined the low ceilings. He handed me a key and a warm pint of lager, and pointed me toward the steep staircase that led to my room.

Before dinner, I walked down a path covered in slugs swollen like blisters. Woods expanded into fields full of sheep that bleated in pitches high and low—short like hiccups, long like pleas. I walked to the gates of the park, which were simple and easily unlatched. A board displayed maps and warnings in English and Welsh—a language I was trying and failing not to find ridiculous for its storybook appearance and sounds. One laminated flyer asked, "Will you go home tonight?" "*A ewch chi adref heno?*" Another detailed weather hazards and dangers hikers might encounter. "Do you have the ability to cope?" it inquired. "If in doubt—TURN BACK." I thought, "I'll find out tomorrow."

Later, I lay on my narrow bed with another lager and wondered why my parents had chosen to spread Yuri's ashes here. Wales was as green and pastoral as promised, and I understood wanting Yuri to be in a place of great beauty. But England was full of beautiful places, many much closer to London. The history of Cader Idris didn't offer an explanation. Cader meant "chair" in Welsh. Idris was a mythical giant who studied the stars as he sat on the mountain like it was his throne; he enjoyed astronomy, poetry, and philosophy. It was said that anyone who slept next to one of the area's three lakes would wake up to find they'd gone mad or become a poet. Both were options parents usually didn't wish for their child.

My breakfast was waiting for me in the dining room the next morning—oily eggs and mushrooms—and my lunch was in a bag behind my white coffee cup. As I was leaving, the owner said I should change into hiking clothes. I told him I was wearing them. In tight jeans and battered orange sneakers, with a leather purse instead of a backpack, I looked ready for a trip to a farmers' market, not a six-mile trek.

When a small sign asked me to pick a trail, I chose the one to my left because it went up the mountain. The other went into a dark forest.

Sheep were everywhere again, scampering over moss and slippery rocks into bushes from which they stuck out their heads to berate me. The hills and peaks that rose around me had large, rocky outcrops and bursts of white and yellow flowers. As I climbed, the grass became a shade lighter and took on the gleam of the towering, silver boulders shaped and smoothed by glaciers that had retreated thousands of years ago.

I came to Tal-y-llyn Lake within an hour, a wide pool that reflected the grays of the rock wall that seemed to prop it up. The lake was as accurate as a mirror until I stood at its edge and the rocks that lay below the surface appeared and mixed with the clouds above.

I placed my hands in the water, which was frigid though it was June. I watched them age and regress as the sun played off them. "Was it here?" I wondered. My parents would have stopped there, too. I didn't know what else I'd see on the hike, but the lake seemed a likely location. Then I remembered that they'd made the trip in early spring. It would have been cold, even snowy, and the lake possibly frozen. I put my hand in my purse, touched my mother's ashes, and thought, "Too soon."

Back on the path, I saw my young parents in front of me, my father taking my mother's hand when the trail was steep or slippery. I saw them separate as my father rushed toward a finish and she lingered behind to stall her arrival.

The path swung to the side of the mountain and became steeper. In some places, rocks grew from the earth in natural steps; in others, they were obstacles. No place seemed right until I came to a grassy spot high above the lake. Ahead of me was a steep drop, but behind me were fields, more rocks, and, eventually, the ocean.

I sat with my bag in my lap, I tugged on some wildflowers, and then clung to a coarse cut of grass until my hand became a fist. I was a third of the way through the hike. I was starting to suspect I wouldn't find one right place to spread my mother's ashes, or one that would make itself known as where they'd scattered Yuri's. I thought of my parents again. The surroundings were gorgeous but also foreboding, and the hike wasn't easy. I stopped to catch my breath many times and twisted my ankle twice while sliding off a rock. They may have felt their journey was a punishment, too difficult to bear physically or emotionally in their raw state and not have even done the full loop.

I tried to see it differently. The loose, overgrown ferns were my mother's optimism, her joy and humor. The silver rocks were scars; the loose pebbles and dry grass, the difficult path she'd had. The wildflowers were what she could have been.

"Yuri," I said out loud, "I'm so sorry you died. Your death extinguished a part of our parents that they dragged with them to their own deaths. What happened to you wasn't fair. I don't know why my parents brought you here, but they did, so that's why I brought Mom here, too."

I took a breath and kept going. "Mom, I hope it's okay you're here. I know it took me a really long time to bring you somewhere, but I'm glad I waited. This makes sense. I'm so sorry for everything that happened to you, and for the things you did to yourself because you were in so much pain. I'm sorry I didn't really know you or understand you. I love you. I love you too, Yuri."

I stood up, opened the bag of ashes, and ran my fingers through them, feeling their softness and coarseness. I turned around in circles, trying to figure out the wind by how it hit my face. I scooped up a small amount of ashes and, without looking, released them. Some of them dropped straight to the ground, while some went a few inches or even a foot away. The lightest bit landed on my shirt. I was looser with my next batch. I let some fall, then tossed the rest to the lake below, and watched them expand until they disappeared.

The air cooled as I gained elevation. Although I hadn't gotten rid of much of my mother, I felt lighter. I looked for other "right" places, and found that everywhere looked right. Every place I saw was pretty enough, grand enough.

I took out clumps of my mother and let her fly from my fingers as I walked. I thought of her dancing as a child, and everything that dancing child wanted. By spreading her ashes, I was throwing flowers at her feet.

When I reached what seemed like the top of the mountain,

I spread the ashes more purposefully. I didn't speak to her or
Yuri again out loud, just in my head, like they were children I
was tucking in together. "There you go," I said.

Again, feeling lighter than I had before, I flung ashes as
I broke into a jog. She flew into in my hair and onto my
tongue, and when I licked my lips, I found her there, too.
"Sorry," I said aloud. "I think I was trying to channel Julie
Andrews in *The Sound of Music*, your favorite movie after *Law-
rence of Arabia* and *Out of Africa*. I know I never wanted you to
visit me in New York, but if I'd let you, as a surprise I would
have taken you to *The Sound of Music* sing-along in Chelsea.
You would have adored that."

I leaned against an improbably large rock and let it cool
my face. I was on a flat part of the trail, the other side of the
mountain sloping into cultivated fields, then a town, then the
light blue rub of the ocean until it blended with the sky. I
reached into my bag and placed some of my mother there,
sprinkling bits directly onto the ground. When a family
walked by, I made sure the bag was concealed. I didn't want
anyone to know what I was doing. I patted the ashes down
and whispered, "I hope you're happy."

Two hours later, I reached the end of the trail, where it
linked up with the start. I was hot, sticky with sweat, but
when a breeze ran up my arms, I shivered. I took out the bag
and saw that much more was left than I'd assumed. The sun
was low and my legs were tired, but I had to finish. I started
on the path again and immediately ran into a family with
three complaining kids. "We're almost done," the mom said
wearily.

"Just starting out?" the dad asked, concerned.

I told him no, I just needed to take a picture.

I went all the way back to the lake, the first place I'd stopped. The mountain was empty, even the sheep had gone home. I said goodbye to the rest of my mother and shook out the bag until it was empty.

My mother was all over me. She was stuck to my cheeks and neck, under my nails, and on my teeth. If I went back to the inn like that, some of her would end up going down the shower drain.

The sky was turning dusky. I peeled off my clothes and tossed them behind me. When I'd put my hands in earlier, the water felt chilly, but on my feet, it was a frigid cold I'd never experienced, metallic and spiky, so sharp it could slice my bones. Goose bumps exploded across my body as I pushed farther in. The water was so clear that I was able to see my feet and shins go from pink to red to a deeper red that felt much worse. I crouched and brought water over my arms, trying to remove as much of the ashes as I could. Then I got lower and let my hair fan out in the water, scratching my head. "You're free" is what I told her, told the mountain. Although parts of her were still in Boston, I believed that she was. I wasn't yet free of my anger and regret, but I was getting there.

At the inn, the owner greeted me and said he'd been worried; I'd been gone much longer than I should have. He took in my muddy sneakers and wild hair. "Bitter or lager?" he asked.

CHAPTER TWELVE

Ukrainian Death: Part Two

I returned to Ukraine in the fall of 2014, a few months after the twentieth anniversary of my father's death. I wanted to see his world, to understand why it and his work had been so important to him, and to learn more about the car crash that had killed him.

There were two competing theories about his death: Either it was a premeditated hit or it was an accident. The majority of Ukrainians or Ukrainian Americans I spoke to heard "murder" when I said "car crash," whether they'd known my father or not. Some people offered vague evidence to support their belief: My father once worked for the government; as a venture capitalist, he could have angered the competitors of one of the business he'd funded; Ukraine was a country where life had little value, and where a hundred dollars—the price of having someone killed in the nineties—was a fortune.

Others said my father wasn't important enough to kill. He wasn't supposed to be traveling that night, no one knew where he was, and coordinating something so complicated would have been close to impossible. When I used the explanations of the second group to counter the arguments of the first, I was interrupted. All of that was irrelevant. They knew it was murder because they knew Ukraine. That's how business was done back then. And, they added, how it was still done today.

Physically, much of Kiev was the same as when I'd first visited as a teenager. Pretty cobblestone streets led to staid squares and wide boulevards lined with government buildings, but modern apartment buildings now towered over them. Kiev had seemed empty when I'd visited at fourteen, with no one on the street and only a few stores with nothing in them. But now the streets were packed with shuffling babushkas and rowdy teenagers crooning into their phones, and there were tons of opportunities to spend money if you had it. You could buy traditional Ukrainian food in cafeterias for a dollar or two, or spend hundreds on a five-course French meal. You could purchase tight dresses for clubbing from the stalls that lined the subterranean walkways of metro stations or in the Givenchy section at the Sanahunt department store. You could continue to repair your old Lada or swap it for an Aston Martin.

It was a warm fall. The autumn light was the kind that could make anything beautiful, even a rusted streetcar, but people wore winter faces. The previous year, President Viktor Yanukovych had failed to sign an agreement with the European Union that many hoped would lead to political and economic reforms and freedoms. There was huge public support for the measure, and when Yanukovych didn't enact it, people responded swiftly and en masse. Protests of up to seven hundred thousand people brought Kiev to a standstill. Peaceful demonstrators camped out for months through a bitter winter in Maidan Nezalezhnosti, a square in the city center, until government forces attacked them in February, killing almost a hundred people and wounding more than a thousand. Amid international outrage, Yanukovych fled to Russia.

By the time I arrived, Kiev was calm, and Maidan Nezalezhnosti had been transformed into a living memorial. The Heavenly Hundred, the civilians who'd died in the February attacks, were commemorated with individual shrines decorated with flowers, helmets, and gas masks, which lined the street that ran between the October Palace and the silver windows of the Globe Shopping Center. The violence had moved east, where ill-equipped Ukrainian soldiers and volunteers fought Russian soldiers and Ukrainian separatists. A Malaysian Airlines passenger flight had recently been shot down as it traveled over the region, and Russia and Ukraine were both saying the other was responsible.

The fiery surges of hope and frustration that fueled the revolution had been dampened back to the despondence I remembered from the nineties. People's fears about their future and that of their country, the safety of their soldiers, and the instability of the hryvnia, which had lost sixty percent of its value since the fighting began, clouded the city's collective brain. I didn't need to speak Ukrainian to know what was discussed on the street. I was exhausted for days after my arrival, and I attributed my lethargy to jet lag until I recognized that I was at the mercy of something heavier. Leaving the apartment meant having to muscle through Ukraine's drab, thick grief, a despair that was both fresh and too familiar to its citizens.

Natasha loaned me her homey apartment for a month, and it became my refuge, even when the kitchen ceiling leaked for a week. The building, like all of the apartment buildings it was connected to along the block, was caked in grime, its European flourishes worn and chipped. On the ground floor was a restaurant badly fashioned after a traditional English pub.

I was under the care of my cousin Larissa, Lana's daughter. She'd gone to Kiev for graduate school a decade earlier and stayed to work in performance art and cultural criticism. She acknowledged that Ukraine could be very frustrating, but said she found the daily struggle of life gratifying and visceral, and felt her work in its small artistic and activist communities was more significant than anything she'd be doing in the States.

I had a list of people to meet who'd known my father or worked with him. Some I'd contacted before I arrived, and others I hoped to find while I was there.

The majority of them were expats from America or Canada who'd come to Ukraine in the early nineties, but others were locals who'd worked with my father at the venture fund. The person I wanted to speak with the most was his driver Vitaliy, who'd survived the crash.

My first week, I met with an American lawyer, Peter, who'd worked with my father at the National Bank of Ukraine. He'd come over at the same time and also left a family behind in America. When I asked why he'd come to work in Ukraine twenty years ago, he told me, "Your father and I grew up with a sense of victimhood, almost a survivor's guilt. We thought, 'We're part of the diaspora; we *have* to go back.' After a certain point in your career," he continued, "you want to leave a mark. You think, 'What can I achieve in my lifetime. What can I do besides being a banker?'" Returning to Ukraine and working toward its success during what everyone thought was a new era was an unexpected opportunity to make such a mark, one with great personal significance.

He leaned forward and became more animated as he went on. "It was a challenging and scary place, but it was also incredibly invigorating. That's part of the drive, too, asking yourself, 'Can I do this?' You had to adapt. You found out you had skills you didn't know you had. It pulled you further away from your comfort zone, but no one ever achieved anything great in their comfort zone."

Peter and my father were very similar. "This," I thought, "is probably as close as I can get to talking to my dad." I believed that he'd felt as Peter had: challenged, powerful, and alive. When I visited Ukraine as a teenager, I couldn't think of one reason why my father wanted to be there. Speaking with Peter, and others like him, allowed me to understand what I hadn't been able to see. The tasks they'd been given, or had asked for, were huge, so even small successes felt momentous. They were a part of history. What could be more rewarding?

"I can see why the environment was seductive," I told him. "I'm drawn to ridiculous challenges as well."

"Obviously," Peter said as he poured me tea. "You're here."

He smiled. "Your father and I talked a lot about family. He was convinced he was doing something he had to do, but he did miss you. He loved you all very, very much. We talked about being torn, being gone, the sacrifice: Was it worth it, how do we explain this to our kids? I'm still asking these questions twenty-three years later. The older kids get it now, but they didn't at the time. At the end of the day, you try to be true to yourself, do your best, and you hope that your wife and children will understand.

"I have tremendous respect for your mother and the sacrifices that she made," he added. " 'Stand by your man.' Smart women realize they're better off letting your husband do what he's got to do, because you'll probably save the marriage and you'll probably save the family. If you fight 'em, like my first wife did, you end up losing everything. I lost everything." He'd gotten a divorce from his first wife and had since married a Ukrainian woman, and they had young twins.

"Your father's death was a real blow," he told me, "a real wake-up call. We realized this place wasn't as benign as we thought it was."

He walked me to the elevator after we finished talking. "You have your father's smile. He had a great smile. Everybody liked him." I thanked him for the compliment, and for his time.

I wandered back to the apartment, thinking about our conversation. I'd enjoyed it so much until he'd said that smart women let their husbands "do what he's got to do." That comment made me furious for my mother, Peter's first wife, and all the women whose partners had left them to pursue their dream. The women weren't given a vote—they were told what was happening. And the men were only able to do what they did because someone was taking care of their children. I didn't know if my mother fought with my father about being in Ukraine, or if she only expressed her frustration and loneliness in boozy outbursts, but I knew she hadn't saved her marriage—it had ended anyway, when my father died. She hadn't divorced him, but she'd lost everything.

When my father went to Ukraine, there was nothing in my mother's life that she found exciting or challenging. The imbalance of their lives—the emptiness of her days, the fullness of his; his fresh start, her inertia—echoed dated patterns of male entitlement and sexism that I imagined she must have wanted to avoid. I was determined to avoid them myself. Fears of having my freedom curtailed by obligations and of being expected to "stand by" someone instead of pursuing my own goals in the same way were huge factors in my persistent distrust of marriage.

With the help of one of my father's coworkers who was still in Ukraine, I got in touch with Vitaliy, and he agreed to come over for tea. I asked Larissa to act as a translator. She arrived with a bag of pastries and arranged them on a plate as I reviewed the information I had about the crash, which I'd gathered from the few newspaper articles about it. Because it was in print, I took the following as fact: As my father, his coworkers, and Vitaliy were returning to Kiev after a day-long visit to a printing facility in Cherkasy, a small city south of the capital, a van veered into their lane on an unlit portion of the road near Kiev and collided with their vehicle. Vitaliy swerved left, and the van hit the passenger side. My father was killed on impact. The other passengers, Serhiy and Yelena, two Ukrainians in their late twenties whom my father was grooming for higher positions at the fund, died soon after. The driver of the van was a construction worker in his thirties; he and his passengers were not seriously injured. Neither he nor Vitaliy were found to have been drinking.

I was fluffing a pillow when Vitaliy knocked. I greeted him in Ukrainian and he greeted me in English. He laughed when I insisted on hugging him and kissing his cheek. He was short, with white hair and a friendly smile. After I made tea, we settled into the living room and chatted, with Larissa's help, about my sister, his family, and the time he'd spent working for my father.

Vitaliy explained that he'd started working as a driver for my father when he was still with the National Bank of Ukraine. As my dad was setting up the venture capital fund and then began working for it full time, Vitaliy also became his assistant, running errands, dealing with the office, and securing various permits.

I figured that he expected me to bring up the accident, but I was worried about how to do it. I wasn't sure how comfortable he'd be discussing something so traumatic. But he brought it up himself after mentioning the printing company they'd visited the day of the crash.

"We were returning very late from a routine visit," he told me. "There were four people in the car: George and two investment officers—Yelena and Serhiy—and myself. It was at one a.m., and we were almost in Kiev. It was a holiday, Ivana Kupala, to honor the summer solstice. People who had been drinking were driving toward us and drove into our lane, and it happened. There was simply no time. There wasn't room to brake because we were going eighty kilometers an hour.

"The thing that saved me was that George always buckled his seat belt. I sometimes used it, sometimes didn't, but he always said, 'Vitaliy, better buckle up.' And that's what saved me. The two people in the back—"

"Wait," I interrupted. "You said that the people in the other vehicle were drinking. Was the driver drinking as well?" When he didn't answer, I read from *The Eastern Economist*'s front-page article about the crash. "Both drivers were checked for blood alcohol content several hours after the incident, and neither registered as having been drinking." I looked at Vitaliy. "Do you think he was?"

"First of all . . ." He sighed. "When they did the blood alcohol content, the results disappeared. Then there was another analysis, a repeat analysis."

"What do you mean, they disappeared?"

"They were gone. The other driver was, by the way, a former policeman. He left the scene very quickly. A car drove up and they got in it. They didn't even wait for the police. He really broke the law."

"This article says that the driver of the van was a 'reinforced concrete worker.' If the other driver left, how would anyone know who he was, or if he'd been drinking or not? How did they find him? How did they figure out that he was a former policeman?"

Instead of answering my question, he said, "There were a lot of inquests and examinations, and the case was transferred."

"But he went to jail." I stared at him. "Right? *Three* people died as a result of the crash."

"No," he said before quickly revising his answer. "The investigation lasted a long time. Honestly, I don't know how it ended."

My voice went tight. "Did the other driver go to jail or not?"

"I don't know."

I'd been cruising until that point, but after hearing that, I felt I'd collided with a van myself. My ribs hurt, my head throbbed. I'd never thought about what happened, or didn't, after the crash. I pressed Vitaliy for more information. "You must have been a part of the investigation," I said. "How do you not know what eventually happened?"

He shifted in his seat. "The driver disappeared, and that's it. Get it? They didn't suffer much damage. They did not wait for the police, they just turned and drove away."

I glanced at Larissa. She repeated what he'd said. I told him that I got it, but I didn't. I hated that I couldn't speak to him directly. There was no way Vitaliy didn't know what happened with that case; claiming ignorance made me think that the other driver had managed to evade conviction. But that line of questioning didn't seem like it was going to produce answers, so I moved on to the question I'd most wanted to ask. "Do you think it was possible that the crash wasn't an accident?"

He shook his head. "George did not have enemies here," he said firmly. "He was a very sincere person. If somebody needed something, they turned to him. He never refused if he could help. And nobody knew where we were. We were supposed to spend the night in Cherkasy. But George had something to do the next day, and he said that we had to be in Kiev by morning. And the other vehicle was driving from some party, maybe singing songs, I don't know, but they obviously distracted the driver, and that's why it happened."

I said, "Do you remember the accident well?"

"I remember this incident very well," he said. "This kind of thing happens only once in one's life."

"You had to see my father, Serhiy, and Yelena. You saw their bodies."

"I saw them. With your father, the lower part of his body was damaged, because he was pressed against the dashboard. The top part was almost not damaged."

"I would have thought he would have hit his head, too."

"No, no, the head not at all. There was no damage. Almost. Maybe a little, yes."

"Was it obvious that they were dead? I'm sorry to ask these gruesome questions. You're the only person who knows these things."

"George died right there. He simply . . . as I now remember . . . how a person takes in air, and he let it out and that was it."

Breath. He was describing breath, the last one that my father took. It should have been difficult for me to hear this information, but it wasn't because I was so upset about everything else I'd learned. A possibly drunk ex-cop fleeing the scene, a lengthy investigation, resolution: unknown. How was all this twenty-year-old information new to me? Would it have been new to my mother?

The crash was an accident. My biggest question had been

answered. But I didn't feel relieved or at peace; I had so many new questions about what had or hadn't happened afterward. The driver who killed my father and two other people had probably walked. That was almost as bad as learning that my father had been murdered.

I lurched through the rest of the conversation. Vitaliy and I made plans for me to meet his wife and sons. They spoke English better than he did, he explained, and it would be nice for us to share a meal.

We hugged and kissed when he left. I told him that for my sister and I, he would always be like family. He nodded and thanked me.

I locked the door behind him. Larissa and I looked at each other. "What the fuck?" I mumbled as we went back to the couch. The newspaper articles I'd used to guide me weren't factual at all. My father and his coworkers had been killed by a drunk ex-policeman who'd likely walked.

I looked at my notes and tried to figure out what I'd learned. Vitaliy said the other driver didn't go to jail, but he also said he didn't know how the investigation had ended. "He said that the people who'd caused the crash had driven away in their van, then later said that they were picked up by another vehicle." My mind started to focus. I remembered my sister telling me that our father's skull had been smashed; Vitaliy had said that it wasn't damaged, then said it was. I asked Larissa unanswerable questions and tried to piece together a satisfying story from what I'd been told. I couldn't. I agonized about not pushing Vitaliy further and failing to make him commit to answers.

"I don't think he's lying," I told Larissa. "But I don't think he's telling us everything. Maybe that means he *is* lying."

I wanted more information about the investigation of the accident but had little idea how to get it. I needed help, and I was willing to pay for it. I googled "Private Investigator Kiev" and read multiple agencies' websites before deciding they were a last resort; I worried how I'd know if they were trustworthy. I reached out to my Eastern European friends to see if anyone had connections with local lawyers or law enforcement.

The next day, a high-school friend put me in touch with Hilb, an ex-cop who'd transitioned to working in HIV prevention. Hilb said I should hire someone to act as a private investigator, and that he knew the perfect person for the job. Her name was Galya, and I could meet them both that afternoon.

I met them in the lobby of a hotel where they were attending a conference. Hilb carried himself like a military man and had a friendly smile. He introduced me to Galya and explained she was a lawyer who worked with HIV-positive women in prisons; she had a lot of police connections. Galya's shiny brown hair fanned past her shoulders. Her bangs were pinned back like a girl's, but her mouth and stare were hard.

I opened a manila folder and spread out on a coffee table the few documents I had about my father: the articles about the crash, his death certificate, a letter from the American embassy. I explained what I had learned so far. I told her about Vitaliy and said he'd probably be willing to speak with her. I knew, I said, that the crash happened twenty years ago, that there were no computers then, and that the people involved might not even be alive. But I needed to find out as much as I could.

Hilb and Galya looked at each other, then at me.

"Why?" Hilb asked.

"Which part?" I said.

"Why do you need to know what happened?"

"Because," I stammered. "This was my father. I should know what happened with his case and to the person who killed him. What if it wasn't handled properly, or the other driver was able to avoid punishment?"

They looked at me with an expression that said "Yeah? So?" There was none of the compassion I got when I talked about having a dead father in America, or the shock and outrage I thought I'd see on someone's face if I said there was a chance that his killer had gotten away with it.

"I can help," Galya said in thickly accented English. "Maybe." She told me that there was an official way to request information from the police, but it was not the best way.

Hilb agreed; it was the *worst* way.

Galya said, "If they know you are looking, and something is there, then that thing is not there anymore." She waved her hands to indicate how things might disappear, and I noticed that she was missing half a finger.

"If something's even there," Hilb added.

"It is very possible there is nothing. But if I talk to the people I know, say I need a favor, make things a bit easier for them, maybe they can get information." She paused and looked at me. "I have to make them want to help."

"Yes," Hilb said. "With favors, that is important."

It took me a moment to understand that "making things

a bit easier" meant offering bribes. I said that I was willing to do whatever was needed.

Galya said that she knew someone in the precinct where my father was killed, and that she was going down there in a few days. She could start there.

I was excited; something was happening. I grinned, but she didn't smile back.

Galya grabbed a pink cane I hadn't noticed and steadied herself with it when we all stood to leave. I told them I was going to call a cab, but Galya insisted on driving me home even though, she said, it was out of her way.

She told me about her work in the prisons as she careened through Kiev in her Mercedes SUV. Every time I asked her a question or responded to something she said, she hunched over the steering wheel and said "No!," which I took to mean that I hadn't understood her. I decided to just repeat a portion of whatever she was saying so I didn't piss her off or sound too stupid, though this approach made me sound, and feel, plenty dumb.

She said her work was very difficult, very awful.

"Very difficult, very awful," I said.

She cursed at other drivers and told me again that she was going out of her way, and, she added, during rush hour. I said, "Rush hour," then, "Thank you."

She dropped me off a few blocks from the apartment, too annoyed by the traffic to take me all the way. I tried to hug her, but she kept both hands on the wheel, so I squeezed her shoulder and gave her a quick kiss on the cheek.

She flinched. "I try," she said, then motioned to my door. "Get out."

A few days later, I met with a Ukrainian American woman who'd started a venture capital fund around the same time as my father. She'd thought she'd only be in Ukraine for few years, but she stayed for twenty and raised her two daughters there on her own.

"Your father was the only person doing venture capital work at that time," she told me, "the only one showing that it could be done, that you could invest in small and medium-size businesses, transparently and legally." A mixture of nostalgia and regret crept into her voice. "We had very lofty goals in the beginning. We all had incredible desire and willpower to make these things work, but the environment was not ready for it."

Inflation, a disastrous government and its disastrous policies, corruption, financial insolvency, and "a neighbor next door who's proven that he's willing to stop us, even when we try to do the right thing" were the most obvious reasons that Ukraine had failed to succeed the way people had hoped. "Ukraine," she said, "is now fighting the war of independence it should have fought in 1991 but didn't have to because Russia was so weak. *This* is really Ukraine becoming a nation. Had your father lived, he would understand this as the existential outcome of what he was trying to do at that time.

"I never thought your father's death was anything but an accident," she continued. "Ukrainians like to believe there's always something behind an accident. But back then, the roads were never lit, people had extremely poor eyesight and poor eyeglasses, and their judgment of distance was bad. Driving was dangerous, especially at night. It's just pitch-black. We hit cows. Somebody hit a horse. I've lost multiple friends in car accidents."

I told her that I'd found out a bit about the investigation, and that it seemed like it hadn't been handled properly. She shook her head with a tired disgust. "There's no justice system here. It comes down to corruption," she said. "What upsets you about your father's case, that some individual could commit a crime and walk away, happens here every single day." I was beginning to understand just how corrupt Ukraine was and why its citizens were so beaten down. The system was rigged and easily manipulated. No one with money or connections was ever accountable.

Later that day, Larissa called Vitaliy to confirm our upcoming lunch. We stood in the middle of the living room and I kept my ear close to the phone even though she was speaking Ukrainian.

She hung up.

"When are we having lunch? Soon?"

"He canceled," she said. "He's moving and he doesn't have time to meet. Maybe he'll be able to near the end of the month. He said he has your number and will call you."

"He never said he was moving." I groaned. "What about Galya?"

"He's willing to speak to her. You can give her his number."

That night, I ate dinner at the twenty-four-hour Italian and sushi restaurant on my block and washed down a bowl of pasta alla carbonara with bitter Moldovan wine as young couples stared at me. Ukraine's currency was so depressed that I could dine out every evening, and at nicer places, too, swapping out carbonara for beef bourguignon and local swill for Châteauneuf-du-Pape. The better restaurants were always nearly empty. When I wasn't spoiling myself, I drank at the bar downstairs or in my bed as I watched television. Instead of sleeping in the middle, I'd chosen the left side. The right side was covered in papers. An article about my father lay on the other pillow: "Fund Director in Highway Tragedy: Foremost American Investor in Small Ukrainian Business Dies." Under the headline was a large black-and-white photo of my father speaking behind a podium. I looked at it before I went to sleep and when I woke up.

I saw my father everywhere in Kiev, in his gray suits and the black wool coat he always wore. I saw him in a little boy on the streetcar who'd wrapped a Ukrainian flag around the arm of his jacket. We were haunting each other, but it was his country. Even if his optimism had soured, as it had for so many, I wanted him to be there.

Galya called to tell me she'd spoken with Vitaliy. As he'd told me, he said that he didn't know what happened with the investigation and had lost his documents from the case. She was indignant. "I don't trust his words, Anichka," she shouted, "I don't trust him."

"So now what?"

She told me she would ask one of her friends to look for the original documents and information about the case, and said, "He will need to be paid." She'd be driving past the apartment that afternoon; she'd pull over wherever she could so I could bring her an envelope full of cash.

I went to meet another of my father's friends, Taras, at the

Natsionalny Hotel, where my father had lived when I'd visited the first time. It had been lavishly remodeled at least once since the nineties. The lobby was done in velvet and marble, and large chandeliers hung from the high ceiling. There was a small bar off in the corner, but there were only a few customers, heavyset men in leather jackets smoking cigars and talking quietly.

Taras was my father's age, but thinner and more handsome than my father had been. He ordered us each small glasses of vodka and bottles of water.

Taras knew my father pre-Ukraine. They'd visited the country together in 1988 and remained friends. "When your father got into venture capitalism in Ukraine," he said, "I don't think he was fully aware of the brutal rules of the game." The game was the criminal system or systems that had always existed but flourished after independence. He gave me an example of how my father, or one of the businesses he funded, might have gotten tangled up in it. "Somebody starts a business, then another person starts a business off of them. They sniff around, 'What are you doing? How can I be a parasite and leech off your company?'"

As he sipped his vodka, I asked about the car crash. Did he think it was an accident or the result of the brutal game, rules maybe misunderstood or ignored? I told him I didn't think that my father would have been unaware of the dangerous extent of corruption. He was optimistic about Ukraine's future, but he wasn't dumb.

He looked at me kindly. "It wasn't an accident. It was definitely connected to your father's work. Even though his company had less than fifteen million dollars under management, in 1994 that was a lot of money. And, as much money as it was in Kiev, it was even more money outside of Kiev."

"I'm trying to learn more about what happened," I told him, "but it's hard. And slow."

"Well," he said, "the only specific I know was that the families of the two other people who died tried to pursue the case and were basically told, 'Drop it.'" He'd heard this from his neighbor, who knew people who knew one of the victim's parents.

I gulped down the rest of my drink. "Shit. That's not good."

I called Vitaliy repeatedly, but he never answered. I made Larissa try him from her phone, but he didn't pick up for her, either. Soon Galya called and told me he'd stopped taking her calls as well. To her this was proof that he was hiding something. Larissa listened to the recording of our conversation with Vitaliy again, and noticed that his speech patterns and sentence construction changed depending on the subject. When he was talking about the current political situation or telling stories about his previous jobs, his speech was easy, and his descriptions had been specific. But when he was answering my questions about the car crash, his thoughts were riddled with filler words like "well" and "you know." He'd been evasive, spoken less confidently, relayed few concrete memories. I thought of how clear he'd been about the other driver taking off instead of waiting for the police. However, everything else he'd said about the accident had been convoluted. He hadn't answered many of my questions directly; he'd skipped between topics, contradicted himself, told me that he didn't know something, then said he did. Even if he'd been in shock immediately after the accident, he'd have remembered the events that followed. I was becoming more and more certain that he wasn't telling me everything that he knew. I didn't like doubting him. When I'd told him that I considered him family, I'd meant it. My father and sister had both been very fond of him. He'd stayed with my father's company after his death, and he'd met with me. I'd taken this all to mean that I could trust him, but maybe I couldn't.

Galya called and told me she was coming over with news. When she arrived, she launched into an explanation of her most recent discovery. She'd spoken with a friend who worked in the police precinct where my father's accident occurred, and he'd told her there were no records of a criminal case related to the crash or against the driver. "Here," she explained, "whenever a case is first opened, it is in the hands of the investigator. This investigator closed the case. For what reason, I don't know, because I can't get to it. The investigator is a very small figure in the system. Maybe he was paid a lot of money, or he was pressured.

"This case never went to court," she continued. "If the investigator states that there was no crime committed, then there is no reason to go to court, and the case is closed. When the investigator makes such a decision, he has to have evidence. This driver who killed your father and his coworkers, he was not currently serving in the police, but he'd had a high position there."

Galya put her hand in my face and counted on her fingers. "One, two, three persons is dead. He should have been tried, he must go stay in the prison, *he must*. But the case did not get to court. The person who did this did not answer for it."

Before I went to Ukraine, one of my friends asked me how I'd feel if I found out that my father's accident was a hit, and what I'd do if I did. "I don't know," I'd said. It seemed so unlikely that I'd discover anything concrete.

But I'd been successful, at least somewhat. And how did I feel? Like I was drowning while knowing no one was coming to save me. I'd softened toward my father, but I hadn't had enough time to get comfortable with liking or sympathizing with him. My teenage self was still convinced that feeling anything other than anger when I thought of him meant weakness or defeat. What I learned pushed me past that. I *was* angry, but not at him. What I'd discovered seemed worse than murder. It offended my privileged American expectations of a criminal justice system. I was furious at everyone who'd been involved and at Ukraine for being so corrupt then, and still. And I was newly grieved. Not for myself but for him and all he lost, as well as for my mother. And I couldn't do anything with what I'd uncovered. I couldn't locate the murderer and avenge my father's death.

Galya interrupted my spinning thoughts. "I don't understand. Your family was in America, yes, but why they don't do anything? If Americans come and ask questions, maybe this would not happen. You want to know now, but now is difficult. Why not then?"

I spoke slowly, trying not to sound as defensive as I felt. "We didn't know what was happening," I said. "We believed what we were told. Well," I conceded, "my mother was suspicious, but she didn't know what to do. She lived in America and she didn't speak Ukrainian. I don't think she knew that the investigation was buried. I don't know why she didn't follow it. Maybe she thought she could trust the system." It was embarrassing, and infuriating, to know that I'd done nothing for reasons far worse than helplessness. I was relieved that my father was dead. People suggested that he might have been murdered, and at sixteen I'd cared so little about anyone other than myself that the idea hadn't made me curious, let alone outraged.

Galya sighed and told me she was seeing another contact tomorrow. "This man may be the miracle, for this man know many men. When I need something, we talk and he help me. But he's policeman and every time need money. Another man, he comes back from vacation soon. I'm meeting him when he returns. Whatever is there, I'll find it."

I gave her the money she needed and asked if it was enough to cover expenses like gas.

"I am woman," she said. "I'm every time needing money, but now you give me money, so it's okay."

After she left, I collapsed on the bed. I pulled the sheets over me, then kicked them off, rubbed my forehead, and chewed my lip. My father had been failed by the country he'd wanted to help for his whole life. It was a place where people had to pay bribes for basic things like medical treatment and having their electricity turned on, where members of parliament could not be convicted of crimes. The country was suffering from an entrenched lawlessness born of decades of oppression and scarcity. But who was I to condemn Ukraine? America, and its government, were plenty corrupt, too.

While I was in Ukraine, I finally connected with a man named Edward who'd worked at the European Bank for Reconstruction and Development, one of the fund's main investors, and who knew my father well. He was now in Nigeria working on infrastructure development. When we finally spoke on the phone, our conversation was intimate and urgent. He spoke to me like he'd been waiting for my call since the day my father died.

He told me that he'd seen my dad two days before the crash, when he'd stopped by the European Bank's London office. My father was in a great mood and was very optimistic about his various projects. As he spoke, he'd leaned back in his chair and propped his feet on Edward's desk. I thought of how unhappy my father had seemed when he was in Boston—our fights, the tension with my mother. How happy he must have been to get back to the work that he loved and the complicated country that was starting to feel like home.

When Edward heard about the crash, he flew to Kiev immediately. It didn't seem possible that my father was dead; he'd just seen him. He went to the site of the accident and left flowers at the base of the tree my father's car hit. The tree was mangled, and its bark had been torn off.

I interrupted his breathless monologue and told him my father's car hadn't collided with a tree. His driver had never said they'd hit anything but the other vehicle, and no one who'd gone to the site had mentioned seeing what he was describing.

Edward said the car had definitely crashed into a tree. He'd examined the area closely because he thought there was a good chance the "accident" had been planned. There was only one set of very black skid marks going toward Kiev. The skid marks showed there was braking, but there weren't swerve marks to match. The marks suggested there had been serious impact to the car on the road when the oncoming vehicle went into my father's car's lane. It must have nicked his car, which sent it into the tree. And if the accident happened as it was reported, why would the people in the backseat of my father's car die?

He said he'd always thought that the crash was a "warning shot" that went wrong. The printing company they were coming from had sophisticated equipment; he suggested it was possible that someone could have been interested in using it to make counterfeit money.

He seemed so certain of his assessment. I explained that while I didn't have a strong grasp of physics, the passengers in the back could have been tossed around or crushed. The person sitting on my father's side would have received impact as well, and neither of them died at the scene.

He tried to disagree with me gently. He explained that if Vitaliy had swerved, there would have been marks on the road, and that the tree appeared freshly damaged. My story of the crash, and the one he'd been told at the time, didn't fit with what he'd seen.

Hearing yet another person say that the crash wasn't an accident, and learning new details about it, was unnerving. Every "truth" I landed on was unsteady. I didn't want what he'd told me to upend the story I'd only just come to believe—but it did.

Galya obtained the personal information of the police officer who oversaw the case regarding my father's accident, and when she got him on the phone, he agreed to meet.

She drove to his house on the outskirts of Kiev with money and a bottle of good cognac, and they took a walk around his property. He was eighty and very ill.

He remembered the case well, and admitted to her that he was responsible for making it disappear. Someone told him to do it. If he refused, he'd have lost his job and maybe his family. It was not the only time he'd covered up a case; such actions were common.

There were two former cops in the van that hit my father, he said, but only one was arrested. The other one was never questioned. He said that the first time Vitaliy was interviewed, he'd told the truth, which implicated the other driver. Vitaliy was forced to change his statement and say that *he* was the one drinking and assume guilt so the cop could get off; he was promised that his admission would be lost, and he would not be tried. The case was archived with the claim that it lacked incriminating evidence, and it was later destroyed. "That's justice in Ukraine for you," the officer said to Galya.

She offered him the money and cognac, but he refused both. "I am guilty," he said. "I realize I will die soon, and I want to apologize to the girl."

She asked, "Can you apologize to her face?"

He said that he couldn't.

"But he is sorry," she told me. "He wanted me to tell you he feels very bad about what he did. I was right. I *knew* Vitaliy was not telling the truth."

He hadn't told the truth, but I understood why. He'd been forced to give a false testimony that helped the perpetrator get off. He wouldn't want to admit that, or that he'd played a role in the man's ability to evade justice.

I'd come to see Ukraine and why my father loved it, but everything I'd learned suggested it was a terrible and cruel country. My father had wanted to be one of the many people who might reform its lawlessness and support its transformation, but he hadn't been able to because the people in power had an interest in keeping things as they were. I admired his devotion and optimism, but I also found it foolish. Why would anyone think they could change such a stubborn place? Yet even when people like him saw the enormity of the fight they'd entered, they hadn't given up. They refused to relinquish their ideals and agendas, which was either admirable or idiotic. It seemed like their love for their country was unconditional.

The last week of my trip, I hired a driver named Oleg to take me to the area where my father had died. I explained what I wanted to do and gave him the location as it had been reported. He said he could take me, no problem.

He picked me up outside of the apartment in a freshly waxed black car. He was smoking when I trotted over to him, but threw down the cigarette when I extended my hand.

As we drove out of Kiev, the city thinned into sprawl, long avenues of small stores and people selling fruit and socks on the sidewalk. I told him about my father's accident, then interrupted myself. "Flowers!" I cried. "I need to get flowers. Is there somewhere we can stop?"

He pulled over under a pedestrian bridge that spanned the

wide highway and parked in front of a woman selling cherries and pale carrots. He ushered me down a flight of stairs that led to an underground arcade of tiny shops.

There were many stalls selling flowers, but he brought me directly to a large one in back. I walked around and examined wreaths made out of lilies and carnations as Oleg followed. I wanted to get something dramatic and reverential. When I found a wreath I liked, I asked a saleswoman how much it cost.

Oleg interjected before she could answer and led me to a tall bucket of red carnations. "There are the flowers people bring to graves and places like that. You need to have an even number in your arrangement since it's for death. In other circumstances, having an even number of flowers is bad luck."

The carnations looked cheap, but I wanted to do what was traditional. I carefully selected ten of the brightest ones and brought them to the counter.

"See," Oleg said, as the saleswoman wound a black ribbon around then. "She knows what they are for."

When we got back in the car, Oleg told me he didn't like the road my father was killed on. "My neighbor's husband died on this road. Many people die in cars all over the country. But this road, it's very bad. No lights, too many cars, crazy drivers. I try to never take it, even during the day."

The road turned into farmland as we got closer to the airport. Both sides were lined with fields and dotted with shrines commemorating the many people who'd lost their lives traveling it.

He slowed down right as we hit the two-kilometer point. "It is here," he said, turning the car around and pointing it toward Kiev. "Where the road turns, that's where it is easy for cars to move into the wrong lane. I think it probably happened there."

I grabbed the flowers, then waited for traffic to whiz past. It was a bright, hot afternoon.

I ran across the road, then slowed down as I moved through a knee-high mess of bushes toward a line of trees that fronted fields of dead sunflowers. When I stumbled over a rock, a flock of brown birds erupted from the ground.

After surveying the trees, I went to the one with the widest trunk. "Hi, Dad," I began. I paused to see if tears would come or my throat would tighten, but neither happened. "I've been here for a month, almost. I learned a bunch of terrible stuff. I'm really angry that the person who killed you got away with it, and I feel so stupid that Mom and I didn't even know. I'm sorry you were stopped when you were doing something that made you so happy and that you believed was important. You'd hate things now. I don't mean it's better that you're dead, just that you'd be disappointed. But I don't think you'd give up. You'd probably work even harder. I still don't feel that sad that you died, because things were awful between us. I wish you hadn't been so scary, and that you could have been yourself with me, or more like the person other people knew." My voice sped up when it hit that truth. A car honked behind me and another honked back. "We have a lot in common. I think we'd understand each other now."

A breeze sprang up, lifted my hair and edged under my clothes. The air was different there; it seemed active, charged. Dead leaves floated inches above the grass. I lay the flowers at the base of the tree, then left.

As Oleg drove us back to Kiev, I said goodbye to Ukraine, although I wasn't leaving for a few more days. This was my father's country. I didn't know how to love such a complicated place, just as I didn't know how to love such a complicated person. But it didn't matter if I loved them or not. They were part of me, either way.

Back in Brooklyn, I reviewed what I'd learned and settled on the story Galya got from the retired police officer, who died a few months after she spoke with him. I felt I was done. The crash was an accident. With the help of colleagues and money, the ex-cop had been able to stop the investigation and shirk responsibility. The only people imprisoned were the families of the victims, still walled in by their grief for those they'd lost and a system that protected only itself.

I was satisfied, but Galya was not. She was still stuck on something Vitaliy had told her. He said the case had been reopened in a different precinct and that there had been multiple investigations. She'd looked at the registers at each precinct and saw the case had been archived in the precinct where the accident occurred. That meant the file should have been there, but it wasn't. If it had been reopened or transferred, there should be a paper trail. She'd hadn't found one.

She told me that the police chiefs all knew one another and that it was common for them to "cover their own." The officer she had spoken with, she said, was the sort who would never reveal the whole truth. He told her a story, said he was guilty, and that he was sorry. But, she reminded me, a person could say anything. You could believe any story you wanted, but documents told what really happened.

When I said we already knew that some, if not all, of the

documents related to the case had been destroyed, and that any she found would probably contain false information, she said she still needed to look. She should be able to find *something*. She wanted to speak with her acquaintance who worked at the Security Service of Ukraine (SBU), the official counterintelligence and surveillance organization that grew out of the Russian State Security Committee (KGB). She hoped he'd agree to look in their archive for documents on my father and the accident. If something was there, he would find it. She didn't ask for money and hadn't for a while.

I didn't hear from her for months and assumed that her acquaintance hadn't found anything. So when I received an email from Larissa saying she'd spoken with Galya and that there'd been a big development, I was surprised. Larissa said she wanted to share it with me in person, and that she'd be in Connecticut in a few weeks for Easter. I refused to wait, and she reluctantly agreed to talk by Skype while she was still in Ukraine.

I sat in my room with my computer on my lap. As she looked at her keyboard, Larissa said that Galya had visited her a few days earlier and had explained that she hadn't been in touch because she'd contracted hepatitis C. While she was in the hospital, her acquaintance from the SBU discovered that Vitaliy had worked for them and for the KGB as well, reporting on a number of people, including my father. This wasn't surprising. All Westerners in Ukraine were under observation in the nineties—my father probably had assumed that Vitaliy was reporting on him if he didn't know for sure. His phone was tapped and he sensed people listening to his conversations in restaurants and elevators; foreigners were innately of interest, but being watched didn't mean you were doing something wrong.

Galya's friend and a companion staked out Vitaliy for months before they finally saw him on his street. They followed him into his house, where they interrogated him and beat him up. Eventually, he'd admitted that the crash was a hit, but said he did not know who'd ordered it or why. Refusing would have cost him his life. He said the accident had been staged and was not a head-on collision as had been reported, but did not say what actually happened.

I blinked at my screen. That the crash could have been a coordinated hit had been believable for so long, but now it seemed impossible, even absurd. As I turned over what Larissa said, I began to panic. I'd justified my participation in Ukraine's pervasive shadow economy by telling myself that bribing people was the only way to get things done. I was told there was a formal way to investigate an old criminal case but that it was not the "best way," and I'd chosen, without even a moment of hesitation, to work outside of the rules and pay to learn what I wanted to know. I hadn't condoned the country's corruption, I told myself, just used it to my advantage. But I'd participated in the same system that helped the person who'd killed my father avoid punishment. And my questions, slick with money, had led to more violence.

If Galya had told me that her guy was going to speak to Vitaliy, I would have insisted he not use any physical force. Since it had been employed, could I trust the confession? Maybe Vitaliy told them what they wanted to hear so their interrogation would end. Confessing didn't have any repercussions; he could no longer be brought to trial.

I threw these doubts and more at Larissa. How could the accident have been coordinated in the middle of the night? If Vitaliy had played a role in my father's death, why would he meet with me? "What if this isn't the truth?" I groaned.

"Why would he lie?"

"Because he was scared! I'm not saying he did, but how can we actually trust this confession. Galya wasn't even there!"

"Vitaliy is the only living witness, and we know that he is capable of telling different things to different people. We know that what was in the articles wasn't true, and he said that the accident didn't happen as it was reported. *He* could have driven into the other car and swerved to protect himself. Maybe the police officer who helped bury that case was just a part of a larger cover-up. He told Galya he never questioned his orders. He could have had no idea what was actually going on." Larissa's jaw tightened with frustration as she continued. "You aggressively pursued the truth, and now you're rejecting it." She told me that I had to stop viewing Ukraine with my American expectations. This was how it worked.

Out of arguments, I said goodbye and closed my computer. Larissa was right. I'd gone after the truth, and now I was determined to discredit it. But wasn't that the right thing to do? Staging accidents was a common way to get rid of people at the time. It seemed so unnecessarily complex, as it killed more people than it needed to, but the more complicated the crash was, the more likely it was to be seen as an accident, and it would arouse less suspicion than other tactics, such as shooting my father, an act that could not have been seen as anything other than murder.

I flipped open my computer and wrote an email to Galya. My fingers were heavy and fast, their taps sounded like gunshots. "I'm sorry to bother you. I'm hoping you can tell me if you think that the confession Vitaliy gave your friends is real. I understand that when they spoke with him, they used physical force. Couldn't that have influenced what he said?"

She replied the next day. "The people who talked to Vitaliy are not my friends. They were doing their job. There was physical pressure. Vitaliy is not an honest man. It's impossible to talk to him adequately without pressure. Vitaliy himself didn't decide to kill. At that time, drivers who worked for people in high positions (your father was one) all went through the KGB/SBU. I told Larissa all this in detail. What other information do you need?"

I needed, or wanted, so much more information. I wanted to be as certain as Galya that Vitaliy was guilty of at least carrying out orders. She'd ignored my question about believing him, which meant she thought that I should, too. She didn't respond to questions that she felt had an obvious answer.

I wandered my room thinking about all the times I'd said my father's death was a gift. That I didn't care how he died. The circumstances of his death seemed so insignificant that I wasn't even sure if I'd ask people about them when I began my research. My interest was only spurred by other people's interest, and by their doubts.

It was scary to think of how close I'd come to never knowing the truth, and how comfortable I'd been with that possibility. I still believed that if he'd lived, I'd have been too afraid to push myself to discover how smart and capable I was, but I could no longer feel happy that he'd died. And I had to acknowledge that my mother's suspicions turned out to be true; they weren't the product of grief-fueled paranoia or a need for sympathy. She was smart to question the story we were given.

I took my passport from my dresser and rubbed its curled edges. I could fly to Ukraine that night, demand Galya or her associates take me to Vitaliy, and question him myself. I grabbed my suitcase from the closet and tossed it on the floor. I threw a pair of jeans in it, then stared at them. What would Vitaliy tell me that he hadn't told Galya's men? What would change if I could hear his confession myself and stare at him while he spoke? I might not even be able to find him; he could have left town, disappeared. And if I returned, I risked putting myself, and Larissa, in danger.

Feeling defeated, I collapsed on my bed and surveyed the piles of papers that stretched across the floor. They were the same piles that I'd created years ago, but the bedroom was different, as was the apartment. I'd moved many times since I'd first examined and organized my parents' things, had unpacked their letters and photographs in different homes, states, and countries, then packed them up again when my search took me to another destination. They'd told me everything that they could, but there was still so much that I wanted to know. If my father hadn't died, would we have found a way to heal our relationship? Would he have apologized for how he'd treated me, and would I forgive him? Who would I be now, and what would have happened to my mother?

I picked up one of my father's early letters to my mother, then quickly put it down. I knew that I wouldn't be able to delight in their young love without thinking of its shaky progression, cheer for their optimism but not lament all that choked it, read about their travels without seeing the limited existence my mother retreated to.

Because I thought that my parents never really cared for each other, I'd believed that if my father had lived, my parents would have divorced, or grown further apart even if they'd remained linked on paper. But I'd been wrong. Perhaps the promises my father made to my mother would have become more important than the ones he'd made to himself, and he'd have returned to America and fought with her to restore her life and their marriage.

When I began investigating their lives, I thought only about getting answers. I didn't consider how I would feel when I got them, or what it would be like to live with the knowledge that they'd been in love, that I was so much like them, and that my father had been murdered. Embracing my parents, their love and catastrophes, meant embracing their pain as well as my own. Acknowledging who I'd lost and all we'd failed to understand.

I placed their letters in a folder, and that folder in a box. Pictures went into bags, and documents were slid into an accordion file. As the piles disappeared, I thought of how relieved I'd been when my mother died, how I'd believed that cleaning out her house would be my final goodbye to my parents and the end of our relationship. It turned out to be the beginning of a new one—one that was vivid and complicated, frustrating and rich. It was the relationship I needed, and the one that I wanted.

$\mathcal{H}$ow often did my parents see each other's best qualities, the ones I'd learned about? They'd seen them when they first met, but these qualities seemed to recede with time. Perhaps my parents stopped noticing what they'd once loved about each other because they lost the ability to truly see someone they'd come to know well or because they'd squashed those parts of themselves when their lives didn't require them. Maybe they were still able to be those people when they were abroad, far from their responsibilities. When my parents returned from trips, I didn't recognize them. But this didn't mean they weren't happy and authentic in those moments or hadn't been while they'd been elsewhere.

When I found my parents' letters, I had to surrender the people I'd constructed from my experiences, observations, and assumptions so I could meet them for the first time. Often I felt overwhelmed by all I didn't know; more frequently, however, I was frustrated by the fact that I'd never be able to know everything that I wanted to. I'd said I wanted to be rid of my parents, and I was. I'd replaced them with Anita and George.

Wanting to know them better was the way I expressed and dealt with my grief. It didn't look like other people's. I wasn't sad that my parents were dead, but I was devastated to grasp that I didn't know them and had never understood who they were or all they'd done. If I truly didn't care, I wouldn't have upended their lives, and mine as well, looking for answers. I would have let us be. I fought to learn who they were, though I knew that it was almost impossible for children to truly know their parents. Children are just one part of their parents' lives; kids cannot understand their parents' depths and dimensions, and parents often cannot be or share all that they are with the young people in their charge.

I didn't expect the pain I'd encounter. The good things I discovered made me feel sad, while the sad things I discovered made me despair. When I read the diary that my mother kept before and after Yuri's death, heard about my father's breakdown upon losing his son, or revisited my mother's self-slaughter, I grieved. Hard. I wept for everything that Anita and George lost, and for the girl I'd been, a trembling child who didn't have the parents she needed.

My parents had fallen in love and committed to sharing their lives with the audacious optimism that compels many couples. They didn't know about the blows they'd suffer as individuals and as a pair, or the sudden end of their relationship. If I'd asked them, at the end of their lives, if they would have chosen someone else, would they have? Or would they tell me that what they'd suffered with each other was not greater than the beauty they'd experienced as well?

I'd come to know George and Anita as well as I could and had so much sympathy and compassion for them. I accepted the people they were and had wanted to be. And acceptance, I knew, was a vital form of love. I realized that a desire to find a way to love them had been hidden in my search all along; it was the need that had fueled all I sought. I would always have questions and always lack certainty, but that was okay, because I'd managed to find peace.

ACKNOWLEDGMENTS

I was privileged to work with an outstanding team at Crown. My editor, Lindsay Sagnette, was a champion of this book from the beginning, and Domenica Alioto and Rose Fox provided invaluable guidance through many drafts and revisions. I received additional support from Leslie Wells, and am grateful to have found her.

My agents, Lane Zachary and Jennifer Gates of Aevitas Creative, were therapists, eagle-eyed readers, and, most important, believers. Their faith was there when mine was not.

Doree Shafrir asked me to write an essay about the original *My Dead Parents* for BuzzFeed, and that essay is a big reason why this book exists at all. I am as thankful for her friendship as I am for her vision.

My writing group provided me with so much cheese and even more encouragement. Emily Gould, Bennett Madison, Lukas Volger, and Lauren Waterman are as patient as they are wise.

Ruchika Tomar, Annie DeWitt, Meaghan Winter, Lauren Spohrer, Eva Lou, Chiwan Choi, Elizabeth Greenwood, Catrin Einhorn, Abby Rabinowitz, and Kristen O'Toole read parts of this book as I was writing and gave me insight and counsel when I was desperate for both. Wei Cho was an excellent research assistant.

I am deeply indebted to Charles Colson, Susan and Martin Davidson, Sally Warren, Sylvia Marich, Jo-Del and Doug Gaeth, Eileen Meny, Anne Carballo, Rita Jeremy, Martha Margowsky, George Gajecky, Justin Dangle, Irene Schmid, Tania D'avignon, Alicia Szendiuch, Zina Kondratiuk, Elizabeth Ames, Peri Onipede, Susan Fenno, Mark Tomlinson, Daniel Bilak, Frank Sysyn, Paul Kenney, Edward Dawson, Mary Ann Nelson, Michael Novack, Mario Inganni, Theo and Annemarie Compernolle, John Khoury, John Boatright, Robert Woods, Robert Cordek, Carl Gage, Thomas and Rachel Claflin, Thomas Ebrey, Nicholas Robinson, Michele Perrault, Lidia Wolanskj, Micheal McCloskey, Patricia Scharlin, Bruce Hamilton, Whit Knapp, Peter Jeton, Sue and Frank Wellington, Bill Baldwin, Jaroslav Kinach, Andriy Masiuk, Katherine Adler, John Zamecnik, William Flemer, Barry Wendell, Valeriy Schekaturov, Kanako Sekine, Abby Sobel, Victoria Vyshenska, Victor Pynzenyk, Bill Hamilton, Lesia Haliv, Osaro Isokpan, Marcel Yondo, Boris Balan, Roman Matkiwsky, Steven Bavaria, Denis Hamboyan, Barbara Neachtain, Annie Crawley, Jerry Bird, Bruce Share, Eduardo Alvarez, Pam Knutson, Frank and Donna Urbia, Piroska Soos, Yuriy Strygun, and Vitaly and Galina Sokirko. Without their stories and memories of my parents, this book would not have been possible. They were generous with their time and ideas and gave me an incredible gift.

Hillary Shugrue Paquette, Tanya Charnis, Alex Runne, Nicole Markoff, Sarah Masters, Maria Biber-Ferro, Tina Darling, Leo Beletsky, Monica Beletsky, Sarah Cohen, Christopher Abraham, Meredith Wu, Eleni Gage, Yng-Ru Chen, Devin Gordon, Gregg Murphy, Madeleine Merchant, Christopher John Williams, Michael Francis Craft, Justin Bergman, Axel Barragan, my Macdowell crew, Stephanie Diani, and Mark Hewko are amazing humans. I am forever grateful for their friendship and all they've brought to my life.

I learned the importance of family during the years it took me to write this book. Alexandra, Lana, Arlene, Christine, Larissa, Gene, Natalie, Susie, Wendy, Raj, Naveen, and Toshi answered hundreds of questions, fed me, housed me, shouldered burdens on my behalf, and barely flinched when I first told them what I was up to. My family is incredible, and I am so lucky to have them.

ABOUT THE AUTHOR

Anya Yurchyshyn's writing has appeared in *Esquire, Granta, N+1,* and *Noon* and was included in *The Best Small Fictions 2015.* She received her MFA from Columbia University.